Related Titles for College-Bound Students

ACT
ACT

Titles for the SAT
SAT 2006 Comprehensive

SAT 2006 Premier

SAT 2400

SAT Critical Reading Workbook

SAT Math Workbook

SAT Writing Workbook

12 Practice Tests for the SAT

SAT Strategies for Super Busy Students

SAT Subject Tests
SAT Subject Test: SAT Biology E/M

SAT Subject Test: SAT Chemistry

SAT Subject Test: SAT Literature

SAT Subject Test: SAT Math IC

SAT Subject Test: SAT Math IIC

SAT Subject Test: SAT Physics

SAT Subject Test: SAT Spanish

SAT Subject Test: SAT U.S. History

SAT Subject Test: SAT World History

Vocabulary-Building for the SAT
Extreme SAT Vocabulary Flashcards Flip-O-Matic, 2nd Ed.

SAT Vocabulary Flashcards Flip-O-Matic, 2nd Ed.

SAT Vocab Velocity

Dr. Jekyll and Mr. Hyde: A Kaplan SAT Score-Raising Classic

Frankenstein: A Kaplan SAT Score-Raising Classic

The Ring of McAllister: A Score-Raising Mystery Featuring 1,046 Must-Know SAT Vocabulary Words

The Scarlet Letter: A Kaplan SAT Score-Raising Classic

The Tales of Edgar Allan Poe: A Kaplan SAT Score-Raising Classic

Wuthering Heights: A Kaplan SAT Score-Raising Classic

SAT for Native Spanish Speakers
Domina el SAT: Prepárate para Tomar el Examen para Ingresar a la Universidad

Test Prep and Admissions

The Procrastinator's Guide to the ACT®

2006 Edition

The Staff of Kaplan, Inc.

Simon & Schuster

NEW YORK · LONDON · SINGAPORE · SYDNEY · TORONTO

Kaplan Publishing
Published by Simon & Schuster
1230 Avenue of the Americas
New York, NY 10020

Contributing Editor: Jon Zeitlin
Editorial Director: Jennifer Farthing
Project Editor: Anne Kemper
Production Manager: Michael Shevlin
Content Manager: Patrick Kennedy
Interior Page Layout: Dave Chipps
Cover Design: Mark Weaver

Manufactured in the United States of America
Published simultaneously in Canada

December 2005

10 9 8 7 6 5 4 3 2 1

ISBN-13: 978-0-7432-6553-9
ISBN-10:   0-7432-6553-X

TABLE OF CONTENTS

Preface ix

Part One: Preparing for the ACT

Step 1: **Introduction to the ACT** 3

What Is the ACT? 5

What Is the ACT Writing Test? 5

How Is the ACT Scored? 6

How Many ACT Scores Will You Get? 6

How Do Colleges Use Your ACT Score? 7

Should You Guess on the ACT? 8

Can You Retake the Test? 8

Step 2: **The Subject Tests** 9

English 10

Math 14

Reading 16

Science 19

Writing 22

Step 3: **The Top Ten Strategies** 23

1. Do Question Triage 24

2. Put the Material into a Form You Can Understand 25

3. Ignore Irrelevant Issues 27

4. Check Back 27

5. Answer the Right Question 28

6. Look for the Hidden Answer 29

7. Guess Intelligently 30

8. Be Careful with the Answer Grid 30

9. Use the Letters of the Answer Choices to Stay on Track 31

10. Keep Track of Time 31

Take Control of Your Test 32

Part Two: The ACT English Test

Step 4: **Basic English Skills** 35

Kaplan's Three-Step Method for ACT English 36

Skimming English Passages 36

Economy Questions 37

Sense Questions 39

Nonstandard-Format English Questions 50

Step 5: **ACT English Strategies** 53

Trusting Your Ear 54

"Listening" Carefully: Practice Passage 55

Twelve Classic Grammar Errors 58

Part Three: The ACT Math Test

Step 6: **Classic Math Strategies** 67

Question Breakdown 68

Be a Thinker—Not a Number Cruncher 68

Kaplan's Three-Step Method for ACT Math 70

Definition Alert 73

Kaplan's Two-Pass Plan for ACT Math 73

Know When to Skip a Question 74

What to Do When You're Stuck 74

Step 7: **Calculator Techniques** 79

Think Before You Calculate 80

Using the Calculator to Save Time 81

Calculators: The Game Plan 82

Step 8: **Algebra, Coordinate Geometry, Percents, and Averages** 85

Textbook Algebra and Coordinate Geometry Questions 86

Complex Algebra and Coordinate Geometry Questions 87

Story Problems 93

Step 9: **Geometry** 97

Textbook Geometry Questions 97

Complex Geometry Questions 98

Part Four: The ACT Reading Test

Step 10: The Key to ACT Reading 109

Know Where You're Going. 110

Kaplan's Three-Step Method for ACT Reading. 111

Creating a Road Map 113

The Fiction and Science Passages 115

Step 11: Reading Question Types and Strategies 119

Specific Detail Questions. 123

Inference Questions 124

Big Picture Questions 125

Proven Reading Strategies 126

Part Five: The ACT Science Test

Step 12: Basic Science Techniques 131

Reading Skills for Science 132

Kaplan's Three-Step Method for ACT Science 132

Reading Tables and Graphs 133

What to Do When You're Running Out of Time 137

Step 13: Experiments 139

How Scientists Think. 139

How Experiments Work. 141

Handling Experiment Questions: Practice Passage. 142

Step 14: The Conflicting Viewpoints Passage 149

Prereading the Conflicting Viewpoints Passage 150

The Real Thing: Practice Passage and Key Strategies 152

Part Six: The ACT Writing Test

Step 15: Write What Counts 159

Just the Facts 160

How the ACT Essay Is Scored 161

Kaplan's Four-Step Method for the ACT Essay. 162

Know the Score: Sample Essays 168

Strategy Recap 174

Part Seven: Practice Test and Explanations

Practice Test 181

Answer Key 249

Answers and Explanations 251

Part Eight: ACT Resources

Last-Minute Tips 279

    Testing Timeframe 280

Stress Management 283

    Making the Most of Your Prep Time 284

pro·cras·ti·na·tor (n): one who puts off intentionally the doing of something that should be done*

Hmmm… sound like anyone you know? Let's face it: We all procrastinate. It's natural to put off doing something boring, difficult, or unpleasant (such as studying for the ACT) in favor of doing something fun. And chances are, between rushing to classes, basketball games, and your part-time job, you have barely enough time to eat or sleep, let alone study material that won't even help you pass tomorrow's biology quiz.

So now you're in a tight spot: The ACT is looming on the horizon, and, true to form, you haven't started studying yet. Wouldn't it be nice if you could use the little bits of free time you have left—the odd hour here, half-hour there—to somehow get in some solid preparation?

Well, now you can. The book you're holding in your hand is designed for the student who wants (or needs) to prepare on the run. Here you'll find just about all of the most important things you need to know before walking in to the test. And all of this information is laid out for you in 15 easy steps, so that you can learn each step fast, move on to the next activity, and get a great score when you actually take the test.

Don't get the wrong idea: This book won't give you comprehensive test preparation. Reaching your maximum score on the ACT will take a thorough, considered effort, and Kaplan publishes other books that provide a more in-depth approach. But you can still benefit from having a guide to basic skills, techniques, and strategies that will make you a better ACT test-taker.

How much of a difference can this last-minute help make? Consider this: You can boost your score just by getting a couple of extra questions correct on each section! But you won't accomplish this by getting bogged down with long vocabulary lists and reams of math principles. You can do it by absorbing our targeted test-taking strategies in the following pages. That way, your energies will be focused on the essential elements of the exam—places where you can really boost your score easily.

So don't panic. You might think you need 25 hours in a day to get everything done, but with *The Procrastinator's Guide to the ACT* in hand, you still have an opportunity to boost your score.

*Merriam-Webster's Collegiate® Dictionary, Eleventh Edition

Test Prep and Admissions

kaptest.com/publishing

The material in this book is up-to-date at the time of publication. However, ACT, Inc. may have instituted changes in the test after this book was published. Be sure to carefully read the materials you receive when you register for the test. If there are any important late-breaking developments—or any changes or corrections to the Kaplan test preparation materials in this book—we will post that information online at **kaptest.com/publishing**.

kaplansurveys.com/books

We'd love to hear your comments and suggestions about this book. We invite you to fill out our online survey form at **kaplansurveys.com/books**. Your feedback is extremely helpful as we continue to develop high-quality resources to meet your needs.

Part One

PREPARING FOR THE ACT

Introduction to the ACT

STEP ONE PREVIEW

What Is the ACT?

What Is the ACT Writing Test?

How Is the ACT Scored?

How Many ACT Scores Will You Get?

How Do Colleges Use Your ACT Score?

Should You Guess on the ACT?

Can You Retake the Test?

You've probably heard rumors to the effect that the ACT is a tough exam. Well, the rumors are true. In fact, the ACT is probably one of the toughest exams you'll ever take.

Should that faze you, given that you have only a few weeks before you take the exam? No. Honestly. For one thing, if you carry out the program outlined in this book, you'll have done more preparation for the ACT than most other people sitting with you in the examination room. And since the test is marked "on a curve," your weeks of preparation will definitely put you at an advantage over your peers.

But you've got some work to do between now and then. That's why it's so important that you take the test in the right spirit. Don't be timid in the face of the ACT. Don't let it bully you. You've got to take control of the test. Our mission in this book is to show you exactly how to do that—in a few short weeks.

Here are the three things you'll learn that will enable you to take control of the ACT.

You'll Learn the Test Format

The ACT is very predictable. You'd think the test makers would get bored after a while, but they don't. The same kinds of questions, testing the same skills and concepts, appear every time the ACT is given. The exception to this rule is the optional Writing test. But don't worry: this book includes many useful tips—including the Kaplan Method for the ACT Essay—that will help you master this portion of the exam should you decide to take it.

Because the test specifications rarely change, you should know in advance what to expect on every section. Just a little familiarity with the directions and common question types can make an enormous difference.

You'll Learn Test Strategies

The ACT isn't a normal exam. Normal exams test mostly your memory. But the ACT tests problem-solving skills as well as memory, and it does so in a standardized test format. That makes the test highly vulnerable to test-smart strategies and techniques.

Most students miss a lot of ACT questions for no good reason. They see a tough-looking question, say to themselves, "Uh-oh, I don't remember how to do that," and start to gnaw on their No. 2 pencils.

But many ACT questions can be answered without complete knowledge of the material being tested. Often, all you need to do to succeed is to think strategically and creatively.

You'll Learn the Concepts Tested

The ACT is designed to test skills and concepts learned in high school and needed for college. Familiarity with the test, coupled with smart test-taking strategies, will take you only so far. For your best score you need to sharpen the skills and knowledge that the ACT rewards. In other words, sometimes you've just got to eat your spinach.

The good news is that most ACT content is pretty basic. You've probably already learned in high school most of what the ACT expects you to know. But you may need help remembering.

In short, follow these three principles:

- Learn the test format
- Learn test strategies
- Learn the concepts tested

If you do, you'll find yourself in full command of your ACT test taking experience.

WHAT IS THE ACT?

Okay, let's start with the basics. The ACT is a three-hour exam (two hours and 55 minutes, to be precise) taken by high school juniors and seniors for admission to college. Contrary to the myths you may have heard, the ACT is not an IQ test. It's a test of problem-solving skills—which means that you can improve your performance by preparing for it.

All students who take the ACT complete four subject tests: English, Math, Reading, and Science. All four subject tests are designed primarily to test skills rather than knowledge, though some knowledge is required—particularly in English, for which knowledge of grammar and writing mechanics is important, and in Math, for which you need to know the basic math concepts taught in a regular high school curriculum.

The ACT:

- Is about three hours long.
- Includes a short break (between the second and third subtests).
- Consists of a total of 215 scored questions.
- Comprises four subject tests:
    English (45 minutes, 75 questions)
    Math (60 minutes, 60 questions)
    Reading (35 minutes, 40 questions)
    Science (35 minutes, 40 questions)
- Includes an optional Writing test:
    Writing (30 minutes, 1 essay question)

WHAT IS THE NEW ACT WRITING TEST?

In early 2005, the ACT added an optional 30-minute Writing test. Colleges and universities have the option to make the Writing test a requirement for admission or to use the results to determine course placement. Students who are applying to college for the fall of 2006 or later can decide whether to take the Writing portion of the ACT based on the requirements of the schools to which they plan to apply. For this optional test, students write an essay in response to a prompt that asks them to take a stand on an issue. The ACT Assessment Plus Writing takes approximately three hours and 40 minutes to complete.

Should You Take the Writing Test?

Find out the requirements of the schools to which you're applying so you can determine whether to complete the essay on test day.

HOW IS THE ACT SCORED?

No, your ACT score is not merely the sum total of questions you get right. That would be too simple. Instead, what the test makers do is add up all of your correct answers to get what they call a "raw score." Then they put that raw score into a very large computer, which proceeds to shake, rattle, smoke, and wheeze before spitting out an official score at the other end. That score—which has been put through what they call a scoring formula—is your "scaled score."

ACT scaled scores range from 1 to 36. Nearly half of all test takers score within a much narrower range: 17 to 23. Tests at different dates vary slightly, but the following data are based on a recent administration of the test and can be considered typical:

Percentile Rank*	Scaled (or Composite) Score	Approximate Percentage Correct
99%	31	90%
90%	26	75%
76%	23	63%
54%	20	53%
28%	17	43%

*Percentage of ACT takers scoring at or below given score

To earn a score of 20 (the national average), you need to answer only about 53 percent of the questions correctly. On most tests, getting only a bit more than half the questions right would be terrible. Not so on the ACT. That fact alone should ease some of your anxiety about how hard this test is. You can miss loads of ACT questions and still get a good score. Nobody expects you to get all of the questions right.

HOW MANY ACT SCORES WILL YOU GET?

The "ACT scaled score" we've talked about so far is technically called the "composite score." It's the really important one. But when you take the ACT, you actually receive 12 (or 14, depending on whether you take the Writing test) different scores: the composite score, four (or five) subject scores, and seven (or eight) subscores.

Students who take the Writing test will receive a combined English-Writing Score in addition to the four regular subject scores. They will also receive a Writing subscore (2–12) for their essay. The English-Writing score will not be factored into the overall composite score, unlike the other four subject test scores.

KAPLAN

Following is a breakdown of the subject scores and subscores. Though the subject scores can play a role in decisions at some schools, the subscores usually aren't important for most people.

1. English Score (1–36)
   - Usage/Mechanics Subscore (1–18)
   - Rhetorical Skills Subscore (1–18)

2. Math Score (1–36)
   - Prealgebra/Elementary Algebra Subscore (1–18)
   - Algebra/Coordinate Geometry Subscore (1–18)
   - Plane Geometry/Trigonometry Subscore (1–18)

3. Reading Score (1–36)
   - Social Sciences/Sciences Subscore (1–18)
   - Arts/Literature Subscore (1–18)

4. Science Score (1–36)
   (There are no subscores in Science.)

5. (Optional) Combined English-Writing Score (1–36)
   - Writing Subscore (2–12)

HOW DO COLLEGES USE YOUR ACT SCORE?

You may have heard that the ACT is really the only thing colleges look at when deciding whether to admit you. Untrue. Most admissions officers say the ACT is only one of several factors they take into consideration. But let's be realistic. Here's this neat and easy way of comparing all students numerically, no matter what their academic backgrounds and no matter how much grade inflation exists at their high schools. You know the admissions people are going to take a serious look at your scores.

The most important score, naturally, is the composite score (which is an average of the four subject scores). This is the score used by most colleges and universities in the admissions process, and the one that you'll want to mention casually at parties during your freshman year of college. The four subject scores and seven subscores on the regular ACT may be used for advanced placement or occasionally for scholarships, but are primarily used by college advisors to help students select majors and first-year courses. Colleges that require the Writing test may use the Writing subscore as part of the admissions process or to determine advanced placement.

Although many schools deny that they use benchmark scores as cutoffs, we're not sure we really believe them. Big Ten universities and colleges with similarly competitive admissions generally decline to accept students with composite scores below 22 or 23. For less competitive schools, the benchmark score may be lower than that; for some very strong schools, the cutoff may be higher.

To be fair, no school uses the ACT score as an absolute bar to admission, no matter how low it is. But for most applicants, a low ACT score is decisive. As a rule, only students whose backgrounds are extremely unusual or who have overcome enormous disadvantages are accepted if their ACT scores are below the benchmark.

SHOULD YOU GUESS ON THE ACT?

The short answer? Yes! The long answer? Yes, of course!

As we said, ACT scores are based on the number of correct answers only. This means that questions left blank and questions answered incorrectly simply don't count. Unlike some other standardized tests, the ACT has no wrong-answer penalty. That's why you should always guess on every ACT question you can't answer, even if you don't have time to read it. Though the questions vary enormously in difficulty, harder questions are worth exactly the same as easier ones, so it pays to guess on the really hard questions and spend your time breezing through the really easy ones. We'll show you just how to do this in the step called "The Top Ten Strategies."

CAN YOU RETAKE THE TEST?

You can take the ACT as many times as you like. You can then select whichever test score you prefer to be sent to colleges when you apply.

When you sign up for the ACT, you have the option of designating colleges to receive your score. Think twice before you do it! Wait until you receive your score, then send it along if you're happy. This may cost you a few extra dollars (since you won't get to take advantage of the three free reports you get if you designate schools on the registration form before the test), but we think it's worth the extra expense. If you hate your score, you can take the test again and send only the new, improved score. (Seniors, beware! Make sure there is enough time to get your scores in by the application deadline.)

Important

Don't automatically designate colleges to receive score reports at the time of registration. If you have time, wait until you're sure you've gotten a score you're proud of.

What this means, of course, is that even if you blow the ACT once, you can give yourself another shot without the schools of your choice knowing about it. The ACT is one of the few areas of your academic life in which you get a second chance.

STEP TWO

The Subject Tests

STEP TWO PREVIEW

English
- Format
- Directions
- To Omit or Not to Omit
- Nonstandard-Format Questions

Math
- Format
- Directions
- Reading and Drawing Diagrams
- How to Approach that Story
- Getting the Concept

Reading
- Format
- Directions
- Reading Passages
- Nailing Down the Details
- Making an Inference
- Getting the Big Picture

Science
- Format
- Directions
- Analyzing Data
- Conducting Experiments
- The Principle of the Thing

Writing
- Format and Directions

Okay, you've seen how the ACT is set up. But to really know the test, you've got to know something about the ACT subject tests (which, by the way, always appear in the following order):

- English
- Math
- Reading
- Science
- Writing (Optional)

As you'll see, the questions in every subject test vary widely in difficulty. Some are so easy that most elementary school students could answer them. Others might give even college students a little trouble. But, again, the questions are not arranged in order of difficulty. That's different from some other tests, in which easier questions come first. Skipping past hard questions is important, since otherwise you may never reach easy ones at the end of the exam.

Don't Get Bogged Down

Skip past hard questions so that you can quickly rack up points on easier questions.

Here's a preview of the types of questions you'll encounter on the subject tests. We'll keep the questions toward the easy end of the difficulty scale here, since you're just becoming familiar with the test. Later, we'll be less kind.

ENGLISH

Statistic

The English test is 45 minutes long and includes 75 questions. That works out to about 30 seconds per question. The test is divided into five passages, each with about 15 questions.

Students nearly always get more questions correct in English than in any other section. That tends to make them think that English is a lot easier than the rest of the ACT. But, alas, it's not that simple. Because most students do well, the test makers have much higher expectations for English than for other parts of the test. That's why, to earn an average English subscore (a 20, say), you have to get almost two-thirds of the questions right, while on the rest of the test you need to get only about half right.

Note too that you have less time per question on the English test than on any of the other three tests. You'll have to move fast.

Keep Moving

Never spend more than 45 seconds or so on an English question.

Format

Almost all of the English questions follow a standard format. A word, phrase, or sentence in a passage is underlined. You're given four options: to leave the underlined portion alone ("NO CHANGE," which is always the first choice), or to replace it with one of three alternatives. For example:

. . . Pike's Peak in Southwest

Colorado is named <u>before Zebulon</u>
                        37
<u>Pike, an early explorer.</u> He traveled
                  37
through the area, exploring . . .

37. **A.** NO CHANGE
         B. before Zebulon Pike became an explorer,
         C. after Zebulon Pike, when,
         D. after Zebulon Pike.

The best answer choice is D. The other choices all have various problems—grammatical, stylistic, logical. They make the passage look and sound as if it were written by your baby brother.

How Does That Sound?

In English, trust your ears. The right answer is usually the one that "sounds right" to you.

Notice that a single question can test different kinds of writing errors. We find that about one-third of the English questions test writing economy (we call them Economy questions), about another third test for logic and sense (Sense questions), and the remaining third test hard-and-fast rules of grammar (Technicality questions). There's overlap between these question types, so don't worry too much about categories. We provide them to give you an idea of the kinds of errors you'll be expected to correct.

Directions

The directions on the English test illustrate why there's an advantage to knowing the directions before test day. The English directions are long and complicated. We're going to show you what they look like, but take our advice: Don't bother reading them. We'll show you exactly what you need to do. Then, while everyone else is reading the directions on the day of the test, you'll be racking up points.

Directions: In the following five passages, certain words and phrases have been underlined and numbered. You will find alternatives for each underlined portion in the right-hand column. Select the one that best expresses the idea, that makes the statement acceptable in standard written English, or that is phrased most consistently with the style and tone of the entire passage. If you feel that the original version is best, select "NO CHANGE." You will also find questions asking about a section of the passage or about the entire passage.

For these questions, decide which choice gives the most appropriate response to the given question. For each question in the test, select the best choice and fill in the corresponding space on the answer folder. You may wish to read each passage through before you begin to answer the questions associated with it. Most answers cannot be determined without reading several sentences around the phrases in question. Make sure to read far enough ahead each time you choose an alternative.

You read the directions anyway, didn't you? Well, that's okay. You'll never have to do it again.

Know the Directions

Don't waste time reading directions on test day.

To Omit or Not to Omit

Some English questions offer, as one alternative, the chance to completely omit the underlined portion, usually as the last of the four choices. For example:

... Later, Pike fell while valiantly defending America in the War of 1812. It goes without saying
that this took place after he
discovered Pike's Peak. He
actually died near York (now called Toronto)....

40. **F.** NO CHANGE
    G. Clearly, this must have occurred subsequent to his discovering Pike's Peak.
    H. This was after he found Pike's Peak.
    J. OMIT the underlined portion.

Nonstandard-Format Questions

Some English questions—usually about 10 per exam—don't follow this standard format. These items pose a question and offer four possible responses. In many cases, the responses are either "yes" or "no," with an explanation. Pay attention to the reasoning.

... Later, Pike fell while valiantly defending America in the War of 1812. [40] He actually died

40. Suppose the author considered adding the following sentence at this point:

"It goes without saying that this occurred after he discovered Pike's Peak." Given the overall purpose of the passage, would this sentence be appropriate?
   F. No, because the sentence adds nothing to the meaning of the passage.
   G. No, because the passage is not concerned with Pike's achievements.
   H. Yes, because otherwise the sequence of events would be unclear.
   J. Yes; though the sentence is not needed, the author recognizes this fact by using the phrase "it goes without saying."

The correct answer for question 40 is F. Though G correctly indicates that the sentence doesn't belong in the passage, it offers a pretty inappropriate reason. Choices H and J, meanwhile, are wrong because they recommend including a sentence that's clearly redundant.

Many of the nonstandard questions occur at the end of a passage. Some ask about the meaning, purpose, or tone of the text. Others ask you to evaluate it, and still others ask you to determine the proper order of words, sentences, or paragraphs that have been scrambled.

We think you'll like the English subject test. It can actually be fun, which is probably why the test makers put it first. We'll cover strategies for the question types in the two English steps later.

MATH

Statistic

The Math test is 60 minutes long and includes 60 questions. That works out to a minute a question, but some will take more time than that, some less.

Format

All of the Math questions have the same multiple-choice format. They ask a question and offer five possible choices (unlike questions on the other three subject tests, which have only *four* choices each).

The questions cover a full range of math topics, from prealgebra and elementary algebra through intermediate algebra, coordinate geometry, plane geometry, and even trigonometry.

Although the Math questions, like those in other sections, aren't ordered in terms of difficulty, questions drawn from the elementary school or junior high curricula tend to come earlier in the section, while those from high school curricula tend to come later. But this doesn't mean that the easy questions come first and the hardest ones come later. We've found that high school subjects tend to be fresher in most students' minds than things they were taught years ago, so you may actually find the later questions easier.

Directions

Here's what the Math directions will look like:

Directions: Solve each of the following problems, select the correct answer, and then fill in the corresponding space on your answer sheet.

Don't linger over problems that are too time-consuming. Do as many as you can, then come back to the others in the time you have remaining.

Calculator use is allowed, but some problems may best be done without a calculator.

Note: Unless otherwise noted, all of the following should be assumed.

1. Illustrative figures are not necessarily drawn to scale.

2. All geometric figures lie in a plane.

3. The term *line* indicates a straight line.

4. The term *average* indicates arithmetic mean.

Again, when it comes to directions on the ACT, the golden rule is: Don't read them! You'll already know what they say by the time you take the test.

Of the four special notes at the end of the Math directions, numbers 2, 3, and 4 almost go without saying. Note 1—that figures are not necessarily drawn to scale—seems pretty scary, but in fact the vast majority of ACT figures are drawn to scale (a fact that, as we'll see, has significant implications for how to guess on geometry questions).

Reading and Drawing Diagrams

We find that about one-third of the Math questions either give you a diagram or describe a situation that should be diagrammed. For these questions, the diagrams are crucial. For example:

1. The figure below contains five congruent triangles. The longest side of each triangle is 4 meters long. What is the area of the whole figure?

    A. 12.5 square meters

    B. 15 square meters

    C. 20 square meters

    D. 30 square meters

    E. Cannot be determined from the given information

The key to this question is to let the diagram tell you what you need to know—that each triangle represents one-quarter of the area of the square, and that the sides of the square are 4 meters (you can figure this out because the top side of the square is the hypotenuse—or longest side—of the triangle that makes the "roof"). Since the area of a square can be found by squaring the side, the area of the square is 16 square meters. Thus, each triangle has an area one-fourth as much—4 square meters. Since the whole figure consists of five triangles, each with area 4, the total area is $5 \times 4 = 20$. The answer is C.

How to Approach that Story

About another third of the Math questions are story problems like the following:

2. Evan drove halfway home at 20 miles per hour, then sped up and drove the rest of the way at 30 miles per hour. What was his average speed for the entire trip?

    F. 20 miles per hour

    G. 22 miles per hour

    H. 24 miles per hour

    J. 25 miles per hour

    K. 28 miles per hour

A good way to comprehend—and resolve—a story problem like this is to think of a real situation that's similar. What if Evan had 120 miles to drive? (It helps to pick a distance that's easily divisible by both rates.) He would go 60 miles at 30 mph, then 60 miles at 20 mph. How long would it take? 60 miles at 30 mph is 2 hours; 60 miles at 20 mph is 3 hours. That's a total of 120 miles in 5 hours; 120 divided by 5 gives an average speed of 24 mph. Thus, the answer is H. (Note: We'll show you alternative ways to answer questions like this later.)

Getting the Concept

Finally, about one-third of the math questions directly ask you to demonstrate your knowledge of specific math concepts.

3. If angles A and B are supplementary, and the measure of angle A is 57°, what is the measure, in degrees, of angle B ?

   A. 33
   B. 43
   C. 47
   D. 123
   E. 147

This question simply requires that you know the concept of "supplementary angles." Two angles are supplementary when they form a straight line—in other words, when they add up to 180°. So, the question boils down to this: What number, added to 57, makes 180? The answer is D.

READING

Statistic

The Reading test is 35 minutes long and includes 40 questions. The test contains four passages, each of which is followed by 10 questions. When you factor out the amount of time you'll initially spend on the passages, this works out to about 30 seconds per question—again, more for some, less for others.

Format

There are four categories of Reading passages: Social Studies, Natural Sciences, Humanities, and Prose Fiction. You'll get one passage in each category. The passages are about 1,000 words long and are written at about the same difficulty level as college textbooks and readings.

The Social Studies, Natural Sciences, and Humanities passages are usually well-organized essays. Each has a very specific theme. Questions expect you to recognize this theme, to comprehend specific facts contained in the passage, and to understand the structure of the essay. Prose Fiction passages require you to understand the thoughts, feelings, and motivations of fictional characters, even when these are not explicitly stated in the passage.

Whatever the type of passage, it's important that you skim it quickly rather than read it carefully. It's crucial not to get bogged down. You can always deal with the details later, if and when they become relevant.

Save Time by Skimming

Skim the passages; do not read them carefully!

After each passage, you'll find 10 questions. There are really only three different categories of Reading questions:

- Specific Detail questions
- Inference questions
- Big Picture questions

Directions

Here's what the Reading directions will look like:

Directions: This test contains four passages, each followed by several questions. After reading a passage, select the best answer to each question and fill in the corresponding oval on your answer sheet. You are allowed to refer to the passages while answering the questions.

Nothing stupefying here. But nothing very substantive, either. We'll be a little more specific and strategic than the test makers are when we suggest a plan of attack in the two Reading steps.

Reading Passages

What follows is a sample minipassage. Note that this passage is much shorter than the ones you'll see on the test. We provide it here to give you an idea of the kind of material you'll see, and to generate material for the three sample reading questions that follow. In the two reading steps later on, we'll give you a full-length Reading passage, with questions.

Recent geological studies have demonstrated the existence of huge deposits of gas hydrate, a frozen compound consisting of flammable methane gas trapped in ice, on continental shelves around the globe. These deposits, which exist under extreme pressure at a depth of 1,500 feet under the ocean floor, are believed to contain twice as much potential carbon energy as all fossil fuels combined. Efforts to mine this "burnable ice," however, will pose one of the great engineering problems of the next century. Ocean floor avalanches, set off by mining activity, could conceivably release vast amounts of methane into the atmosphere, setting off an intensified "greenhouse effect" that could significantly alter the world's climate.

Nailing Down the Details

Here's a Specific Detail question that might come after the minipassage above:

1. According to the passage, a major obstacle to the successful mining of gas hydrate is:

    A. the inaccessibility of the deposits.
    B. recent climatic changes caused by the "greenhouse effect."
    C. the potential of mining accidents to cause environmental harm.
    D. the danger posed by methane gas to the health of miners.

Specific Detail questions ask about things stated explicitly in the passage. The challenge with them is, first, finding the proper place in the passage where the answer can be found (sometimes you'll be given a line reference, sometimes not), and second, being able to match up what you see in the passage with the correct answer, which will probably be worded differently.

The mention of the "major obstacle" in the question stem should have led you to the last sentence in the passage, where the potential problems of gas hydrate mining are specified: Avalanches (mining accidents) could release methane into the atmosphere (environmental harm). That's why C is correct here.

Notice how some wrong choices are designed to trip you up by including details from other parts of the passage, or by using the same wording that the passage uses while distorting the meaning.

Making an Inference

Most Reading passages also include a large number of Inference questions, which require you to make an inference from the passage (to "read between the lines"). They differ somewhat from Specific Detail questions. For one thing, students usually consider them harder.

2. It can be inferred that gas hydrate can be used for energy because it:

    F. is under great pressure.
    G. contains gas that can be burned.
    H. will contribute to the greenhouse effect.
    J. is frozen.

Here you have to put two and two together. You're told that gas hydrate contains "flammable methane gas." Later, the gas hydrate is referred to as "burnable ice." Since ice is not normally burnable, it must be the methane in the ice that allows it to be burned, creating energy. G is correct.

Getting the Big Picture

Although the majority of Reading questions are Specific Detail and Inference questions like those above, some will be what we call Big Picture questions. Some Big Picture questions require you to find the theme, tone, or structure of the passage. Others ask you to evaluate the writing.

3. The author's main purpose in the passage above is to do which of the following?

    A. advocate the mining of gas hydrate deposits
    B. show how scientists are looking for alternatives to fossil fuels
    C. argue that the risks of deep-sea mining are too great
    D. describe a potential new energy source

The best choice here is D, since it is general enough to describe the full passage (the potential new energy source being gas hydrate), but it's not overly general or broad (like B), and it doesn't introduce value judgments that are not really present in the passage (as A and C do, by implying that the author either advocates or condemns gas hydrate mining).

We'll discuss strategies for all passage types and question types in the two Reading steps.

SCIENCE

Statistic

The Science test is 35 minutes long and includes 40 questions. The test contains seven passages, each followed by five to seven questions. Factoring out the amount of time you'll initially spend on the passage leaves you a little more than 30 seconds for each question.

No, you don't have to be a scientist to succeed on this test. All that's required is common sense (though a knowledge of standard scientific processes and procedures sure does help). You'll be given passages containing various kinds of scientific information—drawn from the fields of biology, chemistry, physics, geology, astronomy, and meteorology—that you'll have to understand and use as a basis for inferences.

Format

Three (or so) passages will present scientific data and three passages will discuss specific experiments. There's also usually one passage in which two scientists state opposing views on the same issue. Each passage will generate five to seven questions. A warning: Some of these passages will be very difficult to understand, but to make up for that fact, there will be easy questions attached to them. The test makers do show a little mercy once in a while.

Directions

Here's what the Science directions will look like:

Directions: Each of the following seven passages is followed by several questions. After reading each passage, decide on the best answer to each question and fill in the corresponding oval on your answer sheet. You are allowed to refer to the passages while answering the questions. Calculator use is not allowed on this test.

Sounds a lot like the set of directions for Reading, doesn't it? Not much substance here, either. But don't worry. We'll show you the best strategic way to attack the Science Reasoning subject test in the three Science steps.

Analyzing Data

About one-third of the questions on the Science test require you to read data from graphs or tables. In easier questions, you'll need only to report the information. In harder questions, you may need to draw inferences or note patterns in the data. For example:

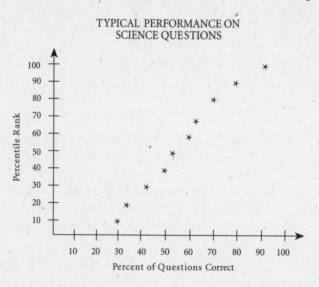

TYPICAL PERFORMANCE ON
SCIENCE QUESTIONS

1. A test taker who scores in approximately the 40th percentile has correctly answered about what fraction of the questions?

   A. $\dfrac{9}{10}$

   B. $\dfrac{2}{3}$

   C. $\dfrac{1}{2}$

   D. $\dfrac{1}{5}$

The correct answer is C. The point with 40th percentile as its *y*-coordinate has an *x*-coordinate approximately above the 50 percent point on the horizontal axis (percent correct). Fifty percent is the same as $\frac{1}{2}$. Note that this question involves a little simple arithmetic (translating a percent into a fraction)—not uncommon for Science questions.

Conducting Experiments

Other Science questions require that you understand how experiments are designed and what they prove.

A scientist adds one drop of nitric acid to beakers A, B, and C. Each beaker contains water from a different stream. The water in beaker A came from Stream A, that in beaker B came from Stream B, and that in beaker C came from Stream C. In beakers B and C, small precipitates form, but not in beaker A.

12. Which of the following could properly be inferred on the basis of the experiment?
   F. Stream A is more polluted than Streams B or C.
   G. Streams B and C are more polluted than Stream A.
   H. Stream A contains material that neutralizes nitric acid.
   J. Streams B and C contain some substance that reacts in the presence of nitric acid.

The answer is J. Since a precipitate forms when nitric acid is added to beakers B and C, which contain water from streams B and C, something in these streams must be involved. However, we don't know that it is pollution, so choices F and G are unwarranted. We also don't know exactly why no precipitate formed in beaker A, so H is also an unwarranted conclusion.

The Principle of the Thing

The remaining Science questions require you either to apply a principle logically, or to identify ways to defend or attack a principle. Some questions will involve two scientists stating opposing views on the same subject. Or, a passage might describe a theory about how "V-shaped" valleys are typically formed on Earth—by water erosion through soft rock. Then the following question might be asked:

16. Which of the following is most likely to be a V-shaped valley?
   F. A valley formed by glaciers
   G. A river valley that is cut into very hard basalt
   H. A valley formed by wind erosion
   J. A river valley in a region of soft shale rocks

The answer is J, since this is consistent with the passage as described.

WRITING

Statistic

The Writing test is 30 minutes long and features one essay question. While it is an optional section on the ACT, many colleges require it.

Format and Directions

The Writing test asks students to take a position on an issue and support it with evidence, in a persuasive essay. The directions will look like this (the final paragraph is always the same):

In many high schools, the administration has provided guidelines for the publication of student newspapers. These guidelines often determine which topics can and cannot be discussed in the newspaper and prohibit what the administration deems inappropriate language. Many administrators and teachers feel that these restrictions enable them to provide a safe learning environment for students. Others feel that any restriction on the student newspaper is a violation of freedom of speech. In your opinion, should high schools place restrictions on student newspapers?

In your essay, take a position on this question. You may write about either one of the two points of view given, or you may present a different point of view on this question. Use specific reasons and examples to support your position.

For more information on the Writing test, turn to Step 15: Write What Counts.

KAPLAN

STEP THREE

The Top Ten Strategies

STEP THREE PREVIEW

1. **Do Question Triage**

2. **Put the Material into a Form You Can Understand**
   - Mark Up Your Test Booklet
   - Reword the Questions
   - Draw Diagrams

3. **Ignore Irrelevant Issues**

4. **Check Back**

5. **Answer the Right Question**

6. **Look for the Hidden Answer**

7. **Guess Intelligently**

8. **Be Careful with the Answer Grid**

9. **Use the Letters of the Answer Choices to Stay on Track**

10. **Keep Track of Time**

Take Control of Your Test

Now that you have some idea of the kind of adversary you face in the ACT, it's time to start developing strategies for dealing with this adversary. Here are the top ten general test strategies for success on the ACT.

1. DO QUESTION TRIAGE

In a hospital emergency room, the triage nurse is the person who evaluates each patient and decides which ones get attention first and which ones should be treated later. You should do the same thing on the ACT.

Performing question triage is one of the most important ways of controlling your test-taking experience. There are some questions on the ACT that most students could never answer correctly, no matter how much time or effort they spent on them. For example:

57. If $\sec^2 x = 4$, which of the following could be $\sin x$?

   A. 1.73205

   B. 3.14159

   C. $\sqrt{3}$

   D. $\dfrac{\sqrt{3}}{2}$

   E. Cannot be determined from the given information.

Clearly, even if you could manage to come up with an answer to this question, it would take some time. But would it be worth the time? We think not.

This question clearly illustrates our point: You should perform question triage on the ACT. The first time you look at each question, make a quick decision about how hard and time-consuming it looks. Then decide whether to answer it now or skip it and do it later. Here's how:

- If the question looks comprehensible and of reasonable difficulty, do it right away.
- If the question looks tough and time-consuming, but ultimately "doable," skip it, circle the question number and come back to it later.
- If the question looks impossible, forget about it. Guess and move on.

For the English, Reading, and Science sections, the best plan of attack is to do each passage as a block. Make a longish first pass through the questions (the "triage" pass), doing the easy ones, guessing on the impossible ones, and skipping any that look like they might cause trouble. Then, make a second pass (the "cleanup" pass) and do those questions you think you can solve with some elbow grease. This will be easier if you've marked these questions in your test booklet. For Math, you use the same two-pass strategy, except that you move through the whole subject test twice.

Kaplan's Two-Pass Plan

Make two passes through each group of questions—a triage pass and a cleanup pass.

Make sure you take pains to grid your answers in the right place. It's easy to misgrid when you're skipping around, so be careful. And of course: Be certain you have an answer gridded for every question by the time the test is over!

2. PUT THE MATERIAL INTO A FORM YOU CAN UNDERSTAND

ACT questions are rarely presented in the simplest, most helpful way. In fact, your main job for many questions is to figure out what the question means so you can solve it.

Since the material is presented in such an intimidating way, one of your best strategies is to recast (reword) the material into a form you can handle.

Mark Up Your Test Booklet

This strategy should be employed on all four subject tests. In Reading, for example, the passages can be overwhelming. There are 85 to 90 lines of dense verbiage for each one! But the secret is to put the passages into a form you can understand and use. Circle or underline the main idea, for one thing. And make yourself a road map of the passage, making brief notes about each paragraph so you understand how it all fits together. That way, you'll also know *where* to find certain types of information you'll need.

Reword the Questions

You'll find that you also need to do some recasting of the questions. For instance, take the following question stem.

15. According to Figure 1, at approximately what latitude would calculations using an estimated value at sea level of $g = 9.80$ m/sec^2 produce the least error?

   A.   0°

   B.   20°

   C.   40°

   D.   80°

Figure 1

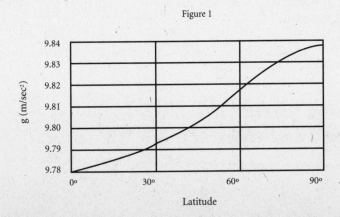

Latitude

At what latitude would the calculations using a value of g = 9.80 m/sec² produce the least error? Yikes! What does that mean?

Take a deep breath. Ask yourself: Where would an estimate of 9.80 m/sec² produce the least error? In a latitude where 9.80 m/sec² is the real value of *g*. If you find the latitude at which the real value of *g* is 9.80 m/sec², then using 9.80 m/sec² as an estimate there would produce no error at all!

So, in other words, what this question is asking is: At what latitude does *g* = 9.80 m/sec²? In that form, you can answer it easily. The answer is choice C, which you can get just by reading the chart.

Draw Diagrams

Sometimes, putting the material into usable form involves drawing with your pencil.

2. Jason bought a painting with a frame 1 inch wide. If the dimensions of the outside of the frame are 5 inches by 7 inches, which of the following could be the length of one side of the painting inside the frame?

   F.   3 inches

   G.   4 inches

   H. $5\frac{1}{2}$ inches

   J. $6\frac{1}{2}$ inches

   K.   7 inches

Just looking at the question the first time, you might be tempted simply to subtract 1 inch from the outside dimensions and think that the inside dimensions are 4 by 6 inches (and pick G). Why isn't this correct? Because the frame goes all the way around—both above and below the painting, both to the right and to the left. This would have been clear if you had put the problem in a form you could understand and use.

You might make the situation graphic by actually sketching out the painting frame:

When you draw the picture frame like this, you realize that if the outside dimensions are 5 by 7 inches, the inside dimensions must be 3 by 5 inches. Thus, the correct answer is F.

What Does That Say?

Put everything into a form you can understand.

---

3. IGNORE IRRELEVANT ISSUES

It's easy to waste time on ACT questions by considering irrelevant issues. Just because an issue looks interesting, or just because you're worried about something, doesn't make it important. For example:

... China was certainly one of

the cradles of civilization. <u>It's</u>
                             14
<u>obvious that, China has a long</u>
            14
<u>history.</u> As is the case with
   14
other ancient cultures, the early

history of China is lost in

mythology. ...

14. F. NO CHANGE
     G. It's obvious that China has a long history.
     H. Obviously; China has a long history.
     J. OMIT the underlined portion.

In this question, the test makers are counting on you to waste time worrying about punctuation. Does that comma belong? Can you use a semicolon here? These issues might be worrisome, but there's a much bigger issue here—namely, does the sentence belong in the passage at all? No, it doesn't. If China has an ancient culture and was a cradle of civilization, it must have a long history, so the sentence really is "obvious." Redundancy is the relevant issue here, not punctuation. Choice J is correct.

4. CHECK BACK

Remember, all of the information you need is in the test itself. You shouldn't be afraid to refer to it.

In Reading and Science, always refer to the place in the passage where the answer to a question can be found (the question stem will often contain a line reference or a reference to a specific table, graph, or experiment to help you out). Your chosen answer should match the passage—not in exact vocabulary or units of measurement, perhaps, but in meaning.

Checking back is especially important in Reading and Science, because the passages leave many people feeling adrift in a sea of details. Often, the wrong answers will be "misplaced details"—details taken from different parts of the passage. These misplaced details don't answer the question properly but might sound good to you if you aren't careful. By checking back with the passage, you can avoid making such wrong choices.

There's another important lesson here: Don't pick an answer just because it contains "keywords" you remember from the passage. Many wrong answer choices are distortions; they use the right words but say the wrong things about them. Look for choices that contain the same ideas you find in the passage.

5. ANSWER THE RIGHT QUESTION

This strategy is a natural extension of the last. As we said, the ACT test makers often include among the wrong answers to a question the *correct answer to a different question*. Under time pressure, it's easy for you to fall for one of these red herrings, thinking that you know what's being asked for when you really don't. For example:

7. What is the value of $3x$ if $9x = 5y + 2$ and $y + 4 = 2y - 10$?

   A. 5
   B. 8
   C. 14
   D. 24
   E. 72

To solve this problem, we need to find y first, even though the question asks about x (because x here is given only in terms of y). You could solve the second equation like this:

$y + 4 = 2y - 10$ given
$4 = y - 10$ by subtracting y from both sides
$14 = y$ by adding 10 to both sides

But C, 14, isn't the right answer here, because the question doesn't ask for y—it asks about x. We can use the value of y to find x, however, by plugging the calculated value of y into the first equation:

$9x = 5y + 2$ given
$9x = 5(14) + 2$ because $y = 14$
$9x = 70 + 2$ $5 \times 14 = 70$
$9x = 72$

But E, 72, isn't the answer either, because the question doesn't ask for $9x$. It doesn't ask for x either, so if you picked B, 8, you'd be wrong as well. Remember to refer to the question! The question asks for $3x$. So we need to divide $9x$ by 3:

$$9x = 72 \qquad \text{from above}$$
$$3x = 24 \qquad \text{dividing by 3}$$

Thus, the answer is D.

Doing all the right work but then getting the wrong answer can be seriously depressing. So be sure to answer the right question.

What Was the Question?

Check the question stem again before choosing an answer.

6. LOOK FOR THE HIDDEN ANSWER

On many ACT questions, the right answer is hidden in one way or another. It might be hidden by being written in a way that you aren't likely to expect. For example, you might work out a problem and get .5 as your answer, but then find that .5 isn't among the answer choices. Then you notice that one choice reads "$\frac{1}{2}$."

But there's another way the ACT can hide answers. Many ACT questions have more than one possible right solution, though only one correct answer choice is given. Often, the ACT will hide that answer by offering one of the less obvious possible answers to a question. For example:

2. If $3x^2 + 5 = 17$, which of the following could be the value of x?

A. -3
B. -2
C. 0
D. 1
E. 4

You quickly solve this very straightforward problem like so:

$$3x^2 + 5 = 17 \qquad \text{given}$$
$$3x^2 = 12 \qquad \text{by subtracting 5}$$
$$x^2 = 4 \qquad \text{dividing by 3}$$
$$x = 2 \qquad \text{taking square root of both sides}$$

Having arrived at an answer, you confidently look for it among the choices. But 2 isn't a choice. The explanation? This question has two possible solutions, not just one. The square root of 4 can be either 2 or –2, so B is the answer.

Keep in mind that though there is only one right answer choice for each question, that right answer may not be the one that occurs to you first. A common mistake is to pick an answer that seems "sort of" like the answer you're looking for even when you know it's wrong. Don't settle for second best.

7. GUESS INTELLIGENTLY

On the ACT, an unanswered question is always wrong, but even a wild guess may be right. In fact, smart guessing can make a big difference in your score. Always guess on every ACT question you can't answer.

You'll be doing two different kinds of guessing during your two sweeps through any subject test:
- Blind guessing (which you do mostly on questions you deem too hard or time-consuming to try)
- Considered guessing (which you do mostly on questions that you do some work on, but can't make headway with)

When you guess blindly, you just choose any letter you feel like choosing. When you guess in a considered way, on the other hand, you've usually done enough work on a question to eliminate at least one or two choices. If you can eliminate any choices, you increase the odds that you'll guess correctly.

8. BE CAREFUL WITH THE ANSWER GRID

Your ACT score is based on the answers you select on your answer grid. Even if you work out every question correctly, you'll get a low score if you misgrid your answers. So be careful! Don't disdain the process of filling in those little "bubbles" on the grid. Sure, it's pretty mindless, but under time pressure it's easy to make mistakes.

It's important to develop a disciplined strategy for filling in the answer grid. We find that gridding the answers in groups rather than one question at a time works best. As you figure out each question in the test booklet, circle the answer choice you come up with. Then transfer those answers to the answer grid in groups of five or more (until you get close to the end of time for the section, when you start gridding answers one-by-one).

In English, Reading, and Science, the test is divided naturally into groups of questions—the passages. For most students, it makes sense to circle your answers in your test booklet as you work them out. Then, when you're finished with each passage and its questions, fill in the answers as a group on your answer grid.

In Math, the strategy has to be different because the Math test isn't broken up into natural groups. The best strategy is to mark your answers in the test booklet and then grid them when you reach the end of each page or two. Since there are usually about five math questions per page, you'll probably be gridding five or ten math answers at a time.

Gridding Strategy

Grid your answers in groups.

No matter what subject you're working on, however, you should start gridding your answers one at a time near the end of the session. You don't want to be caught with ungridded answers when time is called.

During each subject test, the proctor should warn you when you have about five minutes left. But don't depend on that! Rely on your own watch: When there are five minutes left in a subject test, start gridding your answers one-by-one. With a minute or two left, fill in everything you've left blank. Remember: Even one question left blank could cut your score.

9. USE THE LETTERS OF THE ANSWER CHOICES TO STAY ON TRACK

One oddity about the ACT is that even-numbered questions have F, G, H, J (and, in Math, K) as answer choices, rather than A, B, C, D (and E in Math). This might be confusing at first, but you can make it work for you. A common mistake with the answer grid is to enter an answer one row up or down accidentally. On the ACT, that won't happen if you pay attention to the letter in the answer. If you're looking for an A and you see only F, G, H, J, and K, you'll know you're in the wrong row on the answer grid.

10. KEEP TRACK OF TIME

It's important to keep track of time while you take the ACT. During your two passes through each subject test, you really have to pace yourself. On average, English, Reading, and Science questions should take about one-half minute each. Math questions should average less than one minute each.

Set your watch to 12:00 at the beginning of each subject test, so it will be easy to check your time. Again, don't rely on proctors, even if they promise that they'll dutifully call out the time every five, ten, or fifteen minutes. Proctors get distracted once in a while.

For English, Reading, and Science questions, it's useful to check your timing as you grid the answers for each passage. English and Reading passages should take about nine minutes each. Science passages should average about five minutes.

Remember that more basic questions should take less time, and harder ones will probably take more. In Math, for instance, you need to go much faster than one per minute during your first sweep. But at the end, you may spend two or three minutes on each of the hardest problems you work out.

TAKE CONTROL OF YOUR TEST

A common thread in all 10 strategies above is: Take control. You are the master of the test-taking experience. Do the questions in the order you want and in the way you want. Use your time for one purpose—to maximize your score. Don't get bogged down or agonize. Remember, you don't earn points for suffering, but you do earn points for moving on to the next question and getting it right.

Get with the Program

In the remaining steps of your study program, we'll provide you with the arsenal of tools and techniques you'll need to take control of the ACT.

Part Two

THE ACT ENGLISH TEST

STEP FOUR

Basic English Skills

STEP FOUR PREVIEW

Kaplan's Three-Step Method for ACT English
- Step 1: Ask: "Does This Stuff Belong Here?"
- Step 2: Ask: "Does This Stuff Make Sense?"
- Step 3: Ask: "Does This Stuff Sound Like English?"

Skimming English Passages

Economy Questions
- Redundancy, Verbosity, Irrelevance
- When in Doubt . . .

Sense Questions
- Make It Make Sense
- Good Grammar Makes Good Sense

Nonstandard-Format English Questions
- Judging the Passage
- Reading-Type Questions

KAPLAN'S THREE-STEP METHOD FOR ACT ENGLISH

Here's our three-step (or really, three-question) method for ACT English questions.

Step 1: Ask: "Does This Stuff Belong Here?"

Writing economy is very near to the hearts of ACT test makers. So ask yourself: Does the underlined section belong? Is it expressed as succinctly as possible? If the answer is no, choose the answer that gets rid of the stuff that doesn't belong. If the answer is yes, move on to . . .

Step 2: Ask: "Does This Stuff Make Sense?"

The ACT test makers want simple, easy-to-understand prose. They expect everything to fit together logically. Does the underlined part of the passage make logical sense? If the answer is no, select the choice that turns nonsense into sense. If the answer is yes, go on to . . .

Step 3: Ask: "Does This Stuff Sound Like English?"

Many grammar errors will sound wrong to your ear. Even the ones that don't will be recognizable to you if you study our Twelve Classic Grammar Errors (in Step Five: ACT English Strategies) and create a "flag list" of the ones you're shaky on. Choose the answer that corrects the error and makes the sentence sound right.

Most ACT English test takers are so worried about grammar and punctuation that they don't think about anything else. That's the wrong mindset. Don't think too much about technical rules. As indicated in the approach above, the first thing is to get rid of unnecessary or irrelevant words. Only after you've decided that the underlined selection *is* concise and relevant do you go on to Steps 2 and 3. This means that you won't necessarily have to go through all three steps on every English question. The answer can come at any point in the three-step method.

SKIMMING ENGLISH PASSAGES

Before launching in and starting to correct the prose on an ACT English passage, it usually pays to skim each paragraph to get a sense of how it's shaped and what it's about. For most students, that makes correcting the underlined portions a little easier, since you'll have a better sense of the context. The skimming technique is simple: You skim a paragraph, then do the questions it contains, then skim the next paragraph, do the questions it contains, and so forth. Some students even find it helpful to skim the entire passage before starting on the questions.

In this preliminary skim, you needn't read carefully—you'll be doing that when you tackle the questions—but you should get a sense of what the passage is about and, just as important, whether it's written in a formal or informal style.

After your brief skim of a paragraph (it should take only a few seconds), it's time to start work on its questions.

Get the Gist of the Passage

Try skimming an English passage before starting work on the questions.

ECONOMY QUESTIONS

Almost all of us have padded papers at one time or another in our academic careers. The recipe for padding, in fact, is practically universal: You repeat yourself a few times. You trade short phrases for long-winded verbiage. You add a few offbeat ideas that don't really belong. And presto! Your six-page paper is transformed into a ten-page paper.

The ACT test makers know that most students pad when they write. And on the English subject test, they know how to punish you for it. In fact, almost one-third of the English questions on the ACT—we call them Economy questions—are testing for long-windedness, repetition, and irrelevance.

But there's hope. Once you know what ACT English is testing for, you can easily avoid making these common English mistakes. More than any other part of the exam, ACT English is predictable.

Try your hand at the following English minipassage—and pay attention to the message conveyed as well.

On recent ACTs, the shortest answer is

correct and absolutely right, for about
           1
half of all English questions. Because this

1. **A.** NO CHANGE
     B. correct
     C. right, that is,
           correct,
     D. correct, absolutely, and

is true, a student who knew no English
   2

2. **F.** NO CHANGE
     G. truthfully factual
     H. factually correct
     J. factual—and true too—

at all could earn—and justly so—an
           3
English subject score of about 15. Such

3. **A.** NO CHANGE
     B. , and justly so,
     C. and justify
     D. OMIT the
           underlined portion.

a student could compare the choices

carefully, and choose the single
           4
shortest one every time. Where the
  4
answers were same length, the

4. **F.** NO CHANGE
     G. singularly shortest one
     H. uniquely short item
     J. shortest one

student could pick at random. On

recent published ACTs, guessing in this

way would have yielded between 35 and

38 correct answers out of 75 questions

Of course, you're going to do much

better than that. You actually <u>are capable</u>
                                      5
<u>of speaking the English Language</u>. You
          5
may not know every little rule of English

usage, but you certainly know *something*.

Obviously, getting the question right

because you *know* the <u>right answer</u>
                              6
is better than getting it right because

you guessed well. But you should always

remember that the ACT test makers

<u>like</u> the shortest answers.
 7

5. **A.** NO CHANGE
B. possess the capability of speaking that wonderful language called the language of England
C. possess the capability of speaking in the land called England
D. speak English

6. **F.** NO CHANGE
G. best choice to select
H. most correct answer of the choices given
J. answer considered as correct

7. **A.** NO CHANGE
B. have a habit of liking
C. habitually tend to like
D. are in the habit of liking

Answers: 1. B, 2. F, 3. D, 4. J, 5. D, 6. F, 7. A

In case you didn't notice, the shortest answer happens to be correct in all eight of the questions above. OMIT, where it is an option, is the shortest answer, since taking the material out leaves a shorter text than leaving anything in.

Redundancy, Verbosity, Irrelevance

In the passage above, the wrong (long) answers are either redundant, verbose, or irrelevant. This means that they either make the passage say the same thing twice, force the reader to read more words than necessary, or introduce topics that are off the topic being discussed.

The ACT is very strict about redundancy, verbosity, and irrelevance. Wherever these flaws appear, your first impulse should be to correct them.

Remember the Three Rules of Economy:

Redundancy
• Never let the text in a sentence repeat itself.

Verbosity
• Remember that the best way to write something is the shortest way, as long as it's grammatically correct.

Irrelevance
• Omit the ideas that are not directly and logically tied in with the purpose of the passage.

When in Doubt . . .

On a real ACT, more than twenty questions—almost one-third of all the English items—test your awareness of redundancy, verbosity, relevance, and similar issues. For these Economy questions the shortest answer is very often correct. So your best bet is: When in doubt, take it out.

Because these issues of writing economy are so important to English questions of all kinds, we've made them the linchpin for our recommended approach to the English test. When approaching English questions, the first question you should ask yourself is: "Does this stuff belong here? Can the passage or sentence work *without* it?"

SENSE QUESTIONS

Okay, we just saw that the ACT expects you to use words efficiently, and that, in fact, the shortest answer is right remarkably often. But, obviously, the shortest answer is sometimes wrong. What could make it wrong? It may not mean what it says.

Take this example: "Abraham Lincoln's father was a model of hard-working self-sufficiency. He was born in a log cabin he built with his own hands." Well, that's a cute trick, being born in a cabin you built yourself. Presumably the writer means that *Abe* was born in a cabin that his *father* built. But the literal meaning of the example is that the father somehow managed to be born in a cabin that he himself had built.

It's possible, of course, to analyze this example in terms of the rules of apostrophe use and pronoun reference. But that's not practical for the ACT, even for a student who's good at grammar. There isn't time to carefully analyze every question, consider all the rules involved, and decide on an answer. You have to do 75 English questions in only 40 minutes—that's almost two questions per minute.

But there is plenty of time to approach examples like this one in a more pragmatic way. After deciding whether or not the selection in a question is concise and relevant (Step 1 in the three-step method), the next step isn't to remember lots of rules. It's to make sure that the sentence says exactly what it's supposed to *mean*. If not, your job is to fix it.

Make It Make Sense

We at Kaplan have a name for questions that test meaning errors: Sense questions. Once you get the hang of them, these questions can actually be fun. Errors of meaning are often funny once you see them.

Most people—even those who've never

read Daniel Defoe's *Robinson Crusoe*—

are familiar with the strange story of the

sailor shipwrecked on a far-flung Pacific

island. Relatively few of them, however,

know that Crusoe's <u>story. It was actually</u>
                                    1
based on the real-life adventures of a

Scottish seaman, Alexander Selkirk.

Selkirk came to the Pacific as a member

of a 1703 privateering expedition led by a

captain named William Dampier. During

the voyage, Selkirk became dissatisfied

with conditions aboard ship. <u>After a bitter</u>
                                          2
<u>quarrel with his captain, he put Selkirk</u>
                           2
<u>ashore</u> on tiny Mas a Tierra, one of the
    2
islands of Juan Fernandez, off the

coast of Chile. Stranded, Selkirk lived

1. **A.** NO CHANGE
   B. story: was
   C. story, was
   D. story was

2. **F.** NO CHANGE
   G. Quarreling with his captain, the boat was put ashore
   H. Having quarreled with his captain, Selkirk was put ashore
   J. Having quarreled with his captain, they put Selkirk ashore

there alone—in much the <u>same manner</u>
3
<u>as</u> Defoe's Crusoe—until 1709, when ·
3
he was finally rescued by another

English privateer.

  Upon his return to England, Selkirk

found himself a <u>celebrity, his</u> strange tale
4
had already become the talk of pubs and

coffeehouses throughout the British Isles.

The story even reached the ears of

Richard Steele, who featured it in his

periodical, *The Tatler*. Eventually, <u>he</u>
5
<u>became</u> the subject of a best-selling
5
book, *A Cruizing Voyage Round the World*,

by Woodes Rogers. <u>And while</u> there is
6
some evidence that Defoe, a journalist,

may actually have interviewed Selkirk

personally, most literary historians believe

that it was the reprinting of the Rogers

book in 1718 that served as the real

stimulus for Defoe's novel.

  In *Crusoe*, which <u>has been published</u> in
7
1719, Defoe took substantial liberties

with the Selkirk story. For example, while

3. **A.** NO CHANGE
   B. same manner that
   C. identical manner that
   D. identical way as

4. **F.** NO CHANGE
   G. celebrity, but his
   H. celebrity. His
   J. celebrity his

5. **A.** NO CHANGE
   B. Selkirk became
   C. his became
   D. he becomes

6. **F.** NO CHANGE
   G. But since
   H. And therefore
   J. OMIT the underlined portion
       and start the sentence with
       "There."

7. **A.** NO CHANGE
   B. was published
   C. had been published
   D. will have been published

Selkirk's presence on the island was of

course <u>known for many people</u> (certainly
           8
everyone in the crew that stranded him

there), no one in the novel is aware of

Crusoe's survival of the wreck and

presence on the island. Moreover, while

Selkirk's exile lasted just six years,

Crusoe's goes on for a much more

dramatic, though less credible, twenty-eight

<u>(over four times as long)</u>. But Defoe's
      9
most blatant embellishment of the tale

is the invention of the character of Friday,

for whom there was no counterpart

whatsoever in the real-life story.

   <u>Because of</u> its basis in fact, *Robinson*
      10
Crusoe is often regarded as the first

major novel in English literature. <u>Still</u>
                11
<u>popular today, contemporary audiences</u>
         11
<u>enjoyed the book as well.</u> In fact, two
      11
sequels, in which Crusoe returns to the

island after his rescue, were eventually

8. **F.** NO CHANGE
  G. widely known among people
  H. known about many for people
  J. known to many people

9. **A.** NO CHANGE
  B. (much longer)
  C. (a much longer time, of course)
  D. OMIT the underlined portion

10. **F.** NO CHANGE
  G. Despite
  H. Resulting from
  J. As a consequence of

11. **A.** NO CHANGE
  B. Still read today, Defoe's
     contemporaries also enjoyed it.
  C. Viewed by many even then as a
     classic, the book is still popular
     to this day
  D. Read widely in its day, modern
     people still like the book.

published. Though to little acclaim.
12

Meanwhile, Selkirk himself never gave a
13
hoot about returning to the island that
13
had made him famous. Legend has it

that he never gave up his eccentric living

habits, spending his last years in a

cave teaching alley cats to dance in his

spare time. One wonders if even Defoe

himself could have invented a more

fitting end to the bizarre story of his

shipwrecked sailor.

12. **F.** NO CHANGE
     G. published, though
     H. published although
     J. published; although

13. **A.** NO CHANGE
     B. evinced himself as
         desirous of returning
     C. could whip up a head of
         steam to return
     D. expressed any
         desire to return

Items 14 and 15 ask about
the passage as a whole

14. Given the tone and subject matter
     of the text, is the last sentence an
     appropriate way to end the essay?
     F. Yes, because some doubt must
         be shed on Defoe's creativity.
     G. Yes, because the essay is about
         the relationship between the real
         Selkirk and Defoe's fictionalized
         version of him.
     H. No, because there's nothing
         "bizarre" about Selkirk's
         story as it is related here.
     J. No, because the essay focuses
         more on Selkirk than on
         Defoe's fictionalized version of him.

15. This essay would be most
     appropriate as part of a:
     A. scholarly study of 18th-century
         maritime history.
     B. geography study of the islands
         off Chile.
     C. history of privateering in the
         Pacific.
     D. popular history of
         English literature.

Answers:

1. D, 2. H, 3. A, 4. H, 5. B, 6. F, 7. B, 8. J, 9. D, 10. G, 11. C, 12. G, 13. D, 14. G, 15. D

You may have found these Sense questions harder than the Economy questions. The shortest answers here aren't right nearly as often. But, all other things being equal, the shortest answer is still your best bet. In this case, the correct answers for six out of 15 questions (numbers 1, 3, 7, 9, 10, and 13) were the shortest answers.

On some of the questions in the passage above, you may not have gotten past Step 1 ("Does it belong here?") in Kaplan's three-step method. Question 9, for example, presented material that was clearly redundant. We certainly know that 28 years is longer than six (and if we're really up on our math, we can even figure out that 28 is "more than four times" six), so including any parenthetical aside like the one given would be unnecessary. Remember, when in doubt, take it out. As we saw earlier, if a question includes an OMIT option, or if some answers are much longer than others, it is usually testing writing economy.

In the rest of the questions in this passage, the answers differ in other ways. They may join or separate sentences, rearrange things, or add words that affect the meaning of the sentences. When the answers are all about the same length, as in most of the questions here, the question is more likely to test Sense. Consider the shortest answer first, but don't be as quick to select it and move on. Think about the effect each choice has on the *meaning* of the sentence and pick longer answers if the shortest one doesn't make sense.

Good Grammar Makes Good Sense

The ACT test makers include questions like those in the passage above to test many different rules of writing mechanics. Though it's not *necessary* to think about rules to answer the questions, familiarity with the rules can give you an alternative approach. The more ways you have to think about a question, the more likely you are to find the right answer.

We'll discuss some of these examples in groups based on what they're designed to test. That way we can show you how the basic strategic approach of "make it make sense" can get you the answers without a lot of technical analysis. Let's start with question 1:

. . . Relatively few of them, however,

know that Crusoe's <u>story. It was actually</u>
                       1
based on the real-life adventures of a

Scottish seaman, Alexander Selkirk.

1. **A.** NO CHANGE
     B. story: was
     C. story, was
     D. story was

If the underlined section for question 1 were left as it is, the second sentence of the passage would be incomplete. It wouldn't make sense. "Relatively few people know that Crusoe's story" what? To make that make sense, you've got to continue the sentence so that it can tell us what it is that few people know about Crusoe's story. The three alternatives all do that, but B introduces a nonsensical colon, while C adds a comma when there's no pause in the sentence. D, however, continues the sentence—adding nothing unnecessary, but making it complete.

Completeness

What question 1 is testing is something we call *completeness*—the requirement that every sentence should consist of an entire thought. Don't just blindly judge the completeness of a sentence by whether it contains a subject and a verb. The alleged sentence—"Relatively few of them, however, know that Crusoe's story."—actually *does* contain a subject and a verb, but it's still not complete. It leaves a thought hanging. Don't leave thoughts hanging on the ACT. The test makers don't like it one bit.

Question 12 also tests this same concept of completeness.

Sentence Structure

Technically, of course, questions 1 and 12 test the broader topic of sentence structure, of which completeness is one part. The rules of good sentence structure require that every sentence contain a complete thought. A "sentence" without a complete thought is called a *fragment*. A "sentence" with *too many* complete thoughts (usually connected by commas) is called a *run-on*. That's what we find in question 4:

Upon his return to England, Selkirk found

himself a <u>celebrity, his</u> strange tale had   **4. F.** NO CHANGE
                4   **G.** celebrity, but his
already become the talk of pubs and   **H.** celebrity. His
                                            J. celebrity his

coffeehouses throughout the British Isles.

Here we have two complete thoughts: (1) Selkirk found himself a celebrity upon his return, and (2) his tale was bandied about the pubs and coffeehouses. You can't just run these two complete thoughts together with a comma, as the underlined portion does. And you certainly can't just run them together without a comma or anything else, as choice J does. You can relate the two thoughts with a comma and a linking word (*and*, *for instance*), but choice G's inclusion of the word *but* makes no sense. It implies a contrast, while the two complete thoughts are actually very similar. Thus, you should create two sentences, one for each thought. That's what the correct choice, H, does.

Remember

Make sure every sentence contains at least one, but not more than one, complete thought.

Modifiers

Question 2 tests modifier problems:

<u>After a bitter quarrel with his captain, he</u>
             2
<u>put Selkirk ashore</u> on tiny Mas a Tierra,
    2
one of the islands of Juan Fernandez, . . .

2. **F.** NO CHANGE
    G. Quarreling with his captain,
        the boat was put ashore
    H. Having quarreled with his captain,
        Selkirk was put ashore
    J. Having quarreled with his captain,
        they put Selkirk ashore

In a well-written sentence, it must be clear exactly what words or phrases are modifying (or referring to) what other words or phrases in the sentence. In the underlined portion here, the clause "after a bitter quarrel with his captain" should modify the pronoun that follows it—*he*. But it doesn't. The *he* who put Selkirk ashore must be the captain, but it can't be the captain who had "a bitter quarrel with his captain." That doesn't make sense (unless the captain quarrels with himself). So put the thing modified next to the thing modifying it. The person who quarreled with his captain was Selkirk—not the boat and not "they," whoever they are— so H is correct.

If you recognized the problem with question 2 as a "misplaced modifier," that's great. Fantastic, even. But you didn't have to know the technicalities to get the right answer here. You just had to make the sentence make sense.

Question 11, which we won't discuss here, is another question testing modifier placement.

Mind Your Modifiers

Make sure that modifiers are as close as possible to the things they modify.

Idiom

Question 3 tests a rather hazy linguistic concept known as *idiom*. The word *idiomatic* refers to language that, well, uses words in the right way. Many words have special rules. If you're a native speaker of the language, you probably picked up many of these rules by ear before your eighth birthday; if you're not a native speaker, you had to learn them one by one.

Stranded, Selkirk lived there alone—in

much the <u>same manner as</u> Defoe's
              3

Crusoe—until 1709, when he was finally

rescued by another . . .

3. A. NO CHANGE
B. same manner that
C. identical manner that
D. identical way as

The sentence as written actually makes perfect sense. Selkirk lived in "much the same manner as" Defoe's Crusoe. The phrase *much the same* calls for *as* to complete the comparison between Selkirk's and Crusoe's ways of life. Note how B and C would create completeness problems—in much the same (or identical) manner that Defoe's Crusoe what? Choice D, meanwhile, is just plain unidiomatic. In English, we just don't say "in much the identical way," because the word *identical* is an absolute. You can't be more or partially identical; either you are or aren't identical to something else. But even if you didn't analyze D this carefully, it should have just sounded wrong to your ear. (Trusting your ear can be a great way to get correct answers on the English subject test.)

You'll notice that question 8 tests another idiom problem—the phrase *known to*.

Pronouns

Remember, the object of grammar rules is to make sure that the meaning of language is conveyed clearly. Sometimes, the test will throw you a sentence in which the meaning of a pronoun is unclear. You won't be sure to whom or what the pronoun is referring. That's the kind of problem you were given in question 5:

The story even reached the ears of

Richard Steele, who featured it in his

periodical, *The Tatler*. Eventually, <u>he</u>
                                      5
<u>became</u> the subject of a best-selling
   5
book . . .

5. A. NO CHANGE
B. Selkirk became
C. his became
D. he becomes

The intended meaning of the pronoun *he* here is as a substitute for "Selkirk." But what's the closest male name to the pronoun? Richard Steele, the publisher of *The Tatler*. That creates an unclear situation. Make it clear! Choice B takes care of the problem by naming Selkirk explicitly. C would create a Sense problem. His what became the subject of a book? Meanwhile, D shifts the verb tense into the present, which makes no sense since this book was written over 250 years ago.

Make It Clear

Make sure it's perfectly clear to what or to whom all pronouns refer.

Logic

Structural clues are signal words that an author uses to show where he or she is going in a piece of writing. They show how all of the pieces logically fit together. If the author uses the structural clue *on the other hand*, that means a contrast is coming up. If he or she uses the clue *moreover*, that means that a continuation is coming up—an addition that is more or less in the same vein as what came before.

Many ACT English questions mix up the logic of a piece of writing by giving you the wrong structural clue or other logic word. That's what happened in question 10:

<u>Because of</u> its basis in fact, *Robinson*
      10
Crusoe is often regarded as the first

major novel in English literature.

10. **F.** NO CHANGE
      G. Despite
      H. Resulting from
      J. As a consequence of

As written, this sentence means that *Crusoe* was regarded as the first major novel because it was based on fact. But that makes no sense. If it was based on fact (which implies nonfiction), that would contradict its being regarded as a novel (which implies fiction). To show that contrast logically, you need a contrast word like *despite*. That's why G is correct here. G makes the sentence make sense.

Question 6 on page 56 also tests logic. *And while* is the right answer, because it first conveys a sense of continuation with the preceding sentence, and then a sense of contrast with the second half of the sentence.

Where Is It Going?

Make sure structural clues make logical sense.

Verb Usage

Verbs have an annoying habit of changing form depending on who's doing the action and when he or she is doing it. I *hate* verbs, he *hates* verbs, and we both *have hated* verbs ever since we were kids. Verbs must match their subject and the tense of the surrounding context. Take a look at question 7 on the next page.

In *Crusoe*, which <u>has been published</u> in
                                    7
1719, Defoe took substantial liberties

with the Selkirk story.

7. A. NO CHANGE
    B. was published
    C. had been published
    D. will have been published

The publication of *Robinson Crusoe* is something that took place in 1719—the past, in other words. So the underlined portion, which puts the verb in the present perfect tense, is flawed. Choices C and D, meanwhile, would put the verb into several bizarre tenses. C makes it seem as if publication of the book happened before Defoe took his liberties with the story. But that's nonsensical. The liberties were taken in the writing of the book. D, meanwhile, does strange things with the time sequence. But keep things simple. The book was published in the past; Defoe also took his substantial liberties in more or less the same past. So just use the simple past tense. The book *was published* in 1719, choice B.

Actions: Who Did What When?

Make sure all verbs match their subject and the tense of the surrounding context.

Tone

The passages on the English subject test vary in tone. Some are formal; others are informal. Usually, you'll know which is which without having to think about it. If a passage contains slang, a few exclamation points, and a joke or two, the tone is informal. If it sounds like something a Latin instructor would say, it's probably formal.

Good style requires that the tone of a piece of writing be at the same level throughout. Sometimes the underlined portion might not fit the tone of the rest of the passage. If so, it's up to you to correct it.

Look at question 13:

. . . Meanwhile, Selkirk himself never

<u>gave a hoot about returning</u> to the island
                    13
that had made him famous.

13. A. NO CHANGE
     B. evinced himself as desirous
         of returning
     C. could whip up a head of
         steam to return
     D. expressed any desire to return

Selkirk "never gave a hoot" about going back? No way! That's slang (and pretty dorky slang, too). It certainly doesn't belong in this passage. This text isn't the most formally written piece of prose in the world, but it's certainly no place for a phrase like "gave a hoot" or (just as bad) "whip up a head of steam" (choice C). B, meanwhile, goes too far in the opposite direction. "Evinced himself as desirous of returning" sounds like something no human being would say.

But the rest of the passage sounds human. It makes no sense to shift tonal gears in the middle of a passage. Choose D.

Take Care with Tone

Keep the tone consistent with the rest of the text.

NONSTANDARD-FORMAT ENGLISH QUESTIONS

Some questions ask about the passage as a whole. They're looking for the main point—the gist of the passage—as well as the overall tone and style.

Judging the Passage

Question 14 asks you to judge the passage. Was the last sentence an appropriate ending or not? Most passages will have a well-defined theme, laid out in a logical way. Choose the answer that best continues the logical "flow" of the passage. Some questions on the test will ask you if a passage fits a specified requirement, and often the answer is no.

14. Considering the tone and subject matter of the preceding paragraphs, is the last sentence an appropriate way to end the essay?

   F. Yes, because it is necessary to shed some doubt on Defoe's creativity.

   G. Yes, because the essay is about the relationship between the real Selkirk and Defoe's fictionalized version of him.

   H. No, because there is nothing "bizarre" about Selkirk's story as it is related in the essay.

   J. No, because the focus of the essay is more on Selkirk himself than on Defoe's fictionalized version of him.

Think of the passage as a whole. It's been comparing Selkirk's real life with the one that Defoe made up for Robinson Crusoe. Ending in this way, therefore, with an ironic reference to Defoe as writing a more fitting end to Selkirk's life, is perfectly appropriate. The answer to the question, then, should be yes. F says yes, but gives a nonsensical reason for saying yes. Why is it necessary to shed doubt on Defoe's creativity? Does the author hold a grudge against Defoe? Not that we can tell. So G is the best answer here.

Look at the Big Picture

Make sure that your answer is in keeping with the logical "flow" of the passage.

Reading-Type Questions

If you thought question 15 looked like a Reading question hiding in the English part of the exam, you were right. As mentioned earlier, one reason that you should focus on what the passage means, rather than on picky rules of grammar or punctuation, is that the ACT often asks Reading-Type questions.

15. This essay would be most appropriate as part of a:

    A. scholarly study of 18th-century maritime history.

    B. study of the geography of the islands off Chile.

    C. history of privateering in the Pacific.

    D. popular history of English literature.

What was this passage principally about? How Defoe's *Robinson Crusoe* was loosely based on the life of a real shipwrecked sailor, Alexander Selkirk. Would that kind of thing belong in a study of geography (choice B)? No; the focus is on the fictionalization of a historical life, not on the physical features of the islands off Chile. The passage isn't principally about privateering or maritime history either, so C and A are wrong, too. This passage is about the relationship of a true story and a famous fictionalized story. And its tone isn't overly scholarly, either. So it probably belongs in a popular history of English literature (choice D).

In this step, we've introduced you to ACT English questions and talked about the first two question types—Economy and Sense questions. In the next step we'll cover what we call Technicality questions, where it really does help to know a handful of grammar rules. But remember that common sense is your best guide on this subject test, and be sure to follow our two keys to success on ACT English: "When in doubt, take it out," and "Make it make sense."

STEP FIVE

ACT English Strategies

STEP FIVE PREVIEW

Trusting Your Ear
- Formal or Informal?
- Regional and Ethnic Dialects

"Listening" Carefully: Practice Passage

Twelve Classic Grammar Errors
- Error 1: *It* and *They* (Singulars and Plurals)
- Error 2: Commas or Dashes (Parenthetical Phrases)
- Error 3: Run-ons and Comma Splices
- Error 4: Fragments
- Error 5: Misunderstood Punctuation Marks
- Error 6: *-ly* Endings (Adverbs and Adjectives)
- Error 7: *Its* and *It's* (Apostrophe Use)
- Error 8: *There, Their, They're* and *Are, Our* (Proper Word Usage)
- Error 9: *Sang, Sung, Brang, Brung,* etcetera (Verb Forms)
- Error 10: *-er* and *-est, More* and *Most* (Comparatives and Superlatives)
- Error 11: Confusing *Between* and *Among*
- Error 12: Confusing *Less* and *Fewer*

In the first English step, we discussed English questions that hinged mostly on common sense. But there are also some English questions—we call them Technicality questions—that may seem harder because they test for the technical rules of grammar. These require you to correct errors that don't necessarily harm the economy or sense of the sentence. But don't worry. You don't have to be a grammar whiz to get these questions right. Luckily, you can often detect these errors because they "sound funny." Most of the time on the ACT, it's safe to trust your ear.

TRUSTING YOUR EAR

Which of the following "sounds right" and which "sounds funny"?

- Bob doesn't know the value of the house he lives in.
- Bob don't know the value of the house he lives in.

The first sounds a lot better, right? And for many of these questions, all you need to do is to "listen" carefully in this way. You may not know the formal rules of grammar, punctuation, and diction, but you communicate in English every day. You wouldn't be communicating unless you had a decent feel for the rules.

Formal or Informal?

You might have caught an apparent error in *both* of the examples above—ending a sentence with a preposition such as "in." This is undesirable in extremely formal writing. But ACT passages aren't usually that formal. The test makers expect you to have a feel for the level of formality in writing. If the passage is informal, pick informal answers. If the passage is slightly formal (as most ACT passages are), pick slightly formal answers. If the passage is extremely formal, pick extremely formal answers. For example, if the passage starts off with, "You'll just love Bermuda—great beaches, good living . . .," it won't end like this: "and an infinitely fascinating array of flora and fauna which may conceivably exceed, in range and scope, that of any alternative. . . ." That ending is too formal. Pick something like this: "You'll just love Bermuda—great beaches, good living, and a lot of exotic plants and animals."

Make It Match

Choose answers that match the level of formality of the entire passage.

Regional and Ethnic Dialects

Although ACT passages differ in level of formality, they all are designed to test "standard" English—the kind used by middle-class people in most of America. Test takers who speak regional or ethnic dialects may therefore find it more difficult to trust their ears on some ACT questions. In much of the South, for instance, it's common to use the word *in* with the word *rate*, like this: "Mortality declined in a rate of almost 2 percent per year." Most English speakers, however, use the word *at* with *rate*, as in: "Mortality declined at a rate of. . . ." Fortunately, ACT questions testing idioms like this are rare. And even if you do speak a "nonstandard" dialect, you probably know what standard English sounds like. The dialect used on most television and radio shows, for example, would be considered "standard."

Important

If you speak a "nonstandard" dialect, be extra careful with questions that focus on idioms.

"LISTENING" CAREFULLY: PRACTICE PASSAGE

In the following short passage, you may well be able to determine an answer by "listening" carefully to each choice:

Halloween was first celebrated among
<u>among</u>
1
<u>various</u> Celtic tribes in Ireland in the fifth
1
century B.C. It traditionally took place on

the official last day of summer—

October <u>31, and</u> was named "All Hallows
2
Eve." It was believed that all persons

who had died during the previous year

returned on this day to select persons

or animals to inhabit for the next twelve

months, until they could <u>pass peaceful</u>
3
into the afterlife.

   On All Hallows Eve, the Celts <u>were</u>
4
<u>dressing</u> up as demons and monsters
4
to frighten the spirits away, and tried to

make their homes <u>as coldest</u> as possible
5
to prevent any stray ghosts from crossing

their thresholds. Late at night, the

townspeople typically gathered outside the

village, where a druidic priest would light a

huge bonfire to frighten away ghosts and

1. **A.** NO CHANGE
   B. among varied
   C. between the various
   D. between various

2. **F.** NO CHANGE
   G. 31—and
   H. 31. And
   J. 31; and

3. **A.** NO CHANGE
   B. pass peacefully
   C. passed peacefully
   D. be passing peaceful

4. **F.** NO CHANGE
   G. were dressed
   H. dressed
   J. are dressed

5. **A.** NO CHANGE
   B. colder
   C. coldest
   D. as cold

to honor the sun god for the past

summer's harvest. Any villager <u>whom was</u>

6

suspected of being possessed would be

6. F. NO CHANGE
    G. whom were
    H. who was
    J. who were

captured, after which <u>they</u> might be

7

sacrificed in the bonfire as a warning to

other spirits seeking to possess the

living.

7. A. NO CHANGE
    B. it
    C. he or she
    D. those

When the Romans invaded the British

Isles, they adopted Celtic—not Saxon—

Halloween rituals, but outlawed human

sacrifice in A.D. 61. Instead, they used

effigies for their sacrifices. In time, as

<u>belief in</u> spirit possession waned,

8

Halloween rituals lost their serious aspect

8. F. NO CHANGE
    G. belief for
    H. believing about
    J. belief of

and <u>had been</u> instead performed for

9

amusement.

9. A. NO CHANGE
    B. having been
    C. have been
    D. were

Irish immigrants, fleeing from the potato

famine in the 1840s, <u>brought there</u>

10

Halloween customs to the United States.

10. F. NO CHANGE
     G. brought they're
     H. brought their
     J. their brought-in

In New England, Halloween became a night

of costumes and practical jokes. Some

favorite pranks <u>included unhinging</u> front
11
gates and overturning outhouses. The

Irish also introduced the custom of carving

jack-o'-lanterns. The ancient Celts

probably began the tradition by hollowing

out a large turnip, carving its face, and

lighting it from inside with a candle. Since

there were <u>far less</u> turnips in New
12
England than in Ireland, the Irish

immigrants were forced to settle for

pumpkins.

   Gradually, Halloween celebrations

spread to other regions of the United

States. Halloween has been a popular

holiday ever since, <u>although these days</u>
13
<u>it's</u> principal celebrants are children
13

<u>rather than</u> adults.
14

11.
A. NO CHANGE
B. include unhinging
C. had included unhinged
D. includes unhinged

12.
F. NO CHANGE
G. lots less
H. not as much
J. far fewer

13.
A. NO CHANGE
B. although these days its
C. while now it's
D. while not its

14.
F. NO CHANGE
G. rather then
H. rather
J. else then

ANSWER	PROBLEM
1. A	*among/between* distinction (see Classic Grammar Error 11 below)
2. G	commas and dashes mixed (see Classic Grammar Error 2 below)
3. B	use of adjectives and adverbs (see Classic Grammar Error 6 below)
4. H	unnecessary *-ing* ending
5. D	comparative/superlative (see Classic Grammar Error 10 below)
6. H	*who/whom* confusion
7. C	pronoun usage error (see Classic Grammar Error 1 below)
8. F	preposition usage
9. D	tense problem with *to be*
10. H	*they're/there/their* mixup (see Classic Grammar Error 8 below)
11. A	verb tense usage (see Classic Grammar Error 9 below)
12. J	*less/fewer* confusion (see Classic Grammar Error 12 below)
13. B	*it's/its* confusion (see Classic Grammar Error 7 below)
14. F	*then/than* usage

TWELVE CLASSIC GRAMMAR ERRORS

Many students could rely almost exclusively on their ear to correct many of the errors above. But there are a few English questions on the ACT that contain errors your ear probably won't or can't catch. If you have a good ear for English, there may be only a handful of such questions on the test. If not, there may be many more. For these, you'll have to think about the rules more formally. But fortunately, only a small number of rules are typically involved, and we'll discuss the most common ones in this step. Even more fortunately, most of the technicalities tested on the ACT boil down to one general principle: Make it all match.

The rest of this step is designed to help you build your own "flag list" of common errors on the ACT that your ear might not catch. Consider each classic error. If it seems like common sense to you (or, better, if the error just *sounds* like bad English to you, while the correction *sounds* like good English), you probably don't have to add it to your flag list. If, on the other hand, the error doesn't seem obvious, add it to your list.

As we'll see, making things match works in two ways. Some rules force you to match one part of the sentence with another. Other rules force you to match the right word or word form with the meaning intended.

Error 1: *It* and *They* (Singulars and Plurals)

The "matching" rule tested most on the ACT is this: Singular nouns must match with singular verbs and pronouns, and plural nouns must match with plural verbs and pronouns. The most common error in this area involves the use of the word *they*. It's plural, but in everyday speech, we incorrectly use it as singular.

SENTENCE: "If a student won't study, they won't do well."
PROBLEM: A *student* (singular) and *they* (plural) don't match.
CORRECTION: "If students won't study, they won't do well."
                  "If a student won't study, he (or she) won't do well."

Make It All Match

Watch for subject–verb and noun–pronoun agreement.

Error 2: Commas or Dashes (Parenthetical Phrases)

One rule of punctuation is tested far more often than any other on the ACT. Parenthetical phrases must *begin* and *end* with the same punctuation mark. Such phrases can be recognized because without them, the sentence would still be complete. For instance: "Bob, on his way to the store, saw a large lizard in the street." If you dropped the phrase "on his way to the store," the sentence would still be complete. Thus, this phrase is parenthetical. It could be marked off with commas, parentheses, or dashes. But the same mark is needed at both ends of the phrase.

SENTENCE: "Bob—on his way to the store, saw a lizard."
PROBLEM: The parenthetical phrase starts with a dash but finishes with a comma.
CORRECTION: "Bob, on his way to the store, saw a lizard."

Finish What You Started

Make sure parenthetical phrases begin and end with the same punctuation mark.

Error 3: Run-ons and Comma Splices

The ACT test makers expect you to understand what makes a sentence and what doesn't. You can't combine two sentences into one with a comma (though you can with a semicolon or conjunction).

SENTENCE: "Ed's a slacker, Sara isn't."
PROBLEM: Two sentences are spliced together with a comma.
CORRECTION: "Ed's a slacker, but Sara isn't."
                  "Ed's a slacker; Sara isn't."
                  "Ed, unlike Sara, is a slacker."

Usually, only one thing should happen in each sentence. There should be one "major event." There are only a few ways to put more than one event in a sentence. One way is to connect the sentences with a comma and a conjunction (a word such as *and* or *but*), as in the first correction. Or, as in the second, a semicolon can stand in for such a word. The other way is to "subordinate" one event to the other in a clause, as in the third correction.

Error 4: Fragments

This rule goes hand-in-hand with the one above. A "fragment" is writing that could be a subordinate part of a sentence, but not a whole sentence itself.

SENTENCE: "Emily listened to music. While she studied."
PROBLEM: "She studied" would be a sentence, but *while* makes this a fragment.
CORRECTION: "Emily listened to music while she studied."

Make Sure Sentences Are Complete

Look out for sentence fragments and run-on sentences.

Error 5: Misunderstood Punctuation Marks

The test makers don't test tricky rules of punctuation. But they do expect you to know what the punctuation marks mean and to match their use to their meanings. Here are some common ones:

- Period (.)—Means "full stop" or "end of sentence."
- Question mark (?)—Serves the same purpose, but for questions.
- Exclamation mark (!)—Can be used instead of a period, but is generally inappropriate for all but very informal writing because it indicates extreme emotion.
- Comma (,)—Represents a pause. In many cases a comma is optional. But never use a comma where a pause would be confusing, as in: "I want to go, to the, store."
- Semicolon (;)—Used to separate two complete but closely related thoughts.
- Colon (:)—Works like an "=" sign, connecting two equivalent things. Colons are usually used to begin a list.
- Dash (—)—Can be used for any kind of pause, usually a long one or one indicating a significant shift in thought.

Error 6: *-ly* Endings (Adverbs and Adjectives)

The test makers expect you to understand the difference between adverbs (the *-ly* words) and adjectives. The two are similar because they're both modifiers. They modify, or refer to, or describe, another word or phrase in the sentence. But nouns and pronouns must be modified by *adjectives*, while other words, especially verbs and adjectives themselves, must be modified by *adverbs*.

KAPLAN

SENTENCE:	"Anna is an extreme gifted child, and she speaks beautiful, too."
PROBLEM:	*Extreme* and *beautiful* are adjectives, but they're supposed to modify an adjective (*gifted*) and a verb (*speaks*) here, so they should be adverbs.
CORRECTION:	"Anna is an extremely gifted child, and she speaks beautifully, too."

Don't Mix Up Your Modifiers

Nouns and pronouns are modified by adjectives. Verbs and adjectives are modified by adverbs.

Error 7: *Its* and *It's* (Apostrophe Use)

Probably the trickiest rule is the proper use of apostrophes. Apostrophes are used primarily for two purposes: possessives and contractions. When you make a noun (not a pronoun) possessive by adding an *s*, you use an apostrophe. For example: *Bob's, the water's, a noodle's.* But you *never* use an apostrophe to make a pronoun possessive—pronouns have special possessive forms. You would never write *her's.* (One exception is the pronoun *one,* as in, "One's hand is attached to one's wrist.") When you run two words together to form a contraction, you use an apostrophe to join them. For example: *I'm, he's, they're.*

Apostrophes also have a few unusual uses, but luckily they're almost never tested on the ACT. So, master the basics and you'll be in good shape.

The most common apostrophe issue on the ACT is usage of *its* and *it's.* These two words follow the same rule as do *his* and *he's.* Both *its* and *his* are possessive pronouns—so they have no apostrophes. Both *it's* and *he's* are contractions—so they do have apostrophes.

SENTENCE:	"The company claims its illegal to use it's name that way."
PROBLEM:	*It's* is a contraction of *it is*; *its* is the possessive form of *it.*
CORRECTION:	"The company claims it's illegal to use its name that way."

Remember

It's is a contraction for *it is,* while *its* shows possession.

Error 8: *There, Their, They're* and *Are, Our* (Proper Word Usage)

Some students confuse the words *there, their,* and *they're.* Contractions use apostrophes—so *they're* is the contraction for *they are.* You can tell when to use *there* because it's spelled like *here,* and the words *here* and *there* both indicate location. *Their* means "of or belonging to them." You'll just have to remember that one the old-fashioned way.

Students also frequently confuse the words *are* (a verb) and *our* (a possessive). You can remember that *our* is spelled like *your*, another (less confusing) possessive.

> **Location, Possession, Contraction**
> Learn to distinguish the words *there, their,* and *they're.*

Error 9: *Sang, Sung, Brang, Brung,* etcetera (Verb Forms)

When you have to consider different forms of the same verb (for example, *live, lives, lived*), ask yourself who did it and when did they do it? We would say, "I now live" but "he now lives." In these sentences, the *who* is different—and so the verb changes. Similarly, we would say, "I now live" but "I lived in the past." In these sentences, the *when* is different—so the verb changes.

Most verbs are "regular" in this way. You add *s* when the subject is *he, she,* or *it* and the time is now (present tense). You add *d* for times in the past. For times in the future, or several steps back in the past, there are no special endings; you use the words *will, will have, have,* and *had.* I *will* live. I *will have* lived for 25 years by the time the next century begins. I *had* lived in Nebraska, but we moved. I *have* lived in Indiana since then.

But a few verbs are irregular. They have special forms. For example, we say *sang* rather than *singed* and *have sung* rather than *have singed* or *have sang.* Each of these verbs must be learned separately.

One irregular verb commonly tested on the ACT is *bring.*

SENTENCE: "I've brung my umbrella to work."
PROBLEM: *Brang* and *brung* aren't used in standard English.
CORRECTION: "I've brought my umbrella to work."

Error 10: *-er* and *-est, More* and *Most* (Comparatives and Superlatives)

Whenever you see the endings *-er* or *-est,* or the words *more* or *most,* double-check to make sure they're used logically. Words with *-er* or with *more* should be used to compare only two things. If there are more than two things involved, use *-est* or *most.*

SENTENCE: "Bob is the fastest of the two runners."
PROBLEM: The comparison is between just two things, so the *-est* ending is inappropriate.
CORRECTION: "Bob is the faster of the two runners."

Don't use the words *more* or *most* if you can use the *-er* and *-est* endings instead. Say, "I think vanilla is tastier than chocolate," not "I think vanilla is more tasty than chocolate." Never use both *more* or *most* and an *-est/-er* ending. Don't say, "Of the five flavors of frozen yogurt I've eaten, strawberry delight is the most tastiest." Just say it's "the tastiest."

Error 11: Confusing *Between* and *Among*

As a rule of thumb, use the word *between* only when there are two things involved, or when comparisons in a larger group are made between pairs of things. When there are more than two things, or an unknown number of things, use *among*.

SENTENCES:	"I will walk among the two halves of the class."
	"I will walk between the many students in class."
PROBLEM:	Use *between* for two things; *among* for more than two.
CORRECTION:	"I will walk between the two halves of the class."
	"I will walk among the many students in class."

Error 12: Confusing *Less* and *Fewer*

Make sure that you use the word *less* only for uncountable things. When things can be counted, they are *fewer*.

SENTENCE:	"I have fewer water than I thought, so I can fill less buckets."
PROBLEM:	You can count buckets; you can't count water.
CORRECTION:	"I have less water than I thought, so I can fill fewer buckets."

Hint:

People are always countable, so you should always use *fewer* when writing about them.

Part Three

THE ACT MATH TEST

Classic Math Strategies

Question Breakdown

Be a Thinker–Not a Number Cruncher

Kaplan's Three-Step Method for ACT Math
- Step 1: Understand
- Step 2: Analyze
- Step 3: Select

Definition Alert

Kaplan's Two-Pass Plan for ACT Math

Know When to Skip a Question

What to Do When You're Stuck
- Estimates and Guesstimates
- Eyeballing

All that matters on the ACT is correct answers. Your goal on the math subject test is to get as many correct answers as you can in 60 minutes. It doesn't matter what you do (short of cheating, naturally) to get those correct answers. What matters is using quick methods that get you a solid number of correct answers.

The Answer Is What Counts

Worry about right answers, not "right" ways of solving problems.

QUESTION BREAKDOWN

Each ACT Math subject test includes the following:

- 24 pre-algebra and elementary algebra questions
- 10 intermediate algebra questions
- 9 coordinate geometry questions
- 14 plane geometry questions
- 4 trigonometry questions

Nobody needs to get all 60 questions right. The average ACT student gets fewer than half of the math questions right! You need only about 40 correct answers to get your math score over 25—just two right out of every three questions gets you a great score. So if, for instance, you're hopeless in trigonometry, just forget it!

Trouble with Trig?

If you don't know your trig by now, you're probably better off just skipping the four Trigonometry questions on your Math subject test.

As you can see, you get only four trigonometry questions on any test. Those are four points you can sacrifice at this late date—so that you can focus on things such as algebra questions, which account for a much larger portion of the Math subject test.

BE A THINKER—NOT A NUMBER CRUNCHER

One reason you're given limited time for the Math subject test is that the ACT is testing your ability to think, not your willingness to do a lot of mindless calculations. They're looking for creative thinkers, not human calculators. So, one of your guiding principles for ACT Math should be: Work less, but work smarter.

If you want to get the best score you can, you need to be always on the lookout for quicker ways to solve problems. Here's an example that could take a lot more time than it needs to.

1. When $\dfrac{4}{11}$ is converted to a decimal, the 50th digit after the decimal point is

    A. 2
    B. 3
    C. 4
    D. 5
    E. 6

It seems that when you convert $\frac{4}{11}$ to a decimal, there are at least 50 digits after the decimal point. The question asks for the 50th. One way to answer this question would be to divide 11 into 4, carrying the division out to 50 decimal places. That method would work, but it would take forever. It's not worth spending that much time on one question.

No ACT Math question should take more than a minute, if you know what you're doing. There has to be a faster way to solve this problem. There must be some kind of pattern you can take advantage of. And what kind of pattern might there be with a decimal? How about a repeating decimal!

In fact, that's exactly what you have here. The decimal equivalent of $\frac{4}{11}$ is a repeating decimal:

$$\frac{4}{11} = .3636363636....$$

The first, third, fifth, seventh, and ninth digits are each 3. The second, fourth, sixth, eighth, and tenth digits are each 6. To put it simply, odd-numbered digits are 3s and even-numbered digits are 6s. The fiftieth digit is an even-numbered digit, so it's a 6 and the answer is E.

What looked at first glance like a "fractions-and-decimals" problem turned out to be something of an "odds-and-evens" problem.

If you don't use creative shortcuts on problems like this one, you'll get bogged down, you'll run out of time, and you won't get a lot of questions right.

Question 1 demonstrates how the ACT designs problems to reward clever thinking and to punish students who blindly "go through the motions."

But how do you get yourself into a creative mindset on the Math subtest? For one thing, you have to take the time to understand thoroughly each problem you decide to work on. Most students are so nervous about time that they skim each math problem and almost immediately start computing with their pencils. But that's the wrong way of thinking. Sometimes on the ACT, you have to take time to save time. A few extra moments spent understanding a math problem can save many extra moments of computation or other drudgery.

Think About Each Problem

Take time to look for shortcuts that will save time in the long run.

KAPLAN'S THREE-STEP METHOD FOR ACT MATH

At Kaplan, we've developed this take-time-to-save-time philosophy into a three-step method for solving ACT Math problems. The method is designed to help you find the fast, inventive solutions that the ACT rewards. The steps are:

Step 1: Understand

Focus first on the question stem (the part before the answer choices) and make sure you understand the problem. Sometimes you'll want to read the stem twice, or rephrase it in a way you can better understand. Think to yourself: "What kind of problem is this? What am I looking for? What am I given?" Don't pay too much attention to the answer choices yet, though you may want to give them a quick glance just to see what form they're in.

Step 2: Analyze

Think for a moment and decide on a plan of attack. Don't start crunching numbers until you've given the problem a little thought. "What's a quick and reliable way to find the correct answer?" Look for patterns and shortcuts, using common sense and your knowledge of the test to find the creative solutions that will get you more right answers in less time. Try to solve the problem without focusing on the answer choices.

Step 3: Select

Once you get an answer—or once you get stuck—check the answer choices. If you got an answer and it's listed as one of the choices, chances are it's right; fill in the appropriate bubble and move on. But if you didn't get an answer, narrow down the choices as best you can, by a process of elimination, and then guess.

Each of these steps can happen in a matter of seconds. And it may not always be clear when you've finished with one step and moved on to the next. Sometimes you'll know how to attack a problem the instant you read and understand it.

Let's look at a specific problem.

2. If the sum of five consecutive even integers is equal to their product, what is the greatest of the five integers?

   F. 4
   G. 10
   H. 14
   J. 16
   K. 20

Step 1: Understand

Before you can begin to solve this problem, you have to figure out what it's asking, and to do that you need to know the meanings of sum, product, consecutive, even, and integer. Put the question stem into words you can understand. What it's really saying is that when you add up these five consecutive even integers you get the same thing as when you multiply them.

Step 2: Analyze

How are we going to figure out what these five numbers are? We could set up an equation:

$$x + (x - 2) + (x - 4) + (x - 6) + (x - 8) = x(x - 2)(x - 4)(x - 6)(x - 8)$$

But there's no way you'll have time to solve an equation like this! So don't even try. Come up with a better way.

Let's stop and think logically about this. When we think about sums and products, it's natural to think mostly of positive integers. With positive integers, we would generally expect the product to be *greater* than the sum.

But what about negative integers? Hmm. Well, the sum of five negatives is negative, and the product of five negatives is also negative, and generally the product will be "more negative" than the sum, so with negative integers the product will be *less* than the sum.

So when will the product and sum be the same? How about right at the boundary between positive and negative—that is, around 0? The five consecutive even integers with equal product and sum are –4, –2, 0, 2, and 4.

$$(-4) \times (-2) \times 0 \times 2 \times 4 = (-4) + (-2) + 0 + 2 + 4$$

The product and sum are both 0. Ha! We've done it!

Step 3: Select

The question asks for the greatest of the five integers, which is 4, choice F.

Reword the Question

Make sure *you* know what a math question is asking.

Now let's look at a case in which the method of solution is not so obvious.

4. What is the greatest of the numbers $1^{50}, 50^1, 2^{25}, 25^2, 4^{10}$?

    F. 1^{50}

    G. 50^1

    H. 2^{25}

    J. 25^2

    K. 4^{10}

Step 1: Understand

It's not hard to figure out what the question's asking: Which of five numbers is the greatest? But the five numbers are all written as powers, some of which we don't have time to calculate. Yikes! How are we going to compare them?

Step 2: Analyze

If all the powers had the same base or the same exponent, or if they could all be rewritten with a common base or exponent, we could compare all five at once. As it is, though, we should take two at a time.

Compare 1^{50} and 50^1 to start. $1^{50} = 1$, while $50^1 = 50$, so there's no way choice F could be the biggest.

Next compare 50^1 and 2^{25} We don't have time to calculate 2^{25}, but we can see that it doesn't take anywhere near 25 factors of 2 to get over 50. In fact, 2^6 is 64, already more than 50, so 2^{25} is much, much more than 50. That eliminates G.

Choice J, 25^2, doesn't take too long to calculate: $25 \times 25 = 625$. How does that compare to 2^{25}? Once again, with a little thought, we realize that it doesn't take 25 factors of 2 to get over 625. That eliminates J.

The last comparison is easy because choice K, 4^{10}, can be rewritten as $(2^2)^{10} = 2^{20}$, which in that form is clearly less than 2^{25}. That eliminates K.

Step 3: Select

So the answer is H.

DEFINITION ALERT

You've probably encountered every math term that appears on the ACT sometime in high school, but you may not remember what each one means. Here are a few small but important technicalities that you may have forgotten:

- **"Integers" include 0 and negative whole numbers.**

  If a question says, "x and y are integers," it's not ruling out numbers like 0 and -1.

- **"Evens and odds" include 0 and negative whole numbers.**

  0 and -2 are even numbers. -1 is an odd number.

- **"Prime numbers" do not include 1.**

  The technical definition of a prime number is, "a positive integer with exactly two distinct positive integer factors." 2 is prime because it has exactly two positive factors: 1 and 2. 4 is not prime because it has three positive factors (1, 2, and 4) —too many! And 1 is not prime because it has only one positive factor (1)—too few!

- **"Remainders" are integers.**

  If a question asks for the remainder when 15 is divided by 2, don't say, "15 divided by 2 is 7.5, so the remainder is .5." What you should say is: "15 divided by 2 is 7 with a remainder of 1."

- **The $\sqrt{}$ symbol represents the positive square root only.**

  The equation $x^2 = 9$ has two solutions: 3 and -3. But when you see $\sqrt{9}$, it means positive 3 only.

- **"Rectangles" include squares.**

  A rectangle is a four-sided figure with four right angles, whether or not the length and width are the same. When a question refers to "rectangle *ABCD*," it's not ruling out a square.

Know Your Terminology

Learn the small but important technicalities that can help you earn points.

KAPLAN'S TWO-PASS PLAN FOR ACT MATH

We recommend that you plan two "passes" through the Math subtest.

- **First Pass:** Examine each problem in order. Do every problem you understand. Don't skip too hastily—sometimes it takes a few seconds of thought to see how to do something—but don't get bogged down. Never spend more than a minute on any question in the first pass. This first pass should take about 45 minutes.

- **Second Pass:** Use the last 15 minutes to go back to the questions that stumped you the first time. Sometimes a fresh second look is all you need, and you might suddenly see what to do. In most cases, though, you'll still be stumped by the question stem, so it's time to give the answer choices a try. Work by process of elimination, and guess.

Don't plan on visiting a question a third time; it's inefficient to go back and forth that much. Always grid in an answer choice on the second pass; every question should be answered.

Don't worry if you don't work on every question in the section. The average ACT test taker gets fewer than half of the problems right. You can score in the top quarter of all ACT test takers if you can do just half of the problems on the test, get every single one of them right, and guess blindly on the other half. If you did just *one-third* of the problems and got every one right, then guessed blindly on the other forty problems, you would still earn an average score.

KNOW WHEN TO SKIP A QUESTION

At any time during the three-step problem-solving process you could choose to cut bait and skip the question. Almost everyone should skip at least some questions the first time through. (But remember, don't leave these questions blank! Always go back and guess if you have to.)

If you know your own strengths and weaknesses, you can sometimes choose to skip a question while still in Step 1: "Understand." For example, suppose you never studied trigonometry— maybe you think that a secant is something that sailors sing while climbing up the yardarms. Well, the ACT includes four trigonometry questions, and it's not hard to spot them. Why not pass on such questions? You don't need those four measly questions to get a great score. And since you know a second visit later won't help, you might as well go ahead and guess.

It can be harder to decide when to skip a question if you understand it, but then get stuck in Step 2: "Analyze." Suppose you just don't see how to solve it. Don't give up too quickly. Sometimes it takes a half-minute or so before you see the light. But don't get bogged down, either. Never spend more than a minute on a question the first time through. Be prepared to leave a question and come back to it later. Often, on the second try, you'll see something you didn't see earlier.

Eventually, you're going to grid in answer choices for all the questions, even the ones you don't understand. The first time through, though, concentrate on the questions you understand.

WHAT TO DO WHEN YOU'RE STUCK

Let's say you're on your second pass. You've done some good work on a particular question, but you just can't get an answer. What you *don't* want to do is stall and waste time. What you *do* want to do is take your best shot at the question and move on. Guesstimating and eyeballing are two handy methods for doing just that.

Estimates and Guesstimates

Sometimes when you understand a problem but can't figure out how to solve it, you can at least get a general idea of how big the answer is—what is sometimes called a "ballpark estimate," or "guesstimate." You may not know whether you are looking at something the size of an African elephant or the size of an Indian elephant, but you may be pretty sure it isn't the size of a mouse and it isn't the size of a battleship.

Here's a question that's not hard to understand but is hard to solve if you don't remember the rules for simplifying and adding radicals:

5. $\dfrac{\sqrt{32} + \sqrt{24}}{\sqrt{8}} = ?$

    A. $\sqrt{7}$

    B. $\sqrt{2} + \sqrt{3}$

    C. $2 + \sqrt{3}$

    D. $\sqrt{2} + 3$

    E. 7

Step 1: Understand

The question wants you to simplify the given expression, which includes three radicals. In other words, turn the radicals into numbers you can use, then work out the fraction.

Step 2: Analyze

The best way to solve this problem would be to apply the rules of radicals—but what if you don't remember them? Don't give up; you can still guesstimate. In the question stem, the numbers under the radicals are not too far away from perfect squares. You could round $\sqrt{32}$ off to $\sqrt{36}$, which is 6. You could round 24 to $\sqrt{25}$, which is 5. And you could round $\sqrt{8}$ off to $\sqrt{9}$, which is 3. So the expression is now $\dfrac{6+5}{3}$, which is $3\dfrac{2}{3}$. That's just a guesstimate, of course—the actual value might be something a bit less or a bit more than that.

Step 3: Select

Now look at the answer choices. Choice A, $\sqrt{7}$, is less than 3, so it's too small. Choice B, $\sqrt{2} + \sqrt{3}$, is about 1.4 + 1.7, or just barely more than 3, so it seems a little small, too. Choice C, $2 + \sqrt{3}$, is about 2 + 1.7, or about 3.7—that's very close to our guesstimate! We still have to check the other choices. Choice D, $\sqrt{2} + 3$, is about 1.4 + 3, or 4.4—too big. And choice E, 7, is obviously way too big. Looks like our best bet is C—and C, in fact, is the correct answer.

Key Values to Remember

It pays to learn the approximate value of these three irrational numbers:

$$\sqrt{2} \approx 1.4$$

$$\sqrt{3} \approx 1.7$$

$$\pi \approx 3.14$$

Eyeballing

There is another simple but powerful strategy that should give you at least a 50-50 chance on almost every diagram question: When in doubt, use your eyes. Trust common sense and careful thinking; don't worry if you've forgotten most of the geometry you ever knew. For almost half of all diagram questions you can get a reasonable answer without solving anything. Just eyeball it.

The math directions say, "Illustrative figures are NOT necessarily drawn to scale," but in fact they almost always are. You're never really supposed to just eyeball the figure, but it makes a lot more sense than random guessing. Occasionally eyeballing can narrow the choices down to one likely candidate.

Here's a difficult geometry question that you might just decide to eyeball:

6. In the figure below, points *A*, *B*, and *C* lie on a circle centered at *O*. Triangle *AOC* is equilateral, and the length of *OC* is 3 inches. What is the length, in inches, of arc *ABC* ?

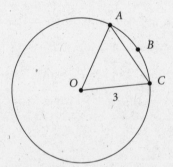

    F.   3

    G.   π

    H.   2π

    J.   3π

    K.   6π

Step 1: Understand

There's an "equilateral" triangle that connects the center and two points on the circumference of a circle. We're looking for the length of the arc that goes from *A* to *C*.

Step 2: Analyze

What you're "supposed" to do to answer this question is recall and apply the formula for the length of an arc. But suppose you don't remember that formula (most people don't). Should you give up and take a wild guess?

No. You can eyeball it. If you understand the question well enough to realize that "equilateral" means that all sides are equal, then you know immediately that side *AC* is 3 inches long. Now look at arc *ABC* compared to side *AC*. Suppose you were an ant, and you had to walk from *A* to *C*. If you walked along line segment *AC*, it would be a 3-inch trip. About how long a walk would it be along arc *ABC*? Clearly more, but not much more, than 3 inches.

Step 3: Select

Now look at the answer choices. Choice F, 3, is no good; we know the arc is more than 3 inches. All the other choices are in terms of π. Just think of π as "a bit more than 3," and you will quickly see that only one answer choice is in the right ballpark. Choice G, π, would be "a bit more than 3," which sounds pretty good. Choice H, 2π, would be "something more than 6"— way too big. Choices J and K are even bigger. It looks like the answer has to be G—and it is.

This is a pretty hard question. Not many ACT students would be able to solve it the textbook way. If you did, great! That's the way to do it if you know how. Solving the problem is always more reliable than eyeballing.

But when you don't know how to solve a diagram problem, or if you think it would take forever to get an answer, eyeballing and eliminating answer choices sure beat wild guessing. Sometimes, as with question 6, you might even be able to narrow down the choices to the one that's probably correct.

When to Eyeball

Eyeball a geometry problem if you don't have the time or knowledge to solve it.

This step has introduced you to the methods for success on ACT Math. In the next Math step we'll give you some advice about calculator use, and in the final two Math steps, we'll talk about specific strategies for the two major areas of ACT Math—algebra and geometry.

Calculator Techniques

Students are permitted to use calculators on the Math section of the ACT. The good news for noncalculator users is that you never absolutely need to use a calculator to answer the questions on the ACT. No Math question will require messy or tedious calculations. But while the calculator can't answer questions for you, it can keep you from making computational errors on questions you know how to solve. The bad news, however, is that a calculator can actually cost you time if you overuse it. Take a look at this example:

1. The sum of all the integers from 1 to 44, inclusive, is subtracted from the sum of all the integers from 7 to 50, inclusive. What is the result?

    A. 6
    B. 44
    C. 50
    D. 264
    E. 300

You could . . . add all the integers from 1 through 44, and then all the integers from 7 through 50, and then subtract the first sum from the second. And then punch all the numbers into the calculator. And then hope you didn't hit any wrong buttons.

But that's the long way . . . and the wrong way. That way involves hitting over 250 keys on your calculator. It'll take too long, and you're too likely to make a mistake. The amount of computation involved in solving this problem tells you that there must be an easier way. Remember, no ACT problem absolutely requires the use of a calculator.

THINK BEFORE YOU CALCULATE

Let's look at that problem again:

1. The sum of all the integers from 1 to 44, inclusive, is subtracted from the sum of all the integers from 7 to 50, inclusive. What is the result?

   A. 6
   B. 44
   C. 50
   D. 264
   E. 300

A calculator can help you on this question, but you have to think first. Both sums contain the same number of consecutive integers, and each integer in the first sum has a corresponding integer 6 greater than it in the second sum. Here's the scratchwork:

$$
\begin{array}{cc}
1 & 7 \\
+2 & +8 \\
+3 & +9 \\
\cdot & \cdot \\
\cdot & \cdot \\
\cdot & \cdot \\
+42 & +48 \\
+43 & +49 \\
+44 & +50 \\
\end{array}
$$

This means there are 44 pairs of integers that are each 6 apart. So the total difference between the two sums will be the difference between each pair of integers, times the number of pairs. Now you can pull out your calculator, punch "6 × 44 =" and get the correct answer of 264 with little or no time wasted. Mark D in your test booklet and move on.

Here's another way to solve it. Both sets of integers contain the integers 7 through 44 inclusive. Think of $7 + 8 + 9 + 10 + \ldots + 50$ as $(7 + 8 + 9 + 10 + \ldots + 44) + (45 + 46 + 47 + 48 + 49 + 50)$. Now think of $1 + 2 + 3 + 4 + \ldots + 44$ as $(1 + 2 + 3 + 4 + 5 + 6) + (7 + 8 + 9 + 10 + \ldots + 44)$.

So $(7 + 8 + 9 + 10 + \ldots + 50) - (1 + 2 + 3 + 4 + \ldots + 44) =$
$(45 + 46 + 47 + 48 + 49 + 50) - (1 + 2 + 3 + 4 + 5 + 6) =$
$(45 - 1) + (46 - 2) + (47 - 3) + (48 - 4) + (49 - 5) + (50 - 6) =$
$44 + 44 + 44 + 44 + 44 + 44 = 6(44) = 264.$

USING THE CALCULATOR TO SAVE TIME

Of course, there will be many questions for which using a calculator can save you time. Here's an ACT trig question that's much easier with a calculator:

2. $\sin 495° =$

   F. $\dfrac{-\sqrt{2}}{2}$

   G. $-\dfrac{1}{2}$

   H. $\dfrac{1}{2}$

   J. $\dfrac{\sqrt{2}}{2}$

   K. $\dfrac{3\sqrt{2}}{2}$

Without a calculator, this is a very difficult problem. To find a trigonometric function of an angle greater than or equal to 90°, sketch a circle of radius 1 and centered at the origin of the coordinate grid. Start from the point $(1, 0)$ and rotate the appropriate number of degrees counterclockwise. When you rotate counterclockwise 495°, you rotate 360° (which brings you back to where you started), and then an additional 135°. That puts you 45° into the second quadrant. Now you need to know whether sine is positive or negative in the second quadrant. Pretty scary, huh?

With a calculator, this problem becomes simple. Just punch in "sin 495°" and you get 0.7071067811865. F and G are negative, so they're out, and 0.7071067811865 is clearly not equal to $\dfrac{1}{2}$, so H is also wrong. That leaves only J or K. Now, $\sqrt{2}$ is greater than 1, so if you multiply it by another number greater than 1 (namely $\dfrac{3}{2}$), the result is obviously greater than 1. So you can eliminate K, leaving J as the correct answer. With a calculator, you can get this question right without really understanding it.

CALCULATORS: THE GAME PLAN

The key to effective calculator use is practice, so don't buy one the night before the test. If you don't already have a calculator (and intend to use one on the test), buy one now. Make sure you buy an extra set of fresh batteries that you can bring with you on test day. You don't want to be stuck with a dead calculator in the middle of a question! Unless you plan to study math or science in college, you won't need anything more complex than trig functions. Bear in mind that you're better off bringing a simple model that you're familiar with than an esoteric model you don't know how to use.

The following calculators are NOT allowed on the test: pocket organizers, computers, models with writing pads, computers with QWERTY keyboards, paper tapes, power cords, wireless transmitters, noisy calculators, Cray supercomputers.

Know Your Calculator

Practicing with your calculator is the best way to get a sense of where it can help and save time.

3. $(7.3 + 0.8) - 3(1.98 + 0.69) =$

   A. -0.99

   B. -0.09

   C. 0

   D. 0.09

   E. 0.99

This problem basically involves straightforward computation, so you'd be right if you reached for your calculator. However, if you just start punching the numbers in as they appear in the question, you might come up with the wrong answer. When you're performing a string of computations you know that you need to follow the right order of operations. The problem is, your calculator might not know this. Some calculators have parentheses keys and do follow PEMDAS, so it's important to know your machine and what its capabilities are. PEMDAS stands for *Parentheses* first, then *Exponents*, then *Multiplication and Division* (left to right), and last, *Addition and Subtraction* (left to right).

If your calculator doesn't follow the order of operations, you'd need to perform the operations within parentheses separately. You'd get $8.1 - 3(2.67)$. Multiplication comes before subtraction, so you'd get $8.1 - 8.01$, and then finally .09, choice D.

4. A certain bank issues 3-letter identification codes to its customers. If each letter can be used only once per code, how many different codes are possible?

   F.   26

   G.   78

   H.   326

   J.   15,600

   K.   17,576

For the first letter in the code you can choose any of the 26 letters in the alphabet. For the second letter, you can choose from all the letters except the one you used in the first spot, so there are 26 − 1 = 25 possibilities. For the third there are 26 − 2 = 24 possibilities. So the total number of different codes possible is equal to 26 × 25 × 24. Using your calculator you find there are 15,600 codes—choice J.

Backsolve

A calculator can help you in backsolving (plugging the answer choices back into the question stem) and picking numbers (substituting numbers for the variables in the question).

5. Which of the following fractions is greater than 0.68 and less than 0.72?

A. $\dfrac{5}{9}$

B. $\dfrac{3}{5}$

C. $\dfrac{7}{11}$

D. $\dfrac{2}{3}$

E. $\dfrac{5}{7}$

Here you have to convert the fractions in the answer choices to decimals and see which one falls in the range of values given to you in the question. If you're familiar with common decimal and fraction conversions, you might know that choice B, $\dfrac{3}{5}$ = .6, is too small and choice D, $\dfrac{2}{3}$, approximately .67, is also too small. But you'd still have to check out the other three choices. Your calculator can make short work of this, showing you that choice A, $\dfrac{5}{9}$ =.5$\overline{5}$, choice C, $\dfrac{7}{11}$ = .$\overline{63}$, and choice E, $\dfrac{5}{7}$, is approximately .71. Only 0.71 falls between 0.68 and 0.72, so E is correct.

STEP EIGHT

Algebra, Coordinate Geometry, Percents, and Averages

STEP EIGHT PREVIEW

Textbook Algebra and Coordinate Geometry Questions

Complex Algebra and Coordinate Geometry Questions
- Restate the Problem
- Remove the Disguise
- Pick Numbers
- Backsolve

Story Problems
- Percent Problems
- Percent Increase/Decrease Problems
- Average Problems
- Weighed Average Problems
- Probability Problems

The main idea of the first Math step was: Don't jump in headfirst and start crunching numbers until you've given the problem some thought. Make sure you know what you're doing, and that what you're doing won't take too long.

As we saw, sometimes you'll know how to proceed as soon as you understand the question. A good number of ACT algebra and coordinate geometry questions are straightforward textbook questions you may already be prepared for.

TEXTBOOK ALGEBRA AND COORDINATE GEOMETRY QUESTIONS

When you take the ACT, you can be sure you'll see some of the following questions with only slight variations. We're assuming that you know how to do these basic kinds of questions. If not, you probably want to pick up Kaplan's larger *ACT* book, which contains a section covering these basic techniques. You might also consider putting off your test, if possible. If you don't know how to multiply binomials, factor a polynomial, or solve a quadratic equation by now, you probably won't be ready to take the test in just a few weeks.

By test day, then, you should know how to do the following:

1. Evaluate an algebraic expression.
   Example: If $x = -2$, then $x^2 + 5x - 6 = ?$

2. Multiply binomials.
   Example: $(x + 3)(x + 4) = ?$

3. Factor a polynomial.
   Example: What is the complete factorization of $x^2 - 5x + 6$?

4. Solve a quadratic equation.
   Example: If $x^2 + 12 = 7x$, what are the two possible values of x?

5. Simplify an algebraic fraction.

   Example: For all $x \neq \pm 3$, $\dfrac{x^2 - x - 12}{x^2 - 9} = ?$

6. Solve a linear equation.
   Example: If $5x - 12 = -2x + 9$, then $x = ?$

7. Solve a system of equations.
   Example: If $4x + 3y = 8$, and $x + y = 3$, what is the value of x?

8. Solve an inequality.
   Example: What are all the values of x for which $-5x + 7 < -3$?

9. Find the distance between two points in the (x, y) coordinate plane.
   Example: What is the distance between the points with (x, y) coordinates $(-2, 2)$ and $(1, -2)$?

10. Find the slope of a line from its equation.
    Example: What is the slope of the line with the equation $2x + 3y = 4$?

These questions are all so straightforward and traditional, they could have come out of a high school algebra textbook. These are the questions you should do the way you were taught.

COMPLEX ALGEBRA AND COORDINATE GEOMETRY QUESTIONS

The techniques you'd use on textbook questions are the techniques you've been taught in high school math classes. We're not so concerned in this book with such problems. Here we're focused on algebra and coordinate geometry situations where the quick and reliable solution method is not so obvious, and where often the best method is one your algebra teacher never taught you.

It's bound to happen at some point during the test. You look at a math problem and you don't see what to do. Don't freak out. Think about the problem for a few seconds before you give up. When you don't see the quick and reliable approach right away, shake up the problem a little. Try one of these "shake-it-up" techniques:

1. Restate the problem.
2. Remove the disguise.
3. Pick numbers.
4. Backsolve.

Restate the Problem

Often the way to get over that stymied feeling is to change your perspective. Have you ever watched people playing Scrabble™? In their search to form high-scoring words from their seven letters, they continually move the tiles around in their racks. Sometimes a good word becomes apparent only after rearranging the tiles. One might not see the seven-letter word in this arrangement:

REBAGLA

But just reverse the tiles and a word almost reveals itself:

ALGABER

The same gimmick works on the ACT, too. When you get stuck, try looking at the problem from a different angle. Rearrange the numbers or change fractions to decimals. Or, factor, multiply out, or redraw the diagram. Do anything that might give you a fresh perspective.

Here's a question you might not know how to handle at first glance:

1. Which of the following is equivalent to $7^{77} - 7^{76}$?

   A. 7
   B. 7^{77-76}
   C. $7^{77} \div 76$
   D. $7(77 - 76)$
   E. $7^{76}(6)$

Here's a hint: Think of an easier problem testing the same principles. The important thing to look for is the basic relationships involved—here, we have exponents and subtraction. That subtraction sign causes trouble, because none of the ordinary rules of exponents seem to apply when there is subtraction of "unlike" terms.

Another hint: How would you work with $x^2 - x$? Most test takers could come up with another expression for $x^2 - x$: They'd factor to $x(x-1)$. So if the problem asked for $x^{77} - x^{76}$, they'd factor to $x^{76}(x-1)$. The rule is no different for 7 than for x. Factoring out the 7^{76} gives you: $7^{76}(7-1)$, which is $7^{76}(6)$, or choice E.

Make Tough Problems Easier

On a complex question, think of how you would handle an easy problem that tests the same principle.

Sometimes an algebra question will include an expression that isn't of much use in its given form. Try restating the expression by either simplifying it or factoring it. For example:

2. If $\dfrac{x}{2} - \dfrac{x}{6}$ is an integer, which of the following statements must be true?

    F. x is positive.

    G. x is odd.

    H. x is even.

    J. x is a multiple of 3.

    K. x is a multiple of 6.

Reexpress it as: $\dfrac{x}{2} - \dfrac{x}{6} = \dfrac{3x}{6} - \dfrac{x}{6} = \dfrac{2x}{6} = \dfrac{x}{3}$

This form of the expression tells us a lot more. If $\dfrac{x}{3}$ is an integer, then x is equal to 3 times an integer:

$$\frac{x}{3} = \text{an integer}$$

$$x = 3 \times (\text{an integer})$$

So x is a multiple of 3, choice J.

Remove the Disguise

Sometimes it's hard to see the quick and reliable method right away because the true nature of the problem is hidden behind a disguise. Look at this example:

3. What are the (x, y) coordinates of the point of intersection of the line representing the equation $5x + 2y = 4$ and the line representing the equation $x - 2y = 8$?

   A. $(2, 3)$
   B. $(-2, 3)$
   C. $(2, -3)$
   D. $(-3, 2)$
   E. $(3, -2)$

This may look like a coordinate geometry question, but do you really have to graph the lines to find the point of intersection? Remember, the ACT is looking for creative thinkers, not mindless calculators! Think about it—what's the significance of the point of intersection, the one point that the two lines have in common? That's the one point whose coordinates will satisfy both equations.

So what we realize now is that this is not a coordinate geometry question at all, but a "system of equations" question. All it's really asking you to do is solve the pair of equations for x and y. The question has nothing to do with slopes, intercepts, axes, or quadrants. It's a pure algebra question in disguise.

Now that we know we're looking at a system of equations, the method of solution presents itself more clearly. The first equation has $x + 2y$, and the second equation has $x - 2y$. If we just "add" the equations, the y terms cancel:

$$5x + 2y = 4$$
$$\underline{x - 2y = 8}$$
$$6x = 12$$

If $6x = 12$, then $x = 2$. Plug that back into either of the original equations and you'll find that $y = -3$. The point of intersection is $(2, -3)$, and the answer is C.

4. A geometer uses the following formula to estimate the area A of the shaded portion of a circle as shown in the figure below when only the height h and the length of the chord c are known:

$$A = \frac{2ch}{3} + \frac{h^3}{2c}$$

What is the geometer's estimate of the area, in square inches, of the shaded region if the height is 2 inches and the length of the chord is 6 inches?

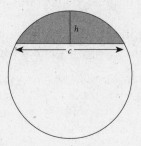

F. 6

G. $6\frac{2}{3}$

H. $7\frac{1}{2}$

J. $8\frac{2}{3}$

K. 12

At first glance this looks like a horrendously esoteric geometry question. Who ever heard of such a formula?

But when you think about the question, you realize that you don't really have to understand the formula. In fact, this is not a geometry question at all; it's really just an "evaluate the algebraic expression" question in disguise. All you have to do is plug the given values $h = 2$ and $c = 6$ into the given formula:

$$A = \frac{2ch}{3} + \frac{h^3}{2c}$$

$$= \frac{2(6)(2)}{3} + \frac{2^3}{2(6)}$$

$$= 8 + \frac{2}{3} = 8\frac{2}{3}$$

Choice J is correct.

The people who wrote this question wanted you to freak out at first sight and give up. Don't give up on a question too quickly just because it looks like it's testing something you never saw before. In many such cases it's really a familiar problem in disguise.

Don't Be Intimidated

A complex problem is often just an easier problem in disguise.

Pick Numbers

Sometimes you can get stuck on an algebra problem just because it's too general or abstract. A good way to get a handle on such a problem is to make it more explicit by temporarily substituting particular numbers for the variables. For example:

5. If a is an odd integer and b is an even integer, which of the following must be odd?

   A. $2a + b$
   B. $a + 2b$
   C. ab
   D. a^2b
   E. ab^2

Rather than try to think this one through abstractly, it's easier to pick numbers for a and b. There are rules that predict the evenness or oddness of sums, differences, and products, but there's no need to memorize those rules. When it comes to adding, subtracting, and multiplying evens and odds, what happens with one pair of numbers generally happens with all similar pairs.

Just say, for the time being, that $a = 1$ and $b = 2$. Plug those values into the answer choices, and there's a good chance only one choice will be odd:

   A. $2a + b = 2(1) + 2 = 4$
   B. $a + 2b = 1 + 2(2) = 5$
   C. $ab = (1)(2) = 2$
   D. $a^2b = (1)^2(2) = 2$
   E. $ab^2 = (1)(2)^2 = 4$

Choice B was the only odd one for $a = 1$ and $b = 2$, so it *must* be the one that's odd no matter *what* odd number a is and even number b is.

Get Specific

Make abstract problems concrete by substituting numbers for variables.

Backsolve

With some Math problems, it may actually be easier to try out each answer choice until you find the one that works, rather than try to solve the problem and then look among the choices for the answer. Since this approach involves working backwards from the answer choices to the question stem, it's called backsolving. Here's a good example:

6. All 200 tickets were sold for a particular concert. Some tickets cost $10 apiece, and the others cost $5 apiece. If total ticket sales were $1,750, how many of the more expensive tickets were sold?

    F.   20

    G.   75

    H.   100

    J.   150

    K.   175

There are ways to solve this problem by setting up an equation or two, but if you're not comfortable with the algebraic approach to this one, why not just try out each answer choice?

The answer choices are generally listed in numerical order, and if the first number you try doesn't work, the process of plugging in that first number might tell you whether you'll need a smaller or a larger number. So when backsolving, start off with the middle choice (choice C or H) to be safe.

So, start with choice H. If 100 tickets went for $10, then the other 100 went for $5. The cost of 100 tickets at $10 is $1,000, and 100 tickets at $5 is $500, for a total of $1,500—too small. There must have been more than 100 $10 tickets.

Try choice J next. If 150 tickets went for $10, then the other 50 went for $5. The cost of 150 tickets at $10 is $1,500, and 50 tickets at $5 is $250, for a total of $1,750—that's it! The answer is J.

Backsolving your way to the answer may not be a method you'd show your algebra teacher with pride, but your algebra teacher won't be watching while you take the test. Remember, all that matters is right answers—it doesn't matter how you get them.

Start in the Middle

When backsolving, start with the middle choice, C (or H).

KAPLAN

STORY PROBLEMS

We find that about one-third of the questions on the Math subtest are story problems. Although some story problems present unique situations that must be analyzed on the spot, others are just variations on familiar themes.

Percent Problems

In percent problems, you're usually given two numbers and asked to find a third. The key is to identify what you have and what you're looking for.

Dealing with Percent Problems

In Percent problems, identify the part, the percent, and the whole, and remember that Part = Percent × Whole.

Put the numbers and the unknown into the general form:

(Usually the part is associated with the word *is* and the whole is associated with the word *of*.)

For example:

7. In a group of 250 students, 40 are seniors. What percentage of the group is seniors?

   A. 1.6 percent
   B. 6.25 percent
   C. 10 percent
   D. 16 percent
   E. 40 percent

The percent is what we're looking for ("What percentage . . ."); the whole is 250 (". . . of the group . . ."); and the part is 40 (". . . is seniors"). Plug these into the general formula:

Part = Percent × Whole

$40 = 250x$

$x = \dfrac{40}{250} = .16 = 16$ percent, choice D

Percent Increase/Decrease Problems

Many ACT percent problems concern percent change. To increase a number by a certain percent, calculate that percent of the original number and add it on. To decrease a number by a certain percent, calculate that percent of the original number and subtract. For example, to answer "What number is 30 percent greater than 80?" find 30 percent of 80—that's 24—and add that to 80: 80 + 24 = 104.

The ACT has ways of complicating percent change problems. Especially tricky are problems with multiple changes, such as a percent increase followed by another percent increase, or a percent increase followed by a percent decrease.

Here's a question, for example, that's not as simple as it seems:

8. If a positive number is increased by 70 percent, and then the result is decreased by 50 percent, which of the following accurately describes the net change?

   F. a 20 percent decrease
   G. a 15 percent decrease
   H. a 12 percent increase
   J. a 20 percent increase
   K. a 120 percent increase

The way to get a handle on this one is to pick a number. Suppose the original number is 100. After a 70 percent increase it rises to 170. That number, 170, is decreased by 50 percent, which means it's reduced by half to 85. The net change from 100 to 85 is a 15 percent decrease—choice G.

Start With 100

Don't just add and subtract percents. Pick 100 as the original number and work from there.

Average Problems

Instead of giving you a list of values to plug into the average formula, ACT average questions often have a slight spin. They tell you the average of a group of terms and ask you to find the value of the missing term. Here's a classic example:

9. To earn a B for the semester, Linda needs an average of at least 80 on the five tests. Her average for the first four test scores is 79. What is the minimum score she must get on the fifth test to earn a B for the semester?

   A. 80
   B. 81
   C. 82
   D. 83
   E. 84

The key to almost every average question is to use the sum. Sums can be combined much more readily than averages. An average of 80 on five tests is more usefully thought of as a combined score of 400. To get a B for the semester, Linda's five test scores have to add up to 400 or more. The first four scores add up to $4 \times 79 = 316$. She needs 84 to get that 316 up to 400. The answer is E.

Weighted Average Problems

Another spin ACT test makers use is to give you an average for part of a group and an average for the rest of the group and then ask for the combined average.

Be Careful

To get a combined average, it's usually wrong just to average the averages.

For example:

10. In a class of 10 boys and 15 girls, the boys' average score on the final exam was 80 and the girls' average score was 90. What was the average score for the whole class?

    F. 83
    G. 84
    H. 85
    J. 86
    K. 87

Don't just average 80 and 90 to get 85. That would work only if the class had exactly the same number of girls as boys. In this case, there are more girls, so they carry more "weight" in the overall class average. In other words, the class average should be somewhat closer to 90 (the girls' average) than to 80 (the boys' average).

As usual with averages, the key is to use the sum. The average score for the whole class is the total of the 25 individual scores divided by 25. We don't have 25 scores to add up, but we can use the boys' average and the girls' average to get two subtotals.

If 10 boys average 80, then their 10 scores add up to 10×80, or 800 total. If 15 girls average 90, then their 15 scores add up to 15×90, or 1,350 total. Add the boys' total to the girls' total: $800 + 1,350 = 2,150$. That's the class total, which can be divided by 25 to get the class average: $\frac{2,150}{25} = 86$. The answer is J.

Probability Problems

Probabilities are part-to-whole ratios. The whole is the total number of possible outcomes. The part is the number of "favorable" outcomes. For example, if a drawer contains two black ties and five other ties, and you want a black tie, the total number of possible outcomes is 7 (the total number of ties) and the number of "favorable" outcomes is 2 (the number of black ties). The probability of choosing a black tie at random is $\frac{2}{7}$.

The Past Doesn't Matter

Remember, the probability of what will happen is not affected by what has happened already.

Because more than half the Math questions on the ACT involve algebra, it's a good idea to take some time before the day of the test to solidify your understanding of the basics. Keep things in perspective. Geometry's important, too, but algebra's more important.

Geometry

STEP NINE PREVIEW

Textbook Geometry Questions

Complex Geometry Questions
- Find the Hidden Information
- Figureless Problems
- Multi-Step Problems

The ACT Math test typically has 14 plane geometry questions and 4 trigonometry questions. Depending on what kind of score you're aiming for, you might be able to blow off those few trigonometry questions. But you probably don't want to blow off many geometry questions.

Fortunately, a good number of the geometry questions are straightforward. Nothing is distorted or disguised. With these questions you know what to do—if you know your geometry—the instant you understand them.

TEXTBOOK GEOMETRY QUESTIONS

When you take the ACT you'll see a few questions requiring you to do some of the actions cited below. These are straightforward geometry tasks, and if you don't know how to do them by now, we recommend that you not take the ACT until you do. Again we refer you to the math review section in Kaplan's more comprehensive prep book, *ACT*.

- **Finding the area of a square or other rectangle**
  The formula for the area of a rectangle is $A = l \times w$.

- **Finding the area of a circle**

  The formula for the area of a circle is $A = \pi r^2$, where r is the radius.

- **Finding the area of a trapezoid**

  The formula for the area of a trapezoid is

  $$A = \left(\frac{b_1 + b_2}{2} \right) h, \text{ where } b_1 \text{ and } b_2 \text{ are the lengths of the parallel sides.}$$

- **Working with isosceles and equilateral triangles**
- **Working with special right triangles**

  $45°–45°–90°$; $30°–60°–90°$; etcetera

- **Using the Pythagorean theorem**

  The Pythagorean theorem says:

  $(\text{leg}_1)^2 + (\text{leg}_2)^2 = (\text{hypotenuse})^2$, or $a^2 + b^2 = c^2$.

- **Working with similar triangles**
- **Working with parallel lines and transversals**
- **Finding the area of a triangle**

  The formula for the area of a triangle is $A = \frac{1}{2} bh$.

- **Figuring the length of an arc**

Know Your Geometry

If you don't know your basic geometry, consider postponing your ACT.

COMPLEX GEOMETRY QUESTIONS

As if it weren't hard enough to remember all the facts and formulas needed for problems like the questions above, the test makers have ways of further complicating geometry questions.

Find the Hidden Information

Some ACT geometry questions are not all that they seem. It's not always obvious what the question's getting at. Sometimes you really have to think about the figure and the given information before that light bulb goes off in your head. Often the inspiration that brings illumination is finding the hidden information.

Here's an example that doesn't come right out and say what it's all about:

1. In the figure below, $\triangle ABC$ is a right triangle and $\overline{AC}$ is perpendicular to $\overline{BD}$. If $\overline{AB}$ is 6 units long, and $\overline{AC}$ is 10 units long, how many units long is $\overline{AD}$?

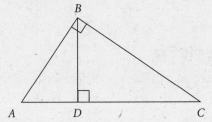

A. 3
B. $2\sqrt{3}$
C. 3.6
D. 4
E. $3\sqrt{2}$

At first this looks like a Pythagorean theorem question. In fact, the two given sides of $\triangle ABC$ identify it as the 6-8-10 version of the 3-4-5 special right triangle. So we know that $BC = 8$. So what? What good does that do us? How's that going to help us find AD ?

The inspiration here is to realize that this is a "similar triangles" problem. We don't see the word *similar* anywhere in the question stem, but the stem and the figure combined actually tell us that all three triangles in the figure—$\triangle ABC$, $\triangle ADB$, and $\triangle BDC$—are similar. We know the triangles are similar because they all have the same three angles. Here are the three triangles separated and oriented to show the correspondences:

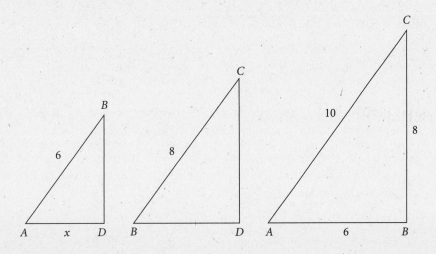

In this orientation it's easy to see the proportion setup that will solve the problem:

$$\frac{10}{6} = \frac{6}{x}$$

$$10x = 36$$

$$x = 3.6, \text{ choice C}$$

More Than Meets the Eye

If you find yourself stuck on a problem, look for hidden information.

Here's another example with hidden information:

2. In the figure below, the area of the circle centered at O is 25π, and $\overline{AC}$ is perpendicular to $\overline{OB}$. If $\overline{AC}$ is 8 units long, how many units long is $\overline{BD}$?

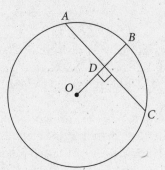

    F.   2
    G.   2.5
    H.   3
    J.   3.125
    K.   4

This is a tough one. It's not easy to see how to get $\overline{BD}$ from the given information. We can use the area—25π—to figure out the radius, and then we'd know the length of $\overline{OB}$:

$$\text{Area} = \pi r^2$$

$$25\pi = \pi r^2$$

$$25 = r^2$$

$$r = 5$$

So we know $\overline{OB} = 5$, but what about $\overline{BD}$? If we knew $\overline{OD}$, we could subtract that from $\overline{OB}$ to get what we want. But do we know $\overline{OD}$? This is where most people get stuck.

The inspiration that will lead to a solution is that we can take advantage of the right angle at D. Look what happens when we take a pencil and physically add $\overline{OA}$ and $\overline{OC}$ to the figure:

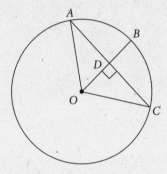

ΔOAD and ΔOCD are right triangles. And when we write in the lengths, we discover some special right triangles:

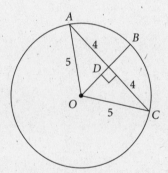

Now it's apparent that $\overline{OD} = 3$. Since $\overline{OB} = 5$, $\overline{BD}$ is $5 - 3 = 2$. The answer is F.

Draw on the Diagrams

Don't be afraid to pencil in additions to the given diagrams.

Figureless Problems

Some ACT geometry problems present an extra challenge because they don't provide a figure. You have to "figure it out" for yourself. Try this one:

3. If one side of a right triangle is 3 units long, and a second side is 4 units long, which of the following could be the length, in units, of the third side?

    A. 1
    B. 2
    C. $\sqrt{7}$
    D. $3\sqrt{2}$
    E. $3\sqrt{3}$

The key to solving most figureless problems is to sketch a diagram, but sometimes that's not so easy because you're given less information than you might like. Question 3 is the perfect example. It gives you two sides of a right triangle and asks for the third. Sounds familiar. And the two sides it gives you—3 and 4—really sound familiar. It's a 3-4-5, right?

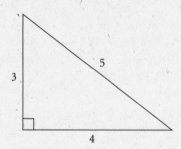

So the answer's 5 . . . whoops! There's no 5 among the answer choices! What's going on?

Better check back. Notice that the question asks, "which of the following could be the length . . . ?" That *could* is crucial. It suggests that there's more than one possibility. Our answer of 5 was too obvious. There's another one somewhere.

Can you think of another way of sketching the figure with the same given information? Who says that the 3 and 4 have to be the two legs? Look at what happens when you make one of them—the larger one, of course—the *hypotenuse*:

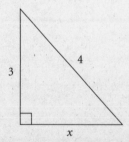

This is not a 3-4-5 triangle, because in a 3-4-5 the 3 and the 4 are the legs. This is not a special right triangle. To figure out the length of the third side, we'll just have to resort to the Pythagorean theorem:

$$(\text{leg}_1)^2 + (\text{leg}_2)^2 = (\text{hypotenuse})^2$$

$$3^2 + x^2 = 4^2$$
$$9 + x^2 = 16$$
$$x^2 = 7$$
$$x = \sqrt{7}$$

The answer is C.

Be an Artist

Sketch your own figures for figureless problems.

Multi-Step Problems

Some of the toughest ACT geometry questions take many steps to solve and combine different geometry concepts. Here's an example:

4. In the figure below, $\overline{AB}$ is tangent to the circle at A. If the circumference of the circle is 12π units and $\overline{OB}$ is 12 units long, what is the area, in square units, of the shaded region?

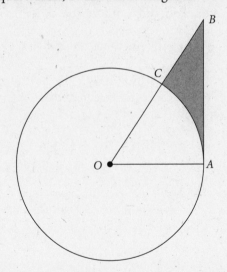

    F. $18\sqrt{3} - 6\pi$

    G. $24\sqrt{3} - 6\pi$

    H. $18\sqrt{3} - 2\pi$

    J. $12\pi - 12$

    K. $24\sqrt{3} - 2\pi$

This is about as hard as they come on the ACT. It's by no means clear how the given information—the circumference of the circle and the length of $\overline{OB}$—will lead us to the area of the shaded region.

So what do you do? Give up? No.

Don't give up immediately unless you're really short on time or you know for sure you can't do the problem. So then should you just plow ahead blindly and figure out every length, angle, and area you can and see where that leads?

Well, *not exactly*. It would be better to be more systematic.

The key to success with a circuitous problem like this is to focus on your destination—what you're looking for—and think about what you need to get there.

Our destination in question 4 is "the area of the shaded region." That region is a shape that has no name, let alone an area formula. Like most shaded regions, this one is the difference between two familiar shapes with names and area formulas. Think of the shaded region in question 4 as:

$$(\text{the area of } \Delta AOB) - (\text{the area of sector } AOC)$$

So, we now know that we need to figure out the area of the triangle and the area of the sector.

First, the triangle. We are explicitly given $\overline{OB} = 12$. We are also given that $\overline{AB}$ is tangent to the circle at A, which tells us that $\overline{OA}$ is a radius and that $\angle OAB$ is a right angle. So if we can figure out the radius of the circle, we'll have two sides of a right triangle, which will enable us to figure out the third side, and then figure out the area.

We can get the radius from the given circumference. Plug what we know into the formula and solve for r:

$$\text{Circumference} = 2\pi r$$

$$12\pi = 2\pi r$$

$$r = \frac{12\pi}{2\pi} = 6$$

$\overline{OA} = 6$. Aha! So it turns out that ΔAOB is no ordinary right triangle. Since one leg—6—is exactly half the hypotenuse—12—we're looking at a 30°-60°-90° triangle. By applying the well-known side ratios ($1:\sqrt{3}:2$) for a 30°-60°-90° triangle, we determine that $\overline{AB} = 6\sqrt{3}$.

Now we can plug the lengths of the legs in for the base and altitude in the formula for the area of a triangle:

$$\text{Area} = \frac{1}{2}bh$$

$$= \frac{1}{2}(6\sqrt{3})(6)$$

$$= 18\sqrt{3}$$

Already it looks like the answer's going to be F or H—they're the choices that begin with $18\sqrt{3}$. We could just guess F or H and move on, but if we've come this far, we might as well go all the way.

Next, the area of the sector. Fortunately, while working on the triangle, we figured out the two things we need to get the area of the sector: the radius of the circle (6) and the measure of the central angle (60°). The radius tells us that the area of the whole circle (πr^2) is 36π. And the central angle tells us that the area of the sector is $\frac{60}{360}$ or $\frac{1}{6}$ of the area of the circle. $\frac{1}{6}$ of 36π is 6π. So the area of the shaded region is $18\sqrt{3} - 6\pi$, choice F.

Break It Down

Break down complex problems into simpler steps.

A final bit of advice: Your goal on the ACT is to get as many points as possible, so focus your studies on the areas that are likely to generate the most points. Together, algebra and plane geometry make up the vast majority of ACT Math questions, so make sure you know how to do the basics in these areas.

Part Four

THE ACT READING TEST

STEP TEN

The Key to ACT Reading

STEP TEN PREVIEW

Know Where You're Going
- Common Structural Clues

Kaplan's Three-Step Method for ACT Reading
- Step 1: Preread the Passage
- Step 2: Consider the Question Stem
- Step 3: Refer to the Passage

Creating a Road Map
- Practicing Prereading
- The General Outline

The Fiction and Science Passages
- The Prose Fiction Passage
- The Natural Sciences Passage

The kind of reading rewarded by the ACT may not be what you expect. You may think that success on a test like this requires that you read very slowly and deliberately, making sure you remember everything. Well, we at Kaplan have found that this kind of reading won't work on the ACT. In fact, it's a sure way to run out of time halfway through the Reading test.

The real key to ACT Reading is to read very quickly but actively, getting a sense of the gist, or "main idea," of the passage and seeing how everything fits together to support that main idea. You should constantly try to think ahead. Look for the general outline of the passage—how it's structured. Don't worry about the details. You'll come back for those later.

Get a Sense of Direction

Read actively, with an eye toward where the author is going.

Fast, active reading, of course, requires a little more mental energy than slow, passive reading. But it pays off. Those who dwell on details—who passively let the passage reveal itself at its own pace—are sure to run out of time. Don't be that kind of reader! Again, the key is *take control.* Make the passage reveal itself to you on *your* schedule by skimming the passage, with an eye on structure rather than detail. Look for keywords that tell you what the author is doing, so that you can save yourself time. For example, read examples very, very quickly, just glancing over the words. When an author says "for example," you know that what follows is an example of a general point. Do you need to understand that specific example? Maybe, maybe not. If you *do,* you can come back and read the verbiage when you're attacking the questions. You'll know exactly where the author gave an example of general point *x* (or whatever). If you *don't* need to know the example for any of the questions, great! You haven't wasted much time on something that won't get you a point.

KNOW WHERE YOU'RE GOING

To help you know where an author is going, pay careful attention to "structural clues" (we discussed these briefly in "Basic English Skills"). Words such as *but, nevertheless,* and *moreover* help you get a sense of where a piece of writing is going. You also should look for signal phrases such as *clearly, as a result,* or *no one can deny that* to determine the logic of the passage. Remember, you can come back for the details later, when you're doing the questions. What's important in reading the passage is to get a sense of how those details fit together to express the point or points of the passage.

For your reference, we've gathered together some important ways in which an author "tells" you where a Reading passage is going.

Common Structural Clues

Indicating a contrast

> *but*
>
> *however*
>
> *on the other hand*
>
> *nevertheless*

Indicating a continuation with a similar or complementary thought

> *moreover*
> *furthermore*
> *; (a semicolon)*

Indicating a conclusion

> *therefore*
> *thus*

Indicating reasons for a conclusion

> *since*
> *because of*
> *due to*

Indicating an example or illustration

> *for instance*
> *for example*

Now let's see how you can use this skill of active reading to develop a plan of attack for the ACT Reading section.

KAPLAN'S THREE-STEP METHOD FOR ACT READING

You must always remember that when reading for the ACT, you have a special purpose: to answer specific multiple-choice questions. And we've found that the best way to do this is initially to read a passage quickly and actively for general understanding, then refer to the passage to answer individual questions. Not everybody should use the exact same strategy, but we find that almost every ACT test taker can succeed by following these three basic steps:

- Preread the passage quickly.
- Consider the question stem.
- Refer to the passage (before looking at the choices).

For most students, these three tasks should together take up about nine minutes per passage. Less than three of those nine minutes should be spent prereading. The remaining time should be devoted to considering the questions and referring to the passage to check your answers. As we mentioned earlier, you probably want to take two sweeps through the questions for each passage, getting the doable ones the first time around, and coming back for the harder ones.

Step 1: Preread the Passage

Prereading means quickly working through the passage before trying to answer the questions. Remember to "know where you're going," using structural clues to anticipate how the parts of the passage fit together. In this prereading, the main goals are:

- To understand the gist of the passage (the "main idea").
- To get an overall idea of how the passage is organized—a kind of road map—so that it will be easier to refer to later.

You may want to underline key points, jot down notes, circle structural clues—whatever it takes to accomplish the two goals above. You may even want to label each paragraph, to fix in your mind how the paragraphs relate to one another and what aspect of the main idea is discussed in each. That could be your road map.

An important reminder: *Don't read slowly, and don't get bogged down in individual details.* Most of the details in the passage aren't required for answering the questions, so why waste time worrying about them?

Get the Main Idea

Don't get bogged down in the details of the passage.

Step 2: Consider the Question Stem

Approaching the Reading questions requires self-discipline. Most test takers have an almost irresistible urge to immediately jump to the answer choices to see what "looks OK." That's not a good idea. The test makers intentionally design the answers to confuse you if they can.

It's All About the Question

Don't let the answer choices direct your thinking.

In Reading, you should think about the question stem (the part above the answer choices) *without looking at the choices.* In most cases, you won't be able to remember exactly what the passage said about the matter in question. That's all right. In fact, even if you do think you remember, don't trust your memory. Instead . . .

Step 3: Refer to the Passage

You won't be rereading the whole passage, of course. But look for the place where the answer to a question can be found (the question stem will sometimes contain a line reference to help you out; otherwise, rely on your road map of the passage). Your chosen answer should match the passage—not in exact vocabulary, perhaps, but in meaning.

The Passage Holds the Answer

Always refer to the passage before choosing an answer.

CREATING A ROAD MAP

Practicing Prereading

Now practice prereading on the full-length ACT passage that follows. We're not going to give you the questions until Step 11, when we'll talk about the different kinds of Reading questions and how to answer them. For now, just worry about the prereading part of the Kaplan Three-Step Method. Take three minutes or so, and preread the passage. Remember to read quickly, with an eye to the structure of the passage. Make yourself a road map for the passage. And—most important of all—keep track of time and don't get bogged down in details!

Tragedy was the invention of the Greeks. In their Golden Age, the fifth century before Christ, they produced the world's greatest
Line dramatists, new forms of tragedy and comedy
(5) that have been models ever since, and a theatre that every age goes back to for rediscovery of some basic principles. . . .

Since it derived from primitive religious rites, with masks and ceremonial costumes,
(10) and made use of music, dance, and poetry, the Greek drama was at the opposite pole from the modern realistic stage. In fact, probably no other theatre in history has made fuller use of the intensities of art. The
(15) masks, made of painted linen, wood, and plaster, brought down from primitive days the atmosphere of gods, heroes, and demons. Our nineteenth- and twentieth-century grandfathers thought masks must have been
(20) very artificial. Today, however, we appreciate their exciting intensity and can see that in a large theatre they were indispensable. If they allowed no fleeting change of expression during a single episode, they could give for
(25) each episode in turn more intense expression than any human face could. When Oedipus comes back with bleeding eyes, the new mask could be more terrible than any facial makeup the audience could endure, yet in its
(30) sculpted intensity more beautiful than a real face.

Most essential of all intensities, and hardest for us to understand, was the chorus. Yet many playwrights today are trying to find
(35) some equivalent to do for a modern play what the chorus did for the Greeks. During

the episodes played by the actors, the chorus would only provide a background of group response, enlarging and reverberating the
(40) emotions of the actors, sometimes protesting and opposing but in general serving as ideal spectators to stir and lead the reactions of the audience. But between episodes, with the actors out of the way, the chorus took over.
(45) We have only the words, not the music or dance, and some translations of the odes are in such formal, old-fashioned language that it is hard to guess that they were accompanied by vigorous, sometimes even
(50) wild dances and symbolic actions that filled an orchestra that in some cities was sixty to ninety feet in diameter. Sometimes the chorus expressed simple horror or lament. Sometimes it chanted and acted out, in
(55) unison and in precise formations of rows and lines, the acts of violence the characters were enacting offstage. When Phaedra rushes offstage in *Hippolytus* to hang herself from the rafters, the members of the chorus,
(60) all fifteen of them, perform in mime and chant the act of tying the rope and swinging from the rafters. Sometimes the chorus tells or reenacts an incident of history or legend that throws light on the situation in the play.
(65) Sometimes the chorus puts into specific action what is a general intention in the mind of the main character. When Oedipus resolves to hunt out the guilty person and cleanse the city, he is speaking
(70) metaphorically, but the chorus invokes the gods of vengeance and dances a wild pursuit.

On the printed page, the choral odes seem static and formal, lyric and philosophical, emotional let-downs that punctuate the
(75) series of episodes, like intermissions between two acts of a play. The reader who skips the odes can get the main points of the play. A few are worth reading as independent poems, notably the famous one in *Antigone*
(80) beginning, "Many are the wonders of the

world, but none is more wonderful than man." Some modern acting versions omit the chorus or reduce it to a few background figures. Yet to the Greeks the odes were
(85) certainly more than mere poetic interludes: the wild Dionysian words and movements evoked primitive levels of the subconscious and at the same time served to transform primitive violence into charm and beauty
(90) and to add philosophical reflections on the meaning of human destiny.

For production today, we can only improvise some partial equivalent. In Athens the entire population was familiar with
(95) choral performances. Every year each of the tribes entered a dithyramb in a contest, rehearsing five hundred men and boys for weeks. Some modern composers have tried to write dramatic music for
(100) choruses: the most notable examples are the French composer Darius Milhaud, in the primitive rhythms, shouts, and chants of his operatic version of the *Oresteia*; George Gershwin, in the Negro funeral scenes of
(105) *Porgy and Bess*; and Kurt Weill, in the African choruses for *Lost in the Stars*, the musical dramatization of Alan Paton's novel, *Cry, the Beloved Country*. For revivals of Greek tragedies we have not dared use much music
(110) beyond a few phrases half shouted, half sung, and drumbeats and suggestive melodies in the background.

From *Invitation to the Theatre*, Copyright 1967 by George Kernodle; Harcourt, Brace, & World Inc., publisher.

The General Outline

Your quick preread of the passage should have given you a sense of its general organization:

- First Paragraph—introduces the topic of Greek tragedy
- Second Paragraph—discusses use of masks (artificial but intense)
- Third Paragraph—discusses use of chorus (also artificial but intense)
- Fourth Paragraph—expands discussion to choral odes
- Fifth Paragraph—concludes with discussion of how Greek tragedy is performed today, and how it has influenced some modern art

And that's really all the road map you need going into the questions. Aside from that, you should take away a sense of the author's main point: Greek tragedy included many artificial devices, but these devices allowed it to rise to a high level of intensity.

You wouldn't need or even want to get more than this on your prereading of the passage. We know it's difficult for many students to accept, but it really is true: *Careful, detail-oriented reading does not pay on the ACT Reading test.* You just don't have the time.

Don't Go Without Your Road Map

Build a mental road map for all nonfiction passages—an outline of the major points covered.

THE FICTION AND SCIENCE PASSAGES

Now that you've learned the general approach, let's look more closely at the two kinds of ACT passage that give students the most trouble—the Prose Fiction passage and the Natural Sciences passage.

The passage breakdown for every ACT Reading test is as follows:

- Prose Fiction—one passage per test
- Nonfiction—three passages per test, one each in:
  —Social Studies
  —Natural Sciences
  —Humanities

Your approach will be essentially the same for all three nonfiction passages, since they're all well-organized essays. We've just seen how to handle passages like this. Your approach to the Prose Fiction passage, however, will be somewhat different.

The Prose Fiction Passage

The Prose Fiction passage is usually a story in which characters, fully equipped with their own motivations and emotions, interact in revealing ways. For that reason, the passage won't break down into an orderly outline or road map, so don't even try to characterize the function of each paragraph. Pay attention instead to the *story*.

A Special Approach

Don't try to construct a mental road map for the Prose Fiction passage. Instead, pay attention to the story and the characters.

In the Prose Fiction passage, almost all the questions relate to the characters. Your job is to find the answers to the following general questions:

- **Who are these people?** What are they like? How are they related to each other?
- **What is their state of mind?** Are they angry, sad, reflective, excited?
- **What's really going on?** What's happening on the surface? What's happening beneath the surface?

Most of the fiction passages focus on one person or are written from the point of view of one of the characters. Figure out who this main character is, and pay special attention to what he or she is like. Read between the lines to determine unspoken emotions and attitudes. Little hints—a momentary pause, a pointed or sarcastic comment—are sometimes all you have to go on, so pay attention. In fact, you probably want to spend more time prereading the Prose Fiction passage than you do any of the other three passages. Get a good feel for the tone and style of the passage as a whole, before going to the questions.

Fortunately, the questions for these passages tend to go more quickly than those for the other passages, so you'll be able to make up some of that lost time you spent reading the text.

Fiction Passage Strategy

When prereading the Fiction passage, ask yourself:

- Who are these people?
- What is their state of mind?
- What's really going on?

The Natural Sciences Passage

The Science passage in the Reading subject test is often similar in outward appearance to a passage on the Science Reasoning subject test. Illustrations, graphs, and tables of information may be included. Usually, though, the emphasis in Reading is more on understanding ideas rather than reading and analyzing experiments and data.

Approaching the Science passage is not very different from approaching the other nonfiction passages, since many of those are well-organized essays laying out ideas in a straightforward, logical way. (However, some nonfiction passages—particularly the Humanities passage—are personal essays that require a focus on the author and tone.) But you may be more likely to find unfamiliar vocabulary in Science passages. Don't panic. Any unfamiliar terms will usually be defined explicitly in the passage, or else will have definitions inferable from context.

In the Science passage, it's extremely easy to lose yourself in complex details. Don't do it. *It's especially important not to get bogged down in the Science passage!* Many students try to understand and remember everything as they read. But that's not the right ACT attitude. In your prereading of the passage, just get the gist and the outline; don't sweat the details. You'd be surprised how many questions you can answer on a passage you don't understand completely.

Get the Big Picture

When prereading the Science passage, you must be even more careful than usual not to get bogged down in details.

As you continue in your ACT training, don't forget the very first piece of Reading advice we offered: Read actively. Always know where a passage is going, and keep an eye on the structure. Use this habit whenever you read on the ACT, not just in the section called Reading. It helps on all of the subject tests.

STEP ELEVEN

Reading Question Types and Strategies

STEP ELEVEN PREVIEW

Specific Detail Questions

Inference Questions

Big Picture Questions

Proven Reading Strategies
- Find and Paraphrase
- Skipping Questions

In the first Reading step, we discussed general strategies for approaching ACT Reading, with a special focus on prereading. Now let's look at the major question types you'll encounter. There are three main types of Reading questions on the test: Specific Detail questions and Inference questions (which make up the bulk), and Big Picture questions (of which there are usually just a few).

The following passage is the same one you already preread. Now, however, you have the questions attached to it, so you can go through the entire process. Remember to use the three-step method:

- Preread the passage quickly.
- Consider the question stem.
- Refer to the passage (before looking at the choices).

We'll discuss selected questions from this set as examples of Specific Detail, Inference, and Big Picture questions.

Tragedy was the invention of the Greeks. In their Golden Age, the fifth century before Christ, they produced the world's greatest dramatists, new forms of tragedy and comedy
(5) that have been models ever since, and a theatre that every age goes back to for rediscovery of some basic principles. . . .

Since it derived from primitive religious rites, with masks and ceremonial costumes,
(10) and made use of music, dance, and poetry, the Greek drama was at the opposite pole from the modern realistic stage. In fact, probably no other theatre in history has made fuller use of the intensities of art. The
(15) masks, made of painted linen, wood, and plaster, brought down from primitive days the atmosphere of gods, heroes, and demons. Our nineteenth- and twentieth-century grandfathers thought masks must have been
(20) very artificial. Today, however, we appreciate their exciting intensity and can see that in a large theatre they were indispensable. If they allowed no fleeting change of expression during a single episode, they could give for
(25) each episode in turn more intense expression than any human face could. When Oedipus comes back with bleeding eyes, the new mask could be more terrible than any facial makeup the audience could endure, yet in its
(30) sculpted intensity more beautiful than a real face.

Most essential of all intensities, and hardest for us to understand, was the chorus. Yet many playwrights today are trying to find
(35) some equivalent to do for a modern play what the chorus did for the Greeks. During the episodes played by the actors, the chorus would only provide a background of group response, enlarging and reverberating the
(40) emotions of the actors, sometimes protesting and opposing but in general serving as ideal spectators to stir and lead the reactions of the audience. But between episodes, with the actors out of the way, the chorus took over.
(45) We have only the words, not the music or dance, and some translations of the odes are in such formal, old-fashioned language that it is hard to guess that they were accompanied by vigorous, sometimes even
(50) wild dances and symbolic actions that filled an orchestra that in some cities was sixty to ninety feet in diameter. Sometimes the chorus expressed simple horror or lament. Sometimes it chanted and acted out, in
(55) unison and in precise formations of rows and lines, the acts of violence the characters were enacting offstage. When Phaedra rushes offstage in *Hippolytus* to hang herself from the rafters, the members of the chorus,
(60) all fifteen of them, perform in mime and chant the act of tying the rope and swinging from the rafters. Sometimes the chorus tells or reenacts an incident of history or legend that throws light on the situation in the play.
(65) Sometimes the chorus puts into specific action what is a general intention in the mind of the main character. When Oedipus resolves to hunt out the guilty person and cleanse the city, he is speaking
(70) metaphorically, but the chorus invokes the gods of vengeance and dances a wild pursuit.

On the printed page, the choral odes seem static and formal, lyric and philosophical, emotional let-downs that punctuate the
(75) series of episodes, like intermissions between two acts of a play. The reader who skips the odes can get the main points of the play. A few are worth reading as independent poems, notably the famous one in *Antigone*
(80) beginning, "Many are the wonders of the world, but none is more wonderful than man." Some modern acting versions omit the chorus or reduce it to a few background figures. Yet to the Greeks the odes were
(85) certainly more than mere poetic interludes: the wild Dionysian words and movements evoked primitive levels of the subconscious

and at the same time served to transform primitive violence into charm and beauty (90) and to add philosophical reflections on the meaning of human destiny.

For production today, we can only improvise some partial equivalent. In Athens the entire population was familiar with (95) choral performances. Every year each of the tribes entered a dithyramb in a contest, rehearsing five hundred men and boys for weeks. Some modern composers have tried to write dramatic music for (100) choruses: the most notable examples are the French composer Darius Milhaud, in the primitive rhythms, shouts, and chants of his operatic version of the *Oresteia*; George Gershwin, in the Negro funeral scenes of (105) *Porgy and Bess*; and Kurt Weill, in the African choruses for *Lost in the Stars*, the musical dramatization of Alan Paton's novel, *Cry, the Beloved Country*. For revivals of Greek tragedies we have not dared use much music (110) beyond a few phrases half shouted, half sung, and drumbeats and suggestive melodies in the background.

From *Invitation to the Theatre*, Copyright 1967 by George Kernodle; Harcourt, Brace, & World Inc., publisher.

1. Combined with the passage's additional information, the fact that some Greek orchestras were sixty to ninety feet across suggests that:

   A. few spectators were able to see the stage.

   B. no one performer could dominate a performance.

   C. choruses and masks helped overcome the distance between actors and audience.

   D. Greek tragedies lacked the emotional force of modern theatrical productions.

2. Which of the following claims expresses the writer's opinion and not a fact?

   F. The Greek odes contained Dionysian words and movements.

   G. Greek theater has made greater use of the intensities of art than has any other theater in history.

   H. Many modern playwrights are trying to find an equivalent to the Greek chorus.

   J. The chorus was an essential part of Greek tragedy.

3. The description of the chorus's enactment of Phaedra's offstage suicide (lines 57–62) shows that, in contrast to modern theater, ancient Greek theater was:

   A. more violent.

   B. more concerned with satisfying an audience.

   C. more apt to be historically accurate.

   D. less concerned with a realistic portrayal of events.

4. It can be inferred that one consequence of the Greeks' use of masks was that:

   F. the actors often had to change masks between episodes.

   G. the characters in the play could not convey emotion.

   H. the actors wearing masks played nonspeaking roles.

   J. good acting ability was not important to the Greeks.

5. Which of the following is supported by the information in the second paragraph (lines 8–31)?

   A. Masks in Greek drama combined artistic beauty with emotional intensity.
   B. The use of masks in Greek drama was better appreciated in the nineteenth century than it is now.
   C. Masks in Greek drama were used to portray gods but never human beings.
   D. Contemporary scholars seriously doubt the importance of masks to Greek theater.

6. The author indicates in lines 68–70 that Oedipus's resolution "to hunt out the guilty person and cleanse the city" was:

   F. at odds with what he actually does later in the performance.
   G. misinterpreted by the chorus.
   H. dramatized by the actions of the chorus.
   J. angrily condemned by the chorus.

7. According to the passage, when actors were present on stage, the chorus would:

   A. look on as silently as spectators.
   B. inevitably agree with the actors' actions.
   C. communicate to the audience solely through mime.
   D. react to the performance as an audience might.

8. The main point of the fourth paragraph (lines 72–91) is that choral odes:

   F. should not be performed by modern choruses.
   G. have a meaning and beauty that are lost in modern adaptations.
   H. can be safely ignored by a modern-day reader.
   J. are worthwhile only in *Antigone*.

9. The passage suggests that modern revivals of Greek tragedies "have not dared use much music" (line 109) because:

   A. modern instruments would appear out of place.
   B. to do so would require a greater understanding of how choral odes were performed.
   C. music would distract the audience from listening to the words of choral odes.
   D. such music is considered far too primitive for modern audiences.

10. *Porgy and Bess* and *Lost in the Stars* are modern plays that:

   F. are revivals of Greek tragedies.
   G. use music to evoke the subconscious.
   H. perform primitive Greek music.
   J. have made use of musical choruses.

Let's remind ourselves of the passage's general outline:

- First Paragraph—introduces the topic of Greek tragedy
- Second Paragraph—discusses use of masks (artificial but intense)
- Third Paragraph—discusses use of chorus (also artificial but intense)
- Fourth Paragraph—expands discussion to choral odes
- Fifth Paragraph—concludes with discussion of how Greek tragedy is performed today, and how it has influenced some modern art

Don't forget to phrase in your mind the author's main point: Greek tragedy included many artificial devices, but these devices allowed it to rise to a high level of intensity.

SPECIFIC DETAIL QUESTIONS

Questions 6 and 7 above are typical Specific Detail questions. As you've seen, some Specific Detail questions (such as 6) give you a line reference to help you out; others (such as 7) don't, forcing you either to start tearing your hair out (if you're an unprepared test taker) or else to seek out the answer based on your own sense of how the passage is laid out (one of the two key reasons to preread the passage). With either type of Specific Detail question, once you've found the part of the passage that a question refers to, the answer is often (though not always) pretty obvious.

Look for the Answer in the Passage
Always refer to the passage before answering a question.

Question 6 provides a line reference (lines 68–70), but to answer the question confidently, you should have also read a few lines before and a few lines after the cited lines. There you would have read: "Sometimes the chorus puts into action what is a general intention in the mind of the main character. When Oedipus resolves. . . ." Clearly, the Oedipus example is meant to illustrate the point about the chorus acting out a character's intentions. So H is correct—it is "dramatizing" (or acting out) Oedipus's resolution. (By the way, G might have been tempting, but there's no real evidence that the chorus is "misinterpreting," just that it's "putting a general intention into specific action.")

Question 7 is a Detail question *without* a line reference. Such questions are common on the ACT. This question's mention of the chorus should have sent you to the third paragraph, but that's a long paragraph, so you probably had to skim it to find the answer in lines 42–43, where the author claims that the chorus serves to "lead the reactions of the audience"— captured by correct choice D.

Context Matters

When given a specific line reference, always read a few sentences before and after the cited lines, to get a sense of the context.

INFERENCE QUESTIONS

For Inference questions, your job is to combine ideas logically to make an inference—something that's not stated explicitly in the passage but that is definitely said *im*plicitly. Often, Inference questions have a word like *suggest, infer, inference,* or *imply* in the question stem to tip you off.

To succeed on these, you have to "read between the lines." Common sense is your best tool here. You use various bits of information in the passage as evidence for your own logical conclusion.

Like Specific Detail questions, Inference Questions only sometimes contain line references. Question 9 does, referring you to line 109, but you really have to keep the context of the entire paragraph in mind when you make your inference. Why would modern revivals not have "dared" to use much music? Well, the paragraph opens by saying that modern productions "can only improvise some partial equivalent" to the choral odes. Inferably, since we can only improvise the odes, we don't understand very much about them. That's why the use of music would be considered daring, and why choice B is correct.

Question 4 provides no line reference, but the mention of masks should have sent you to the second paragraph of the passage, where (according to your trusty road map) masks are discussed. Lines 23–24 explain that masks "allowed no fleeting change of expression during a single episode." Treat that as your first piece of evidence. Your second comes in lines 24–26: "[T]hey [the masks] could give for each episode in turn more intense expression than any human face could." Put those two pieces of evidence together—masks can't change expression during a *single* episode, but they can give expression for each episode *in turn*.

Clearly, the actors must have changed masks between episodes, so that they could express the different emotions that different episodes required. Choice F is correct.

Be a Detective

Making inferences requires that you combine bits of information from different parts of the passage.

One warning: Be careful to keep your inferences as "close" to the passage as possible. Don't make wild inferential leaps. An inference should seem to follow naturally and inevitably from the evidence provided in the passage.

No Flights of Fancy

Don't make your inferences too extreme.

BIG PICTURE QUESTIONS

There are a few questions on the Reading section that test your understanding of the theme, purpose, and organization of the passage. For these Big Picture questions, your main task is different from what it is for Specific Detail or Inference questions, though you should still plan to find the answer in the passages. Big Picture questions tend to focus on:

- The main point or purpose of a passage or part of a passage
- The author's attitude or tone
- The logic underlying the author's argument
- How ideas in different parts of the passage relate to each other
- The difference between fact and opinion

One way to see the Big Picture is to read actively. As you read, ask yourself, "What's the point of this? Why is the author saying this?"

Find Clues from Other Questions

If you're still stumped after reading the passage, try doing the Detail and Inference questions first—to help you fill in the Big Picture.

Question 8 asks for the main idea of a particular paragraph—namely, the fourth, which our general outline indicates as the paragraph about choral odes. Skimming that paragraph, you find reference to how the odes seem to us modern people—"static and formal" (line 73), "like intermissions between two acts of a play" (lines 75–76). Later, the author states, by way of contrast (note the use of the clue word *yet*): "Yet to the Greeks the odes were certainly more than mere poetic interludes" (lines 84–85). Clearly, the author in this paragraph wants to contrast our modern static view of the odes with the Greeks' view of them as something more. That idea is best captured by choice G.

Question 2, meanwhile, is another common type of Big Picture question—one that requires that you distinguish between expressions of fact and opinion in the passage. A simple test for fact (versus opinion) is this: Can it be proven objectively? If so, it's a fact.

The content of Greek odes (choice F) is a matter of fact; you can go to a Greek ode and find out whether it does or doesn't contain Dionysian words. Similarly, the efforts of modern playwrights to find an equivalent to the Greek chorus (choice H), and the central importance of the chorus to Greek tragedy (choice J) can be factually verified.

But the "intensities of art" are a subjective matter. What one person thinks is intense might strike another as simply boring. So G is the expression of opinion the question is looking for.

PROVEN READING STRATEGIES

Find and Paraphrase

The examples above show that your real task in Reading is different from what you might expect. Your main job is to *find* the answers. In other words, "find and paraphrase." But students tend to think that their task in Reading is to "comprehend and remember." That's the wrong mindset.

Here's a key to the Greek tragedy passage, so that you can check the answers to the questions not discussed above.

(Nonfiction—Humanities)

	ANSWER	REFER TO	TYPE	COMMENTS
1.	C	Lines 14–26, 36–43	Inference	Q-stem emphasizes distance between audience and stage; masks and choruses help to "enlarge" the action, so that it can be understood from a distance.
2.	G	Throughout	Big Picture	Discussed above.
3.	D	Lines 57–62	Inference	Combine info from lines 8–12, 54–62, 84–91.
4.	F	Lines 22–26	Inference	Discussed above.
5.	A	Lines 8–31	Inference	Combine info from lines 26–31, 14–22, 22–26.
6.	H	Lines 68–71	Detail	Discussed above.
7.	D	Lines 36–43	Detail	Discussed above.
8.	G	Lines 72–91	Big Picture	Discussed above.
9.	B	Lines 108–112	Inference	Discussed above.
10.	J	Lines 98–108	Detail	"Some modern composers have tried to write dramatic music for choruses." (lines 98–100)

Skipping Questions

Now that you've done a full-length passage and questions, you've probably encountered at least a few questions that you found unanswerable. What do you do if you can't find the answer in the passage, or if you *can* find it but don't understand, or if you *do* understand but can't see an answer choice that makes sense? Skip the question. Skipping is probably more important in Reading than in any other ACT subject test. Many students find it useful to skip as many as half of the questions on the first pass through a set of Reading questions. That's fine.

Come Back to Difficult Questions

Answer the easy questions for each passage first. Skip the tough ones and come back to them later.

When you come back to a Reading question the second time, it usually makes sense to use the process of elimination. The first time around, you tried to find the *right* answer but you couldn't. So, now try to identify the three *wrong* answers. Eliminating three choices is slower than finding one right choice, so don't make it your main strategy for Reading. But it's a good way to try a second attack on a question.

Another thing to consider when attacking a question for a second time is that the right answer may have been hidden. Maybe it's written in an unexpected way, with different vocabulary. Or maybe there is another good way to answer the question that you haven't thought of. But remember not to get bogged down when you come back to a question. Be willing to admit that there are some questions you just can't answer. Guess if you have to.

Part Five

THE ACT
SCIENCE TEST

STEP TWELVE

Basic Science Techniques

STEP TWELVE PREVIEW

Reading Skills for Science

Kaplan's Three-Step Method for ACT Science
- Step 1: Preread the Passage
- Step 2: Consider the Question Stem
- Step 3: Refer to the Passage

Reading Tables and Graphs
- Look for Patterns and Trends

What to Do When You're Running Out of Time

Many ACT takers worry about "not knowing enough science" to do well on the Science test. But the fact of the matter is, you really don't need to be a science whiz to do well on the ACT. Knowing science is a plus, of course, and it certainly can help your work in the Science subject test. But you don't need to know a truckload of scientific facts to answer these science questions. The questions are answerable from the information in the passage.

READING SKILLS FOR SCIENCE REASONING

ACT Science requires many of the same skills that ACT Reading does. The difference between Reading and Science, however, is that the "details" you have to find in the Science passages almost all relate to numbers or scientific processes or both, and they are often contained in graphs and tables rather than in paragraph form. The secret to finding most of these details is:

- **Learn to "read" graphs, tables, and research summaries.**
  Some questions involve only accurately retrieving data from a single graph or table, while others involve combining knowledge from two graphs or tables. Still others involve understanding experimental methods well enough to evaluate information.

- **Learn to look for patterns in the numbers that appear.**
  Do these numbers get bigger or smaller? Where are the highest numbers? Where are the lowest? At what point do the numbers change? A little calculation is sometimes required, but not much. In Science, you won't be computing with numbers so much as thinking about what they mean.

KAPLAN'S THREE-STEP METHOD FOR ACT SCIENCE

In Science, you have 35 minutes to complete seven short passages. Each passage with questions should average five minutes. We recommend using just about one minute to preread, and then a total of about four minutes to consider the questions and refer to the passage (that's about 40 seconds per question). Here's a three-step method that you can use as a guide for attacking passages in the Science section:

Step 1: Preread the Passage

It's especially important in Science not to get tied up in the details. Some of the material covered is extremely technical, and you'll just get frustrated trying to understand it completely. So it's crucial that you skim, to get a general idea of what's going on and—just as important—to get a sense of where certain types of data can be found.

Almost all Science passages have the same basic structure. They begin with an introduction. Always read through the introduction first to orient yourself and get a sense of the overall situation.

After reading the introduction, quickly scan the rest of the passage. How is the information presented? Graphs? Diagrams? Are there experiments? What seems to be important? Size? Shape? Temperature? Speed? Chemical composition? Don't worry about details and don't try to remember it all. Plan to refer to the passage when answering the questions. Remember, your goal is to answer questions, NOT to learn and remember everything that goes on in the passage.

Don't Be Delayed by Details

Don't worry about details on your initial read-through.

Step 2: Consider the Question Stem

Most of your time in Science will be spent considering questions and referring to the passage to find the answers. Here's where you should do most of your really careful reading. It's essential that you understand exactly what the question is asking. Then, go back to the passage and get a sense of what the answer should be before looking at the choices.

Step 3: Refer to the Passage

You have to be diligent about referring to the passage. Your preread should have given you an idea of where particular kinds of data can be found. Sometimes the questions themselves will direct you to the right place.

Be careful not to mix up units when taking information from graphs, tables, and summaries. Make sure you don't confuse opposites. The difference between a correct and an incorrect answer will often be a "decrease" where an "increase" should be. Always look for words like *not* and *except* in the questions.

Find the Answer in the Passage First

Always refer to the passage and the question stem before selecting an answer.

READING TABLES AND GRAPHS

Most of the specific information in ACT Science passages is contained in tables or graphs, usually accompanied by explanatory material. *Knowing how to read data from tables and graphs is critical to success on the Science subject test!*

In order to read most graphs and tables, you have to do four things:
- Determine what is being represented.
- Determine what the axes (or columns and rows) represent.
- Take note of units of measurement.
- Look for trends in the data.

Let's say you saw the following graph in a Science passage:

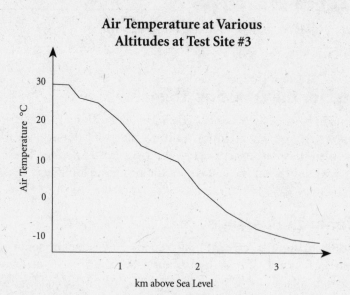

Air Temperature at Various Altitudes at Test Site #3

- **Determine what is being represented.** Most graphs and tables have titles that tell you what they represent. For some, though, you may have to get that information from the introduction. Here, the graph is representing how cold or hot the air is at various altitudes at Test Site #3.
- **Determine what the axes represent.** These, too, are usually labeled. In this graph, the *x*-axis represents kilometers above sea level, while the *y*-axis represents the air temperature in degrees Celsius.
- **Take note of units of measurement.** Note that distance here is measured in *kilometers*, not miles or feet. Temperature is measured in degrees *Celsius*, not Fahrenheit.
- **Look for trends in the data.** The "pattern" of the data in this graph is pretty clear. As you rise in altitude, the temperature drops—the higher the altitude, the lower the temperature.

The sloping line on the graph represents the various temperatures measured at the various altitudes. To find what the measured temperature was at, say, 2 km above sea level, find the 2 km point on the *x*-axis and trace your finger directly up from it until it hits the line. It does so at about the level of 3° C. In other words, at an altitude of 2 km above sea level at Test Site #3, the air temperature was about 3° C.

You should follow a similar procedure with tables of information. For instance, in the introduction to the passage in which the following table might have appeared, you would have learned that scientists were trying to determine the effects of two pollutants (Pb and Hg, lead and mercury) on the trout populations of a particular river.

Location	Water temperature (°C)	Presence of Pb (parts per million)	Presence of Hg (parts per million)	Population Density of Speckled Trout (# per 100 m³)	Population Density of Brown Trout (# per 100 m³)
1	15.4	0	3	5.5	7.9
2	16.1	0	1	12.2	3.5
3	16.3	1	67	0	0
4	15.8	54	3	15.3	5.7
5	16.0	2	4	24	9.5

- **Determine what is being represented.** There's no informative title for this table, but the introduction would have told you what the table represents.
- **Determine what the columns and rows represent.** In tables, you get columns and rows instead of x- and y-axes. But the principle is the same. Here, each row represents the data from a different numbered location on the river. Each column represents different data—water temperature, presence of the first pollutant, presence of the second pollutant, population of one kind of trout, population of another kind of trout.
- **Take note of units of measurement.** Temperature is measured in Celsius. The two pollutants are measured in parts-per-million (or ppm). The trout populations are measured in number per 100 cubic meters of river.
- **Look for trends in the data.** Glancing at the table, it looks like locations where the Hg concentration is high (as in Location 3), the trout population is virtually nonexistent. This would seem to indicate that trout life and a high Hg concentration are incompatible. But notice the location where the other pollutant is abundant—in Location 4. Here, both trout populations seem to be more in line with other locations. That would seem to indicate that this other pollutant—Pb—is NOT as detrimental to trout populations as Hg is.

Look For Patterns and Trends

When you first examine a graph or table, don't focus on exact numbers. Look for patterns in the numbers. Don't assume that there is always a pattern or trend. Finding that there isn't a pattern is just as important as finding that there is one. Let's look at the three characteristic patterns in graphs and tables.

Extremes

Extremes—or maximums and minimums—are merely the highest and lowest points that things reach. In tables, the maximums and minimums will be represented by especially high and low numbers. In graphs, they will be represented by high and low *x*- and *y*-coordinates. In bar charts, they will be represented by the tallest and shortest bars.

In discussing the extremes in the trout populations table, we saw how isolating the locations at which trout populations and chemical concentrations were at their maximum and minimum values led us to a conclusion about the compatibility of trout and water containing high concentrations of Hg.

Critical Points

Critical points—or points of change—are values at which something dramatic happens. For example, at atmospheric pressure water freezes at 0° C and boils at about 100° C. If you examined water at various temperatures below the lower of these two critical points, it would be solid. If you examined water at various temperatures between the two points, it would be liquid. If you examined water above the higher critical point, it would be a gas.

When you scan the numbers in a chart or points on a graph, look for places where values bunch together, where an increasing trend switches to a decreasing trend, or where suddenly something special happens. At atmospheric pressure, 0° C is a critical point for water—as is 100° C—since something special happens: The substance changes form.

To find out how critical points can help you evaluate data, let's look at a graph representing the concentration of *E. coli* (a common type of bacterium) in a location called Cooling Pool B.

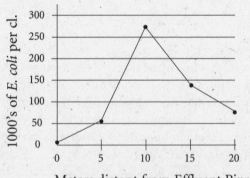

Meters distant from Effluent Pipe 3

Notice how the concentration is low very near Effluent Pipe 3. From there, it rises until about 10 meters away from the pipe, then it falls again, tapering off the farther you get from the pipe. There's a critical point, then, right around 10 meters from Effluent Pipe 3. Somehow, that vicinity is most conducive to the growth of *E. coli*. As you move closer to or farther away from that point, the concentration falls off. So, in looking to explain the data, you'd want to focus on that location—10 meters from the pipe. What is it about that location that's so special? Why is it that more *E. coli* grows there?

Variation

Variation is a bit more complex than extremes or critical points. Variation refers to the way two different things change *in relation to each other*. Direct variation means that two things vary in the same way: When one gets bigger, the other does too; when one gets smaller, so does the other. Inverse variation means that two things vary in *opposite* ways: When one gets bigger the other gets smaller, and vice versa. We saw an example of inverse variation in the air temperature graph, in which altitude and air temperature varied inversely—as altitude *in*creased, air temperature *de*creased. Observing this inverse variation allowed us to draw conclusions about the relationship between altitude and air temperature.

When reading data, you should be on the lookout for the three characteristic patterns or trends:

- Extremes (maximums and minimums)
- Critical points (or points of change)
- Direct or inverse variation (or proportionality)

To do well on Science, you have to be able to read graphs and tables, paying special attention to trends and patterns in the data. And sometimes, that's all you need to do to get most of the points on a passage.

WHAT TO DO WHEN YOU'RE RUNNING OUT OF TIME

Let's conclude now with another quick point about getting quick points. If you're nearly out of time and you still have a whole Science passage left, you need to shift to last-minute strategies. Don't try to preread the passage, or you'll just run out of time before you answer any questions. Instead, scan the questions without reading the passage and look first for the ones that require only reading data off of a graph or table. You can often get a couple of quick points just by knowing how to find data quickly.

> ### Last-Minute Strategy: Do the Data Questions
>
> When you're running out of time, go right to the questions without reading the passage and do as many data interpretation questions as you can.

Again, the most important thing is to make sure you have gridded in at least a random guess on every question.

Experiments

To succeed on the ACT Science test, you must learn how to think like a scientist. You don't have to know very much science (although it certainly helps), but you should at least be familiar with how scientists go about getting and testing knowledge.

HOW SCIENTISTS THINK

Scientists use two very different kinds of logic, which (to keep things nontechnical) we'll call:

- General-to-Specific Thinking
- Specific-to-General Thinking

General-to-Specific

In some cases, scientists have already discovered a law of nature and wish to apply their knowledge to a specific case. For example, a scientist may wish to know how fast a pebble (call it Pebble A) will be falling when it hits the ground three seconds after being dropped. There is a law of physics that says on Earth, falling objects accelerate at a rate of about 9.8 m/sec^2. The scientist could use this known general law to calculate the specific information she needs: After three seconds, the object would be falling at a rate of about 3 sec $\times$ 9.8 m/sec^2, or roughly 30 m/sec. You could think of this kind of logic as *general-to-specific*. The scientist uses a *general* rule (the acceleration of any object falling on Earth) to find a *specific* fact (the speed of Pebble A).

Specific-to-General

But scientists use a different kind of thinking in order to discover new laws of nature. In these cases, they examine many facts and then draw a general conclusion about what they've seen. For example, a scientist might watch hundreds of different kinds of frogs live and die, and might notice that all of them developed from tadpoles. She might then announce a theory: All frogs develop from tadpoles. You could think of this kind of logic as specific-to-general. The scientist looks at many specific frogs to arrive at a general rule about all frogs.

This conclusion is called a "hypothesis," not a fact or a "truth," because the scientist has not checked every single frog in the universe. She knows that theoretically there *could* be a frog somewhere that grows, say, from pond scum or from a Dalmatian puppy. But until she finds such a frog, it is reasonable to think that her theory is correct. Many hypotheses, in fact, are so well documented that they become the equivalent of laws of nature.

Which Direction?

For Science questions, ask yourself whether you should be doing general-to-specific or specific-to-general thinking.

In your science classes in school, you mostly learn about general-to-specific thinking. Your teachers explain general rules of science to you and then expect you to apply these rules to solve problems. Some ACT Science questions are like that, too, but most are not. Most of the questions on the ACT test specific-to-general thinking. They test your ability to see the kinds of patterns in specific data that, as a scientist, you would use to formulate your own general hypotheses. We did something like this in Step Twelve, when we theorized—based on the trends we found in a table of data—that the pollutant Hg was in some way detrimental to trout populations.

HOW EXPERIMENTS WORK

Many ACT passages describe experiments and expect you to understand how they're designed. Experiments help scientists do specific-to-general thinking in a reliable and efficient way. Consider the tadpole researcher above. In a real-world situation, she would probably notice that some frogs develop from tadpoles and wonder if maybe they all did. Then she'd know what to look for and could check many frogs systematically. This process contains the two basic steps of any experiment:

- Form a hypothesis (guessing that all frogs come from tadpoles), and
- Test a hypothesis (checking frogs to see if this guess was right).

Scientists are often interested in cause-and-effect relationships. Having formed her hypothesis about tadpoles, a scientist might wonder what causes a tadpole to become a frog, for instance. To test causal relationships, a special kind of experiment is needed. She must test one possible cause at a time in order to isolate which one actually produces the effect in question. For example, the scientist might inject tadpoles with several kinds of hormones. Some of these tadpoles might die. Others might grow into frogs normally. But a few—those injected with Hormone X, say—might remain tadpoles for an indefinite time. One reasonable explanation is that Hormone X in some way inhibited whatever causes normal frog development. In other words, the scientist would hypothesize a causal relationship between Hormone X and frog development.

A Controlled Situation

The relationship between Hormone X and frog development, however, would not be demonstrated very well if the scientist also fed different diets to different tadpoles, kept some in warmer water, or allowed some to have more room to swim than others—or if she didn't also watch tadpoles that were injected with no hormones at all but that were otherwise were kept under the same conditions as the treated tadpoles. Why? Because if the "eternal tadpoles" had a diet that differed from that of the others, the scientist wouldn't know whether it was Hormone X or the special diet that kept the eternal tadpoles from becoming frogs. Moreover, if their water was warmer than that of the others, maybe it was the warmth that somehow kept the tadpoles from developing. And if she didn't watch untreated tadpoles (a "control group"), she couldn't be sure whether, under the same conditions, a normal, untreated tadpole would also remain undeveloped.

Thus, a scientist creating a well-designed experiment will:

- Ensure that there's a single variable (like Hormone X) that varies from test to test, or group to group.
- Ensure that all other factors (diet, temperatures, space, etcetera) remain the same.
- Ensure that there is a control group (tadpoles who don't get any Hormone X at all) for comparison purposes.

Find What Varies

One advantage to knowing how experiments work is that *you can tell what a researcher is trying to find out about by checking to see what she allows to vary.* That is what's being researched—in this case, Hormone X. Data about things other than hormones and tadpole-to-frog development would be outside the design of the experiment. Information about other factors might be interesting, but could not be part of a scientific proof.

For example, if some of the injected tadpoles that did grow into frogs later turned into princes, the data about the hormone they were given would not prove what causes frogs to become princes. However, the data could be used to design another experiment intended to explore what could make a frog into a prince.

Whenever you see an experiment in Science, therefore, ask yourself three things:

1. What's the factor that's being varied?—That is what's being tested.

2. What's the control group?—It's the group that has nothing special done to it.

3. What do the results show?—What differences exist between the results for the control group and those for the other group(s)? Or between the results for one treated group and those for another, differently treated group?

HANDLING EXPERIMENT QUESTIONS: PRACTICE PASSAGE

On the next page is a full-fledged Science passage organized around two experiments. Use the three-step method (preread the passage, consider the question stem, refer to the passage before looking at the choices), but this time, since this is a passage that centers on experiments, remember to ask yourself the three questions above. Take five or six minutes to do the passage and its questions.

Passage II

A mutualistic relationship between two species increases the chances of growth or survival for both of them. Several species of fungi form mutualistic relationships called *mycorrhizae* with the roots of plants. The benefits to each species are shown in the figure below.

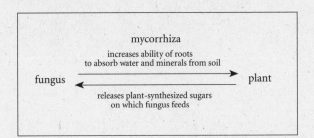

Some of the plant species that require or benefit from the presence of mycorrhizal fungi are noted below.

Cannot survive without mycorrhizae	Grow better with mycorrhizae
All conifers Some deciduous trees (e.g. birch, beech) Orchids	Citrus trees Ericaceae (heath, rhododendrons, azaleas) Grapes Soy beans

Agronomists investigated the effects of mycorrhizae on plant growth and survival in the following studies.

Study 1

Three 4-acre plots were prepared with soil from a pine forest. The soil for Plot A was mixed with substantial quantities of cultured mycorrhizal fungi. The soil for Plot B contained only naturally occurring mycorrhizal fungi. The soil for Plot C was sterilized in order to kill any mycorrhizal fungi. Additionally, Plot C was lined with concrete. After planting, Plot C was covered with a fabric that filtered out microorganisms while permitting air and light to penetrate, as shown below. Two hundred-fifty pine seedlings were planted in each of the three plots. All plots were treated to the same environmental conditions. The six-month survival rates were recorded in the table below.

	# Seedlings alive after 6 months	Utilization of available K (average)	Utilization of available P (average)
Plot A	107	18%	62%
Plot B	34	10%	13%
Plot C	0	N/A	N/A

N/A = not applicable

Study 2

The roots of surviving seedlings from Plots A and B were analyzed to determine how efficiently they absorbed potassium (K) and phosphorus (P) from the soil. The results were added to the table above.

1. The most likely purpose of the concrete liner was:

    A. to block the seedlings from sending out taproots to water below the plot.

    B. to prevent mycorrhizal fungi in the surrounding soil from colonizing the plot.

    C. to absorb potassium and phosphorus from the soil for later analysis.

    D. to provide a firm foundation for mycorrhizal fungi in the plot.

2. Mycorrhizae are highly susceptible to acid rain. Given the information from the passage, acid rain is probably most harmful to:

    F. wheat fields.

    G. birch forests.

    H. orange groves.

    J. grape vines.

3. In a third study, pine seedlings were planted in soil from a different location. The soil was prepared as in Study 1. This time, the survival rates for seedlings planted in Plot A and Plot B were almost identical to each other. Which of the following theories would NOT help to explain these results?

   A. Sterilization killed all the naturally occurring mycorrhizal fungi in the new soil.

   B. The new soil was so mineral deficient that it could not sustain life.

   C. The new soil was naturally more fertile than that used in Study 1.

   D. Large quantities of mycorrhizal fungi occurred naturally in the new soil.

4. According to the passage, in which of the following ways do plants benefit from mycorrhizal associations?

   I. More efficient sugar production
   II. Enhanced ability to survive drought
   III. Increased mineral absorption

   F. I only
   G. III only
   H. II and III only
   J. I, II, and III

5. Which of the following generalizations is supported by the results of Study 2?

   A. Mycorrhizal fungi are essential for the survival of pine seedlings.

   B. Growth rates for pine seedlings may be improved by adding mycorrhizal fungi to the soil.

   C. Mycorrhizal fungi contain minerals that are not normally found in pine forest soil.

   D. Pine seedlings cannot absorb all the potassium that is present in the soil.

Answers: 1. B, 2. G, 3. A, 4. H, 5. D

Approaching the Passage

What's the Topic?

Notice how many diagrams and tables were used here. That's common in experiment passages, where information is given to you in a wide variety of forms. Typically, however, the experiments themselves are clearly labeled, as Study 1 and Study 2 were here.

A quick prereading of the introduction would have revealed the topic of the experiments here—the "mutualistic relationship" between some fungi and some plant roots, the relationship called *mycorrhiza* ("myco" for short). The first diagram just shows you who gets what out of this relationship. The benefit accruing to the plant (the arrow pointing to the word *plant*) is an increased ability to absorb water and minerals. The benefit accruing to the fungus (the other arrow) is the plant-synthesized sugars on which the fungus feeds. That's the mutual benefit the myco association creates.

Notice, by the way, that reading this first diagram alone is enough to answer question 4, which we'll do right now. The question is asking, essentially, what do the plants get out of the association? And we just answered that: increased ability to absorb water and minerals. Statement III is obviously correct, but so is Statement II, since increased water absorption would indeed enhance the plant's ability to survive drought (a drought is a shortage of water, after all). Statement I, though, is a distortion. We know that the fungi benefit from sugars produced by the plants, but we don't have any evidence that the association actually causes plants to produce sugar more efficiently. So I is out; II and III are in, making H the answer to Question 4.

Data Analysis

But let's get back to the passage. We've just learned who gets what out of the myco association. Now we get a chart that shows what *kind* of plants enter into such associations. Some (those in the first column) are so dependent on myco associations that they can't live without them. Others (those in the second column) merely grow better with them; presumably they could live without them.

Here again, there's a question we can answer based solely on information in this one table. Question 2 tells us that mycos are highly susceptible to acid rain, and then asks what kind of plant communities would be most harmed by acid rain. Well, if acid rain hurts mycos, then the plants that are most dependent on myco fungi (that is, the ones listed in the first column) would be the most harmed by acid rain. Of the four choices, only birch forests, choice G, corresponds to something in column 1 of the table. Birch trees can't even survive without myco fungi, so anything that hurts myco fungi would inferrably hurt birch forests. (Grape vines and orange groves—which are citrus trees—would also be hurt by acid rain, but not as much, since they can survive without myco fungi. We're told nothing about wheat in the passage.)

Well, we've answered two of the five questions already and we haven't even gotten to the first experiment. That brings up an important point—namely, that even in passages that center around experiments, there are plenty of Data Analysis questions.

Analyzing Study 1

Now look at the first experiment. Three plots, each with differently treated soil, are planted with pine seedlings. Plot A gets soil with cultivated myco fungi; Plot B gets untreated soil with only naturally occurring myco fungi; and Plot C gets no myco fungi at all, since the soil has been sterilized and isolated (via the concrete lining and the fabric covering). Now ask yourself the three important experiment questions:

- **What factor is being varied?**

  The factor being varied is the amount of myco fungi in the soil. Plot A gets a lot; Plot B gets just the normal amount; Plot C gets none at all. It's clear, then, that the scientists are testing the effects of myco fungi on the growth of pine seedlings.

- **What's the control group?**

  The plants in Plot B, since they get untreated soil. To learn the effects of the fungi, then, the scientists will compare the results from fungi-rich Plot A with the control, and the results from fungi-poor Plot C with the same control.

- **What do the results show?**

  The results are listed in the first column of the table below the illustration of Plot C. And they are decisive: No seedlings at all survived in Plot C; 34 did in Plot B; and 107 did in Plot A. The minimums and maximums coincide. Minimum fungi = minimum number of surviving seedlings; maximum fungi = maximum number of surviving seedlings. Clearly there's a cause-and-effect relationship here. Myco fungi probably help pine seedlings survive.

Questions 1 and 3 can be answered solely on the basis of Study 1. Question 1 is merely a procedural question: Why the concrete liner in Plot C? Well, in the analysis of the experiment above, we saw that the factor being varied was amount of myco fungi. Plot C was designed to have none at all. It follows, then, that the concrete liner was probably there to prevent any stray myco fungi from entering the sterilized soil—choice B.

Question 3 actually sets up an extra experiment based on Study 1. The soils were prepared in the same way, except that the soil came from a different location. The results? The number of surviving seedlings from Plots A and B were almost identical. What can that mean? Well, Plot A was supposed to be the fungi-rich plot, whereas Plot B (the control) was supposed to be the fungi-normal plot. But here they have the same results (but notice that we're not told what those results are; it could be that no seedlings survived in any plots this time around.)

The question is phrased so that the three wrong choices are things that could explain the results; the correct choice will be the one that can't. Choices B, C, and D all can explain the results, since they all show how similar results could have been derived from Plots A and B. If the new soil just couldn't support life—fungi or no fungi—Plots A and B would have produced similar results, namely, no seedlings surviving. On the other end of the spectrum, choices C and D show how the two plots might have produced similar high survival rates. If there were many myco fungi naturally in this soil (that's choice D), then there wouldn't be all that much difference between the soils in Plots A and B. And if the soil were naturally extremely fertile (that's choice C), there might be perfect survival rates no matter what the fungi situation. So all three of these answers would help to explain similar results in Plots A and B.

Choice A, however, wouldn't help, since it talks about the sterilized soil that's in Plot C. The soil in Plot C won't affect the results in Plots A and B, so choice A is the answer here—the factor that doesn't help to explain the results.

Analyzing Study 2

This study takes the surviving seedlings from Plots A and B in Study 1 and just tests how much potassium (K) and phosphorus (P) the roots have used. The results are listed in the second and third columns of the table. (Notice the N/A—not applicable—for Plot C in these columns, since there were no surviving seedlings to test in Plot C!) The data show much better utilization of both substances in the Plot-A seedlings, the seedlings that grew in a fungi-rich soil. This data would tend to support a theory that the myco fungi aid in the utilization of K and P, and that this in turn aids survival in pine seedlings.

The only question that hinges on Study 2 is question 5. It asks what generalization would be supported by the specific results of Study 2. Well, notice that Study 2 involved only measuring K and P. It did not involve survival rates (that was Study 1), so Choice A can't be right. And neither study measured growth rates, so B is out. As for C, the minerals K and P were in the control group's soil, which was natural, untreated pine forest soil, so the results in choice C are clearly unsupported. But the data *did* show that not all of the potassium (K) could be absorbed by pine seedlings. Only 18 percent was absorbed in Plot A, while only 10 percent was absorbed in Plot B. That's a long way from 100 percent, so choice D seems a safe generalization to make.

Of course, not all experiments on the ACT Science subject test are specific-to-general experiments; some are general-to-specific procedures, with scientists making specific predictions based on accepted general premises. But the same kind of strict thinking—manipulating factors to narrow down possibilities—can get you points, no matter in what direction your thinking goes.

STEP FOURTEEN

The Conflicting Viewpoints Passage

STEP FOURTEEN PREVIEW

Prereading the Conflicting Viewpoints Passage

The Real Thing: Practice Passage and Key Strategies
- Identifying the Conflict
- Attacking the Questions
- Countering Evidence
- Keeping Your Scientists Straight

On every Science subject test you'll find one "Conflicting Viewpoints" passage, in which two scientists propose different theories about a particular scientific phenomenon. Often, the two theories are just differing interpretations of the same data. Other times, each scientist offers his own data to support his own opinion. In either case, it's essential that you know more or less what theory each scientist is proposing, and that you pay careful attention to how and where their theories differ.

In the second Science step, we talked about how scientists think, and you should bring all of that learning to bear on the Conflicting Viewpoints passage. Since the scientists are disagreeing on interpretation, it's usually the case that they're engaging in specific-to-general thinking. They're each using specific data, sometimes the same specific data, but they're coming to very different general conclusions.

It's important to remember that your job is not to figure out which scientist is right and which is wrong. Instead, you'll be tested on whether you understand each scientist's position and the thinking behind it. That's what the questions will hinge on.

Don't Judge the Viewpoints

Don't waste time trying to figure out which scientist is "right." Just understand their different viewpoints.

PREREADING THE CONFLICTING VIEWPOINTS PASSAGE

When tackling the Conflicting Viewpoints passage, you'll probably want to spend a little more time than usual on the prereading step of the three-step method. On other Science passages, as we saw, your goal in prereading is to get a general idea of what's going on, so that you can focus when you do the questions. But we find that it pays to spend a little extra time with the Conflicting Viewpoints passage in order to get a clearer idea of the opposing theories and the data behind them.

Remember the Three-Step Method

- Preread the passage.
- Consider the question stem.
- Refer to the passage (before looking at the choices).

The passage will usually consist of a short introduction laying out the scientific issue in question, followed by two different viewpoints on that issue. Sometimes these viewpoints are presented under the headings Scientist 1 and Scientist 2, or the headings might be Theory 1 and Theory 2, Hypothesis 1 and Hypothesis 2, or something similar.

A scientific viewpoint on the ACT usually consists of two parts:

- A statement of the general theory
- A summary of the data behind the theory

Usually, the very first line of each viewpoint expresses the general theory. So, for instance, Scientist 1's first sentence might be something like, "The universe will continue to expand indefinitely." That's Scientist 1's viewpoint boiled down to a single statement. Scientist 2's first sentence might then be, "The forces of gravity will eventually force the universe to stop expanding and to begin contracting." That's Scientist 2's viewpoint, and it is clearly in direct contradiction to Scientist 1's.

If You're Confused

Don't panic if you don't understand both scientists' positions. Many questions will hinge on just one of the scientist's arguments.

It's very important that you understand these basic statements of theory, and, just as important, that you see how they're opposed to each other. In fact, you might want to circle the theory statement for each viewpoint, right there in the test booklet, to fix the two positions in your mind.

After each statement of theory will come the data that's behind it. As we said, sometimes the scientists are just drawing different interpretations from the same data. But usually, each will have different supporting data. There are two different kinds of data:

- Data that support the scientist's own theory
- Data that weaken the opposing scientist's theory

It's normally a good idea to identify the major points of data for each theory. You might underline a phrase or sentence that crystallizes each, or even take note of whether it primarily supports the scientist's own theory or shoots holes in the opposing theory.

Once you understand each scientist's theory and the data behind it, you'll be ready to move on to the questions. Remember that some of the questions will refer to only one of the viewpoints. Whatever you do, *don't mix up the two viewpoints!* A question asking about, for example, the data supporting Theory 2 may have wrong answers that perfectly describe the data for Theory 1. If you're careless, you can easily fall for one of these wrong answers.

Don't Mix Up the Viewpoints:

Always double-check to make sure you haven't assigned Scientist 1's ideas to Scientist 2, and vice versa.

THE REAL THING: PRACTICE PASSAGE AND KEY STRATEGIES

What follows is a full-fledged ACT-style Conflicting Viewpoints passage. Take six minutes or so to read the passage and do all seven questions.

Passage III

Tektites are natural, glassy objects that range in size from the diameter of a grain of sand to that of a human fist. They are found in only a few well-defined areas, called *strewn fields*. Two theories about the origin of tektites are presented below.

Scientist 1:

Tektites almost certainly are extraterrestrial, probably lunar, in origin. Their forms show the characteristics of air-friction melting. In one study, flanged, "flying saucer" shapes similar to those of australites (a common tektite form) were produced by ablating lenses of tektite glass in a heated airstream that simulated atmospheric entry.

Atmospheric forces also make terrestrial origin extremely improbable. Aerodynamic studies have shown that because of atmospheric density, tektite-like material ejected from Earth's surface would never attain a velocity much higher than that of the surrounding air, and therefore would not be shaped by atmospheric friction. Most likely, tektites were formed either from meteorites or from lunar material ejected in volcanic eruptions.

Analysis of specimen #14425 from the *Apollo 12* lunar mission shows that the sample strongly resembles some of the tektites from the Australasian strewn field. Also tektites contain only a small fraction of the water that is locked into the structure of terrestrial volcanic glass. And tektites never contain unmelted crystalline material; the otherwise similar terrestrial glass produced by some meteorite impacts always does.

Scientist 2:

Nonlocal origin is extremely unlikely, given the narrow distribution of tektite strewn fields. Even if a tightly focused jet of lunar matter were to strike Earth, whatever was deflected by the atmosphere would remain in a solar orbit. The next time its orbit coincided with that of Earth, some of the matter would be captured by Earth's gravity and fall over a wide area.

There are striking similarities, not only between the composition of Earth's crust and that of most tektites, but between the proportions of various gases found in Earth's atmosphere and in the vesicles of certain tektites.

Tektites were probably formed by meteorite impacts. The shock wave produced by a major collision could temporarily displace the atmosphere above. Terrestrial material might then splatter to suborbital heights and undergo air-friction melting upon reentry. And tektite fields in the Ivory Coast and Ghana can be correlated with known impact craters.

1. The discovery that many tektites contain unmelted, crystalline material would:

   A. tend to weaken Scientist 1's argument.
   B. tend to weaken Scientist 2's argument.
   C. be incompatible with both scientists' views.
   D. be irrelevant to the controversy.

2. Which of the following is a reason given by Scientist 2 for believing that tektites originate on Earth?

   F. The density of Earth's atmosphere would prevent any similar lunar or extraterrestrial material from reaching Earth's surface.
   G. Tektites have a composition totally unlike that of any material ever brought back from the Moon.
   H. Extraterrestrial material could not have been as widely dispersed as tektites are.
   J. Material ejected from the moon or beyond would eventually have been much more widely distributed on Earth.

3. Scientist 1 could best answer the point that some tektites have vesicles filled with gases in the same proportion as Earth's atmosphere by:

    A. countering that not all tektites have such gas-filled vesicles.

    B. demonstrating that molten material would be likely to trap some gases while falling through the terrestrial atmosphere.

    C. suggesting that those gases might occur in the same proportions in the moon's atmosphere.

    D. showing that similar vesicles, filled with these gases in the same proportions, are also found in some terrestrial volcanic glass.

4. How did Scientist 2 answer the argument that tektitelike material ejected from Earth could not reach a high enough velocity relative to the atmosphere to undergo air-friction melting?

    F. By asserting that a shock wave might cause a momentary change in atmosphere density, permitting subsequent aerodynamic heating.

    G. By pointing out that periodic meteorite impacts have caused gradual changes in atmospheric density over the eons.

    H. By attacking the validity of the aerodynamic studies cited by Scientist 1.

    J. By referring to the correlation between tektite fields and known impact craters in the Ivory Coast and Ghana.

5. The point of subjecting lenses of tektite glass to a heated airstream was to:

    A. determine their water content.

    B. see if gases became trapped in their vesicles.

    C. reproduce the effects of atmospheric entry.

    D. simulate the mechanism of meteorite formation.

6. Researchers could best counter the objections of Scientist 2 to Scientist 1's argument by:

    F. discovering some phenomenon that would quickly remove tektite-sized objects from orbit.

    G. proving that most common tektite shapes can be produced by aerodynamic heating.

    H. confirming that active volcanoes once existed on the moon.

    J. mapping the locations of all known tektite fields and impact craters.

7. Which of the following characteristics of tektites is LEAST consistent with the theory that tektites are of extraterrestrial origin?

    A. Low water content

    B. "Flying saucer" shapes

    C. Narrow distribution

    D. Absence of unmelted material

Answers: 1. A, 2. J, 3. B, 4. F, 5. C, 6. F, 7. C

Identifying the Conflict

Your prereading of the introduction should have revealed the issue at hand—namely, tektites, which are small glassy objects found in certain areas known as *strewn fields*. The conflict is about the *origin* of these objects; in other words, where did they come from?

Scientist 1's theory is expressed in his first sentence: "Tektites almost certainly are extraterrestrial, probably lunar, in origin." Put that into a form you can understand. Scientist 1 believes that tektites come from space, probably the moon. Scientist 2, on the other hand, has an opposing theory, also expressed in her first sentence: "Nonlocal origin is extremely unlikely." In other words, it's unlikely that tektites came from a nonlocal source. Instead, they probably came from a *local* source—right here on Earth. The conflict is clear. One says that tektites come from space; the other says they come from Earth itself. You might have even labeled the two positions "space origin" and "Earth origin."

But how do these scientists support their theories? Scientist 1 presents three points of data:

- Tektite shapes show characteristics of air-friction melting (supporting the theory of space origin).
- Atmospheric forces wouldn't be great enough to shape tektitelike material ejected from Earth's surface (weakening the theory of Earth origin).
- Tektites resemble moon rocks gathered by *Apollo 12* but not Earth rocks (strengthening the theory of space origin).

Scientist 2 also presents three points of data:

- Any matter coming from space would fall over a wide area instead of being concentrated in strewn fields (weakening the theory of space origin).
- There are striking similarities between tektites and the composition of Earth's crust (strengthening the theory of Earth origin).
- Meteorite impacts could create shock waves, explaining how terrestrial material could undergo air-friction melting (strengthening the theory of Earth origin by counteracting Scientist 1's first point).

Obviously, you wouldn't want to write out the supporting data for each theory the way we've done above. But it probably would be a good idea to underline the key phrases in the data descriptions ("air-friction melting," "*Apollo 12*," etcetera) and number them. What's important is that you have an idea of what data supports which theory. The questions will then force you to focus, once you get to them.

Attacking the Questions

Now let's quickly attack the questions:

Question 1 asks how it would affect the scientists' arguments if it were discovered that many tektites contain unmelted crystalline material. Well, Scientist 1 says that tektites *never* contain unmelted crystalline material, and that the terrestrial glass produced by some meteorite impacts *always* does. Therefore, by showing a resemblance between tektites and Earth materials, this discovery would weaken Scientist 1's argument for extraterrestrial origin. Choice A is correct.

For question 2, you had to identify which answer choice was used by Scientist 2 to support the argument that tektites are terrestrial in origin. You should have been immediately drawn to choice J, which expresses what we've identified above as Scientist 2's first data point. Notice how choice F is a piece of evidence that Scientist 1 cites—remember not to confuse the viewpoints! As for G, Scientist 2 says that tektites do resemble Earth materials, but never says that they *don't* resemble lunar materials. And choice H gets it backwards; Scientist 2 says that extraterrestrial material *would* be widely dispersed, and that the tektites are *not* widely dispersed.

Countering Evidence

For question 3, you need to find the best way for Scientist 1 to counter the point that some tektites have vesicles filled with gases in the same proportion as Earth's atmosphere. First, make sure you understand the meaning of that point. The idea that these gases must have been trapped in the vesicles—little holes—while the rock was actually being formed is being used by Scientist 2 to suggest that tektites are of terrestrial origin. Scientist 1 *could* say that not all tektites have such gas-filled vesicles (choice A) but that's not a great argument. If any reasonable number of them *do,* Scientist 1 would have to come up with an alternative explanation (Scientist 2 never claimed that *all* tektites contained these vesicles).

But if, as B suggests, Scientist 1 could demonstrate that molten material would be likely to trap some terrestrial gases while falling through Earth's atmosphere, that would explain how tektites might have come from beyond the Earth and still contain vesicles filled with Earthlike gases. Choice C is easy to eliminate if you know that the moon's atmosphere is extremely thin—almost nonexistent—and totally different in composition from Earth's atmosphere, so it doesn't make much sense to suggest that those gases might occur in the same proportions in the moon's atmosphere. Finally, since it's Scientist 2 who claims that tektites are terrestrial in origin, showing that similar gas-filled vesicles occur in some terrestrial volcanic glass (choice D) wouldn't help Scientist 1 at all.

In question 4, you're asked how Scientist 2 answered the argument that tektitelike material ejected from Earth could not reach a high enough velocity to undergo air-friction melting. Well, that was Scientist 2's third data point. The shock wave produced by a major meteorite collision could momentarily displace the atmosphere right above the impact site—just move the air out of the way for a very brief time—and so when the splattered material reentered the atmosphere, it would undergo air-friction melting. That's basically what choice F says, so F is correct.

Question 5: Subjecting lenses of tektite glass to a heated airstream was mentioned toward the beginning of Scientist 1's argument. The point was to simulate the entry of extraterrestrial tektite material through Earth's atmosphere, and that's closest to choice C.

Keeping Your Scientists Straight

Question 6 shows again why it pays to keep straight whose viewpoint is whose. You can't counter the objections of Scientist 2 to Scientist 1's argument unless you know what Scientist 2 was objecting to. Scientist 2's first data point is the only one designed to shoot holes in the opposing viewpoint. There, Scientist 2 takes issue with the idea that lunar material could strike Earth without being dispersed over a far wider area than the known strewn fields. But if, as correct choice F says, researchers found some force capable of removing tektite-sized objects from orbit *quickly,* it would demolish the objection that Scientist 2 raises in her first paragraph. The tektite material would strike Earth or be pulled away quickly instead of remaining in a solar orbit long enough to get captured by Earth's gravity and subsequently get distributed over a wide area of Earth.

Question 7 wasn't too tough if you read the question stem carefully. You want to find the tektite characteristic that is *least* consistent with the theory that tektites came from the moon or beyond. That's Scientist 1's theory, so you want to pick the answer choice that doesn't go with his argument. Scientist 1's evidence *does* include tektites' low water content, "flying saucer" shapes, and absence of unmelted material. The only answer choice that he didn't mention was the narrow distribution of the strewn fields. And with good reason. That's part of Scientist 2's argument *against* an extraterrestrial origin. So the correct answer is choice C.

Identify the Evidence

Always be careful to take note of the evidence (data) each scientist uses.

Part Six

THE ACT WRITING TEST

STEP FIFTEEN

Write What Counts

STEP FIFTEEN PREVIEW

Just the Facts
- How Will Schools Use the Writing Test?
- Who Should Take the Writing Test?

How the ACT Essay Is Scored
- What Skills Are Tested?
- Do You Need to Prepare for the Essay?

Kaplan's Four-Step Method for the ACT Essay
- Step 1: Pause to Know the Prompt
- Step 2: Plan
- Step 3: Produce
- Step 4: Proofread

Know the Score: Sample Essays
- Turning a 4 into a 6

Strategy Recap
- Information Banks
- Outside Reading
- Establish and Adhere to a Practice Schedule
- Self-Evaluation
- Get a Second Opinion
- If You're Not a "Writer"
- If English is a Second Language

A growing number of colleges want an assessment of your written communication skills. If you consider yourself a good writer and are accustomed to scoring well on essays, there may be a temptation to skip this chapter. Don't. Top scores are not given out easily, and writing a scored first draft in under a half hour is unlike most of your past writing experiences.

Let's start with the facts.

JUST THE FACTS

Writing has always been an essential skill for college success. Technological advances have now made it possible to add an optional 30-minute Writing test to the ACT Assessment beginning in February 2005, for students entering colleges in fall 2006.

The ACT English test already measures knowledge of effective writing skills, including grammar, punctuation, organization, and style. The Writing test will complement that evaluation of technical skill with an example of your simple, direct writing.

How Will Schools Use the Writing Test?

The ACT Writing test may be used for either admissions or course placement purposes, or both. About one-third of the schools using the ACT require the Writing test, and another 20 percent recommend but don't require it. As the Writing test becomes better known, we can assume more schools will elect to rely on the ACT essay as an important assessment of student writing.

Students who take the Writing test will receive an English score, a Writing subscore, and a combined English-Writing score on a 1–36 scale. Copies of the essay (with the graders' comments) will also be available online for downloading. Schools that do not require the Writing test will also receive the Combined English-Writing score for students who have taken the Writing test, unless the school specifically asks *not* to receive those results.

Who Should Take the Writing Test?

You should decide whether to take the ACT Writing test based on the admissions policies of the schools you will apply to and on the advice of your high school guidance counselors. A list of colleges requiring the test is maintained on the ACT website, www.act.org/aap/writing. If you are unsure about what schools you will apply to you should plan to take the Writing test. However, testing will be available later if you decide not to take the Writing test and discover later that you need it.

HOW THE ACT ESSAY IS SCORED

Your essay will be graded on a holistic scale of 1–6 (6 being the best). Graders will be looking for an overall sense of your essay, not assigning separate scores for specific elements like grammar or organization. Two readers read and score each essay; then those scores are added together. If there's a difference of more than a point, your essay will be read by a third reader.

Statistically speaking, there will be few 6 essays. If each grader gives your essay a 4 or 5, that will place you at the upper range of those taking the exam.

What Skills Are Tested?

The readers realize you're writing under time pressure and expect you to make some mistakes. The content of your essay is not relevant; readers are not checking your facts (so go ahead and make them up if you have to). Nor will they judge you on your opinions. What they want is to see how well you can communicate a relevant, coherent point of view.

The test makers identify the following as the skills tested in the Writing test:

- Stating a clear perspective on an issue—that is, answering the question in the prompt
- Providing supporting evidence and logical reasoning—building an argument
- Maintaining focus and organizing ideas logically
- Writing clearly

The Writing test is not principally a test of your grammar and punctuation (which are tested in the English test)—colleges want a chance to see your reasoning and communication skills.

The skill they didn't mention is speed. The skills they list would be relevant if you were writing an essay over the course of several weeks. On the ACT, you have to do all this in 30 minutes. This *cannot* be done using the process you learned for essay writing in the past. There is no time to write and rewrite, no choice of topic, no opportunity to do research.

Do You Need to Prepare for the Essay?

So, the ACT essay is not like other writing experiences. It's a first draft that will be graded. Not only must it be complete and well organized, but it must also be easy for a grader to see that it is complete and well organized (and the grader may spend as little as a minute reading your essay). That's a lot to do in 30 minutes, so preparation and practice are a good idea.

KAPLAN'S FOUR-STEP METHOD FOR THE ACT ESSAY

Step 1: Pause to Know the Prompt

Step 2: Plan

Step 3: Produce

Step 4: Proofread

If you plan your essay and adhere to your plan when you write, the result will be solidly organized. Between now and test day, you can't drastically change your overall writing skills—and you probably don't need to. If your plan is good, all you need to do in the writing and proofreading steps is draw on your strengths and avoid your weaknesses. Get to know what those are as you practice.

Write What Counts: To maximize your score, use the Kaplan Method to help you focus on writing what the scorers will look for—*and nothing else*.

Step:	An upper-level essay:	A lower-level essay:
Prompt	clearly develops a position on the prompt	does not clearly state a position
Plan	supports with concrete, detailed examples	is general or repetitious
Produce	maintains clear focus and organization	digresses or has weak organization
Proofread	shows competent use of language	contains errors that reduce clarity

Kaplan has found this approach useful in its many years of experience with hundreds of sample essay statements on a wide range of tests. Let's look at what the test makers tell you about how the essays are scored.

To score Level 4, you must:

- Answer the question.
- Support ideas with examples.
- Show logical thought and organization.
- Avoid major or frequent errors that make your writing unclear.

Organization and clarity are key to an above-average essay. If the reader can't follow your train of thought—if ideas aren't clearly organized or if grammatical errors, misspellings, and incorrect word choices make your writing unclear—you can't do well.

Remember the Requirements

You can't earn a 5 or 6 if you haven't met the basic requirements for a 4, so think of the requirements as building blocks and be sure you have the foundation in place.

To score Level 5, all you have to add to a 4 is:

- Address the topic in depth.

That is, offer more examples and details. The test makers' graders love specific examples, and the more concrete your examples are the more they clarify your thinking and keep you focused.

To score Level 6, all you have to add to a 5 is:

- Make transitions smoother and show variety in syntax and vocabulary.

Use words from the prompt to tie paragraphs together, rather than relying exclusively on connectors like "however" and "therefore." Vary your sentence structure, sometimes using simple sentences and other times using compound and complex ones. Adding a few college-level vocabulary words will also boost your score.

Now let's apply the Kaplan Method to a practice prompt:

Step 1: Pause to Know the Prompt

Spend less than a minute on this.

Know the General Directions: Before Test Day, you should be familiar with the general directions, which will look like this:

> In many high schools, the administration has provided guidelines for the publication of student newspapers. These guidelines often determine which topics can and cannot be discussed in the newspaper and prohibit what the administration deems inappropriate language. Many administrators and teachers feel that these restrictions enable them to provide a safe learning environment for students. Others feel that any restriction on the student newspaper is a violation of freedom of speech. In your opinion, should high schools place restrictions on student newspapers?
>
> In your essay, take a position on this question. You may write about either one of the two points of view given, or you may present a different point of view on this question. Use specific reasons and examples to support your position.

The final paragraph is always the same. Notice that there are two distinct parts to the assignment: (1) state a position and (2) provide support for your position.

Know Your Task

The assignment is *not* to write something vaguely inspired by the information given—that's where many good, creative writers go wrong.

Many scores are lower than they could be simply because these standard directions are ignored: the writer does not present a point of view or does not provide support for it.

Answer the Question: There is no right or wrong answer, and you don't have to respond to the points of view offered in the prompt. Just decide what you will choose as your position, and then back it up with reasoning and examples. Highlight key words in the prompt and use them in your paragraphs to show how your ideas relate to the prompt. You can also add depth by defining or providing background about these words. Terms that might be explored in this statement include: *topic, inappropriate language, safe,* and *free speech.*

Step 2: Plan

Take 5 minutes or less to build a plan before you write. Focus on what kinds of reasoning and examples you can use to support your position. If you find you have more examples for a position different from the one you thought you would take, change your position.

Subject Matter: Avoid highly emotional examples that will tend to reduce your clarity and organization. Avoid potentially offensive examples or extreme positions that are hard to defend.

A 6 essay can have a single well-developed example; two or more can make strong essays, but won't guarantee a 5 or 6. However, an abundance of undeveloped examples makes weak, low-scoring essays.

Literary or historical examples won't necessarily do better than personal experience. Choose examples that you can write about with confidence; don't try to impress the readers with your content—it doesn't count. If you do choose personal experiences, choose self-improvement, positive acts, or creative work. Remember that colleges may use these essays as additional personal statements.

Controlled Brainstorming: In your high school classes, many of you learned to "brainstorm"—perhaps using a "clustering" approach to organize your ideas. These are excellent strategies if you have the luxury of days or weeks to write your essay. They lead to unbalanced, disorganized essays if you have to write in 30 minutes.

The Kaplan Method is designed to produce balanced and integrated essays in the 30 minutes allotted. Controlled brainstorming means staying very focused on coming up with workable examples and arguments as quickly as possible, and then moving on. You aren't looking for the perfect argument or example—just ones that you can write about with clarity and detail.

Information Banks: Refresh your memory about your favorite or most memorable books, school subjects, historical events, personal experiences, activities—anything you can use as examples in your essay. By doing so, you strengthen mental connections to those ideas and details—that will make it easier to connect to the right examples on test day.

Structure Your Essay: Plan a clear introduction, a distinct middle section, and a strong conclusion. Choose your best examples, decide in what order you'll handle them, and plan your paragraphs.

With that in mind, we suggest:

- Use an effective *hook* to bring the reader in.
- Regular *transitions* provide the glue that holds your ideas together.
- End with a *bang* to make your essay memorable.

A "hook" means avoiding an essay that opens (as thousands of other essays will): "In my opinion, …, because…." Try a more general statement that introduces one or more of the key words you will use from the prompt.

A "bang" means a closing that ties the three paragraphs together. Good choices can be a clear, succinct statement of your thesis in the essay or a vivid example that's right on point.

Let's look at a plan for our prompt. The answer we've chosen is:

> I agree that restrictions on student newspapers violate freedom of speech and I also believe restrictions impede student learning.

This position clearly responds to the assignment, and adding some reasoning *not* taken directly from the prompt immediately tells the reader, "I have ideas of my own."

Next, working with our proposed response, comb your memory or your imagination for supporting reasons and examples to use. We'll use:

> Point: student newspapers should mimic real life newspapers
>
> Point: not being in the school paper doesn't mean it's not discussed
>
> Point: students can avoid "harming" others as well as adults
>
> Point: censorship is anti-democratic

Fill in the details mentally. Jot down any notes you need to ensure that you use the details you've developed, but don't take the time to write full sentences. When you have enough ideas for a few supporting paragraphs, decide what your introduction and conclusion will be and the order in which you'll discuss each supporting idea.

Ending with a Bang

Save your best example for last and stress its relative importance.

Here's our sample plan:

Para 1: I agree with "free speech." Student newspapers should prepare for real life.

Para 2: Press is treated specially in real life

Para 3: Potential harm not a good argument

Para 4: Censorship vs. democracy

Para 5: Better to have discussion out in the open

Para 6: Restate thesis

If you take our advice and use examples that are very familiar to you, you won't have to write much in your plan in order to remember the point being made. Learn how brief you can make your notes and still not lose sight of what you mean to say.

A good plan:

- Responds to the prompt
- Has an introduction
- Has strong examples, usually one per paragraph
- Has a strong conclusion

Step 3: Produce

Timing:

You'll have at least 22 minutes for this step. If you want to make test day seem easy, practice writing in only 20 minutes.

Appearances Count: In purely physical terms, your essay will make a better impression if you fill a significant portion of the space provided, and write three to five reasonably equal paragraphs (the final paragraph can be short). Use one paragraph for your introduction, one for each example or line of reasoning, and one for your conclusion so your essay will be easy for readers to follow.

Write neatly: graders can't help but feel negative about your essay if it's hard to decipher—and negative feelings affect holistic scoring. If your handwriting is a problem, print.

Stick With the Plan: Given the short time you have for the essay, it's vital to the clarity of your writing that you use the ideas and organization you established in your plan. Resist any urge to introduce new ideas—no matter how good you think they are—or to digress from the central focus or organization of each paragraph.

Write Carefully: If your essay is littered with misspellings and grammatical mistakes, you may get a low score simply because the reader cannot follow what you are trying to say.

Each paragraph should be organized around a topic sentence that you should finish in your mind before you start to write. For example:

> *I believe …*
> *One example …*
> *Another example …*
> *Another example …*
> *Therefore we can conclude …*

Stay on Task

This isn't the place for creative flights of fancy. Make your writing direct, persuasive, and grammatical.

Choose your words carefully. Use some college-level vocabulary, but only words you know are correct. If you are trying to impress the reader, you may *obfuscate* more than *elucidate* what you are *articulating*.

Vary your sentence structure. A couple of common weaknesses to keep in mind:

- Avoid using "I" excessively.
- Avoid slang.

Transitions: Think about the relationship between ideas as you write, and spell them out clearly. This makes it easy for the readers to follow your reasoning, and they'll appreciate it. Use key words from the prompt as well as the kinds of words you've learned about in Reading and English that indicate contrast, opinion, relative importance, and support.

Essay Length: The length of an essay is no assurance of its quality. However, it's hard to develop an argument in depth—something the graders look for—in one or two short paragraphs. Practice writing organized essays with developed examples, and you'll find yourself writing more naturally. Aim for 350–450 words.

Don't Sweat the Small Stuff: Even the top scoring essays can have minor errors. The essay readers understand that you are writing first drafts and have no time for research or revision.

Step 4: Proofread

Always leave yourself at least two minutes to review your work—the time spent will definitely pay off. Very few of us can avoid the occasional confused sentence or omitted word when writing under pressure. Quickly review your essay to be sure your ideas are on the page, not just in your head.

Take the Time to Proofread

In addition to checking the quality of your writing, saving time to proofread also helps ensure that you will complete your essay on test day. An incomplete essay will undermine your confidence.

Don't hesitate to make corrections on your essay—these are timed first drafts, not term papers. But keep it clear: Use a single line through deletions and an asterisk to mark where text should be inserted.

You don't have time to look for every minor error or to revise substantially. Learn the types of mistakes you tend to make and look for them. Some of the most common mistakes in students' essays are those found in the English test questions. Refer to Part Two of this book to review these common errors.

KNOW THE SCORE: SAMPLE ESSAYS

The best way to be sure you've learned what the readers will look for is to try scoring some essays yourself.

You Make the Call

Don't cheat yourself by reading our explanation without first deciding what holistic grade you would give the essay.

The graders will be scoring holistically, not checking off "points"—but to learn what makes a good essay, it may help to consider these questions, based on the test makers' scoring criteria:

- Does the author answer the question?
- Is the author's position clearly stated?
- Does the body of the essay support and develop the position taken?
- Are there at least three supporting paragraphs?
- Is the relevance of each supporting paragraph clear?
- Is the essay a reasonable length?

- Is the essay organized, with a clear introduction, middle, and end?
- Did the author use one paragraph for each new idea?
- Is each sentence in a paragraph relevant to the point made in that paragraph?
- Are transitions clear?
- Is the essay easy to read? Is it engaging?
- Are sentences varied?
- Is vocabulary used effectively? Is college-level vocabulary used?

Don't just answer "yes" or "no"—locate specific text in the essay that answers the question.

Let's look at a sample essay based on the prompt and plan we've been looking at.

Here's the prompt:

> In many high schools, the administration has provided guidelines for the publication of student newspapers. These guidelines often determine which topics can and cannot be discussed in the newspaper and prohibit what the administration deems inappropriate language. Many administrators and teachers feel that these restrictions enable them to provide a safe learning environment for students. Others feel that any restriction on the student newspaper is a violation of freedom of speech. In your opinion, should high schools place restrictions on student newspapers?
>
> In your essay, take a position on this question. You may write about either one of the two points of view given, or you may present a different point of view on this question. Use specific reasons and examples to support your position.

Sample Essay 1

In many high schools, the administration has provided guidelines for the publication of student newspapers. These guidelines often determine which topics can and cannot be discussed in the newspaper, and prohibit what the administration deems inappropriate language. Many administrators and teachers feel that these restrictions enable them to provide a safe, appropriate learning environment for students. Others feel that any restriction on the student newspaper is a violation of freedom of speech. In my opinion, students should be free to write on any topic.

Firstly, restrictions will not stop certain topics being talked about. Students will always discuss topics that they are interested in. Second, students are more aware of what is or is not appropriate than the administration might think. A newspaper is there to tell news and students will therefore write about the news.

Finally and most importantly, a right such as freedom of speech should not be checked at the school door. Students not being able to cognizant and value rights such as these if they are not taught their importance in school. So high schools should not place restrictions on student newspapers.

Score: _____/6

It should have been fairly easy to see that this isn't a strong essay. The author does state a clear opinion, but half of the essay is a direct copy of the prompt—something the graders will notice and, if anything, be annoyed by. The time and space spent just quoting the prompt was completely wasted—it earned the writer zero points.

Originality Counts

This doesn't mean you shouldn't quote from the prompt. On the contrary, you should use as much language from the prompt as possible, but always tie language from the prompt to your own ideas.

The rest of the essay is organized and uses transition words ("firstly" and "finally"). The author states her thesis, follows with three supporting reasons, and then a conclusion. However, none of this is discussed fully enough—no concrete details or examples are given. In the second paragraph, for instance, the author should have added an example demonstrating that students are aware of what is appropriate or an example of topics that students will discuss.

The language is understandable but there are significant errors affecting clarity. For instance, the second sentence of paragraph three is a fragment—there is no verb. Some vocabulary words are clearly plugged in without a clear understanding of their meaning: In paragraph three "not being able to cognizant" is incorrect; perhaps the student meant, "not being able to understand."

This essay looks like the writer couldn't think of "good" ideas, waited too long, and had to write in a hurry.

Plan Efficiently

Never spend more than 5 minutes planning, no matter how much you wish you could think of "better" ideas. The content doesn't count; fullness of communication does.

Let's look at another essay. Read it quickly and decide how you would score it.

Sample Essay 2

School administrations and teachers who support restrictions believe that these restrictions are needed to form an appropriate learning environment. But I agree with those who oppose such restrictions because they violate freedom of speech and these limits impede student progress and success after high school.

Despite the true need for rules in high schools, newspapers should be exempt. Students need discipline in the form of detention for misbehavior or demerits for poor study, but the student newspaper should not be a part of that system. Rather, it should mimic "real world" journalism.

Student editors, usually seniors aged seventeen or eighteen, are well aware of the overall environment in which they publish, and understand what is or is not appropriate. High school should give students practice at being cognizant of the larger arena in which they act. The few negative incidents that free press will admittedly cause will teach students that in life, one must take responsibility for one's actions.

Therefore, the argument for freedom of speech in student newspapers advances substantial educational goals for students, as well as our unalienable right of freedom of speech. This right, however, is paramount. The American public school is an extension of the American government and community, and censorship is inconsistent with American democracy. Again, students need to be prepared for the world they will live in; depriving them of rights that are promoted in the greater community prepares students poorly for life after high school.

Finally, censoring information in the student newspaper will not remove the subject from student discussion. Rather, it will remove a balanced, informative viewpoint, and often make the "inappropriate" action more desirable and "cool." Placing restrictions on student newspapers would be a serious mistake that would hinder students from learning what it is to participate in a free society.

Score: _____/6

Did you recognize this as an essay based on the plan we did earlier?

Para 1: I agree with "free speech." Student newspapers should prepare for real life.

Para 2: Press is treated specially in real life

Para 3: Potential harm not a good argument

Para 4: Censorship vs. democracy

Para 5: Not discussing in press doesn't mean not discussing in school

This essay is pretty good—it would earn a 4. The position is clearly stated, and some supporting reasoning is given. There is some good vocabulary here (for example, "impede" in paragraph one, "cognizant" in paragraph three, and "paramount" and "inconsistent" in paragraph four).

However, the reasoning is too general and the writing is too ordinary to earn a top score. Let's see how it could be improved.

Turning a 4 into a 6

The essay plunges right into the two points of view offered in the prompt. It could be improved by introducing the issue with a general statement, like:

There seems to be considerable debate nationwide over the role and proper control of student newspapers.

In the last sentence of the first paragraph, the writer introduces some additional reasoning *not* included in the prompt. That's excellent, but it would be better to make it clear where the position from the prompt ends and the author's position begins, as shown in the following example.

But I agree with those who oppose such restrictions because they violate freedom of speech. <u>I would further argue that</u> these limits impede student progress and success after high school.

The second paragraph is relevant and organized—it covers one of the two positions offered in the prompt. But it would be better if the writer tied this argument more clearly to something specific in the prompt, perhaps with an opening sentence using language from the prompt, like:

Some people claim that high school students need strict guidelines in order to prepare for life after school.

Moreover, at the end of the paragraph the reference to mimicking "real world" journalism would be improved by telling the reader what "real world" journalism is:

Rather, it should mimic "real world" journalism, which strives to provide valid, balanced reporting on events important to the public, or in this case the student body.

The third paragraph addresses the view in the prompt that students can cause harm by printing inappropriate articles. But, again, it should be made clearer what part of the prompt this paragraph is responding to, with a first sentence like:

Others believe that students may cause unintended harm with newspaper articles written on controversial subjects. I think that is laughable.

Paragraph four is pretty good, as is. It states clearly what the author considers the most important argument. The fifth paragraph raises good arguments, but leaves them undeveloped. It would be best to provide an example of what type of story would help promote "balanced, informative" discussion to counteract "inappropriate...cool" actions, like:

For instance, a reporter for my high school paper researched and wrote an in-depth story on the increasing drug problem among students. The administration quickly intervened and stopped the story, declaring that drugs were an inappropriate topic for student discussion. This story, however, would have focused discussion on a crucial issue for students, so that they can make the right choice when offered drugs or when they see friends using drugs. Unfortunately, this is a situation most students will face, and they need to be prepared. Suppressing the story made drugs seem even more rebellious and mysterious and most importantly did not give students facts with which they could prepare.

This makes it clear why the writer saved this argument for the last—an important, detailed example.

Finally, since this writer offers a fair number of supporting ideas, it would also be a good idea to add some transitions that establish the relative importance of those ideas. For example, in the third paragraph:

<u>First of all,</u> student editors, usually seniors aged seventeen or eighteen, are well aware of the overall environment in which they publish, and understand what is or is not appropriate. <u>But even more importantly,</u> high school should give students practice at being cognizant of the larger arena in which they act.

Here's how this essay would look with the improvements we've suggested.

There seems to be considerable debate nationwide over the role and proper control of student newspapers. School administrations and teachers who support restrictions believe that these restrictions are needed to form an appropriate learning environment. But I agree with those who oppose such restrictions because they violate freedom of speech. I would further argue that these limits impede student progress and success after high school.

Some people claim that high school students need strict guidelines in order to prepare for life after school. Despite the true need for rules in high schools, newspapers should be exempt. Students need discipline in the form of detention for misbehavior or demerits for poor study, but the student newspaper should not be a part of that system. Rather, it should mimic "real world" journalism, which strives to provide valid, balanced reporting on events important to the public, or in this case the student body.

Others believe that students may cause unintended harm with newspaper articles written on controversial subjects. I think that is laughable. First of all, student editors, usually seniors aged seventeen or eighteen, are well aware of the overall environment in which they publish, and understand what is or is not appropriate. But even more importantly, high school should give students practice at being cognizant of the larger arena in which they act. The few negative incidents that free press will admittedly cause will teach students that in life, one must take responsibility for one's actions.

Therefore, the argument for freedom of speech in student newspapers advances substantial educational goals for students, as well as our unalienable right of freedom of speech. This right, however, is paramount. The American public school is an extension of the American government and community, and censorship is inconsistent with American democracy. Again, students need to be prepared for the world they will live in; depriving them of rights that are promoted in the greater community prepares students poorly for life after high school.

Finally, censoring information in the student newspaper will not remove the subject from student discussion. Rather, it will remove a balanced, informative viewpoint, and often make the "inappropriate" action more desirable and "cool." For instance, a reporter for my high school paper researched and wrote an in-depth story on the increasing drug problem among students. The administration quickly intervened and stopped the story, declaring that drugs were an inappropriate topic for student discussion. This story, however, would have focused discussion on a crucial issue for students, so that they can make the right choice when offered drugs or when they see friends using drugs. Unfortunately, this is a situation most students will face, and they need to be prepared. Suppressing the story made drugs seem even more rebellious and mysterious and most importantly did not give students facts with which they could prepare.

Placing restrictions on student newspapers would be a serious mistake that would hinder students from learning what it is to participate in a free society.

Remember

There are no right or wrong opinions. You can earn a 6 with an essay for or against the issue raised in the prompt.

This is now a 6 essay. It addresses the task both fully and concretely. It addresses both sides of the argument, refutes two opposing arguments, and then moves to the bulk of the author's own reasoning. The first paragraph introduces all the lines of reasoning that will be used, demonstrating to the reader that the writer knew right from the start where this essay was headed. The development of ideas is clear and logical and the paragraphs reflect this organization.

The author shows a high level of skill with language. The transitions between paragraphs are clear and guide the reader through the reasoning. The sentence structure varies throughout the passage, and is at times complex.

So what did we do to our 4 to make it a 6?

- We added examples and detail.
- We varied sentence structure and added more college-level vocabulary ("strives," "laughable," "intervened," and "suppressing").
- While length alone doesn't make a 6, we've added significantly to our original essay. Those extra words provide more room for detail and the "superior language" the test maker is looking for in a 6 essay.
- The conclusion, rather than being lost in the fifth paragraph, is now a strong, independent statement that concisely sums up the writer's point of view.

Remember that your graders will be reading holistically. They will not be grading you by assigning points to particular aspects of your writing. However, as you practice essay writing, you can build an otherwise humdrum essay into a 6 by working on specific elements, with the net effect of giving your essay that 6 glow.

STRATEGY RECAP

Information Banks

Don't wait until test day to think about what subjects you can draw on for your examples to create animated and engaging essays. Examples can be drawn from anywhere: your life experience, a story you saw on the news, literature, history, or other subjects.

Outside Reading

The outside reading you do for Reading will also help develop your writing skills for the essay. Adopt persuasive language that you find in articles you read. After reading them, flex your own persuasive capacities by asking yourself:

- What is the author's point?
- How is it supported?
- What kinds of people would disagree, and why?

Establish and Adhere To a Practice Schedule

Even if you've waited until the last minute to prepare for the ACT Writing test, you can still use the Kaplan method to practice the writing skills you will need on test day. Practice writing one essay per day (except for the day before the test, when you should focus on relaxing for the exam) at the same time of day you will be writing on test day. Be sure to adhere to a strict time schedule in order to mimic the real conditions of the test.

Self-Evaluation

After each practice essay, score yourself based on the guidelines provided. Then analyze how well you followed the Kaplan Method in constructing your essay, and what you might focus on to improve.

Get a Second Opinion

Ask someone else to read and critique your practice essays. Knowing whether another person can follow your reasoning is the single most important learning aid you can have for the essay.

If You're Not a "Writer"

Writing essays may not be your favorite pastime, but you can still succeed on the ACT essay. If your writing is weak, focus on building a well-supported argument—if you have that, weaknesses and errors in writing will be less important.

If English is a Second Language

The ACT essay can be a special challenge for the international student or ESL student here in the United States. Make a special point of spending time proofreading your practice essays when you finish them, and edit anything that makes your writing unclear. There's a strong connection between your English reading skills and your writing skills, so keep reading as well.

Emergency Plan

It's difficult to create a good essay in the last few minutes. If you're down to the wire, allow yourself a few minutes to plan and then write, based on that plan, no matter how much you wish you could think of other ideas. Remember that the essay tests your ability to convey those ideas—not the quality of the ideas.

Section Four

PRACTICE TEST AND EXPLANATIONS

ACT Practice Test
Answer Sheet

English Test

	10. Ⓐ Ⓑ Ⓒ Ⓓ	20. Ⓐ Ⓑ Ⓒ Ⓓ	30. Ⓐ Ⓑ Ⓒ Ⓓ	40. Ⓐ Ⓑ Ⓒ Ⓓ	50. Ⓐ Ⓑ Ⓒ Ⓓ	60. Ⓐ Ⓑ Ⓒ Ⓓ	70. Ⓐ Ⓑ Ⓒ Ⓓ
1. Ⓐ Ⓑ Ⓒ Ⓓ	11. Ⓐ Ⓑ Ⓒ Ⓓ	21. Ⓐ Ⓑ Ⓒ Ⓓ	31. Ⓐ Ⓑ Ⓒ Ⓓ	41. Ⓐ Ⓑ Ⓒ Ⓓ	51. Ⓐ Ⓑ Ⓒ Ⓓ	61. Ⓐ Ⓑ Ⓒ Ⓓ	71. Ⓐ Ⓑ Ⓒ Ⓓ
2. Ⓕ Ⓖ Ⓗ Ⓙ	12. Ⓕ Ⓖ Ⓗ Ⓙ	22. Ⓕ Ⓖ Ⓗ Ⓙ	32. Ⓕ Ⓖ Ⓗ Ⓙ	42. Ⓕ Ⓖ Ⓗ Ⓙ	52. Ⓕ Ⓖ Ⓗ Ⓙ	62. Ⓕ Ⓖ Ⓗ Ⓙ	72. Ⓕ Ⓖ Ⓗ Ⓙ
3. Ⓐ Ⓑ Ⓒ Ⓓ	13. Ⓐ Ⓑ Ⓒ Ⓓ	23. Ⓐ Ⓑ Ⓒ Ⓓ	33. Ⓐ Ⓑ Ⓒ Ⓓ	43. Ⓐ Ⓑ Ⓒ Ⓓ	53. Ⓐ Ⓑ Ⓒ Ⓓ	63. Ⓐ Ⓑ Ⓒ Ⓓ	73. Ⓐ Ⓑ Ⓒ Ⓓ
4. Ⓕ Ⓖ Ⓗ Ⓙ	14. Ⓕ Ⓖ Ⓗ Ⓙ	24. Ⓕ Ⓖ Ⓗ Ⓙ	34. Ⓕ Ⓖ Ⓗ Ⓙ	44. Ⓕ Ⓖ Ⓗ Ⓙ	54. Ⓕ Ⓖ Ⓗ Ⓙ	64. Ⓕ Ⓖ Ⓗ Ⓙ	74. Ⓕ Ⓖ Ⓗ Ⓙ
5. Ⓐ Ⓑ Ⓒ Ⓓ	15. Ⓐ Ⓑ Ⓒ Ⓓ	25. Ⓐ Ⓑ Ⓒ Ⓓ	35. Ⓐ Ⓑ Ⓒ Ⓓ	45. Ⓐ Ⓑ Ⓒ Ⓓ	55. Ⓐ Ⓑ Ⓒ Ⓓ	65. Ⓐ Ⓑ Ⓒ Ⓓ	75. Ⓐ Ⓑ Ⓒ Ⓓ
6. Ⓕ Ⓖ Ⓗ Ⓙ	16. Ⓕ Ⓖ Ⓗ Ⓙ	26. Ⓕ Ⓖ Ⓗ Ⓙ	36. Ⓕ Ⓖ Ⓗ Ⓙ	46. Ⓕ Ⓖ Ⓗ Ⓙ	56. Ⓕ Ⓖ Ⓗ Ⓙ	66. Ⓕ Ⓖ Ⓗ Ⓙ	
7. Ⓐ Ⓑ Ⓒ Ⓓ	17. Ⓐ Ⓑ Ⓒ Ⓓ	27. Ⓐ Ⓑ Ⓒ Ⓓ	37. Ⓐ Ⓑ Ⓒ Ⓓ	47. Ⓐ Ⓑ Ⓒ Ⓓ	57. Ⓐ Ⓑ Ⓒ Ⓓ	67. Ⓐ Ⓑ Ⓒ Ⓓ	
8. Ⓕ Ⓖ Ⓗ Ⓙ	18. Ⓕ Ⓖ Ⓗ Ⓙ	28. Ⓕ Ⓖ Ⓗ Ⓙ	38. Ⓕ Ⓖ Ⓗ Ⓙ	48. Ⓕ Ⓖ Ⓗ Ⓙ	58. Ⓕ Ⓖ Ⓗ Ⓙ	68. Ⓕ Ⓖ Ⓗ Ⓙ	
9. Ⓐ Ⓑ Ⓒ Ⓓ	19. Ⓐ Ⓑ Ⓒ Ⓓ	29. Ⓐ Ⓑ Ⓒ Ⓓ	39. Ⓐ Ⓑ Ⓒ Ⓓ	49. Ⓐ Ⓑ Ⓒ Ⓓ	59. Ⓐ Ⓑ Ⓒ Ⓓ	69. Ⓐ Ⓑ Ⓒ Ⓓ	

Math Test

	9. Ⓐ Ⓑ Ⓒ Ⓓ Ⓔ	18. Ⓐ Ⓑ Ⓒ Ⓓ Ⓔ	27. Ⓐ Ⓑ Ⓒ Ⓓ Ⓔ	36. Ⓐ Ⓑ Ⓒ Ⓓ Ⓔ	45. Ⓐ Ⓑ Ⓒ Ⓓ Ⓔ	54. Ⓐ Ⓑ Ⓒ Ⓓ Ⓔ
1. Ⓐ Ⓑ Ⓒ Ⓓ Ⓔ	10. Ⓐ Ⓑ Ⓒ Ⓓ Ⓔ	19. Ⓐ Ⓑ Ⓒ Ⓓ Ⓔ	28. Ⓐ Ⓑ Ⓒ Ⓓ Ⓔ	37. Ⓐ Ⓑ Ⓒ Ⓓ Ⓔ	46. Ⓐ Ⓑ Ⓒ Ⓓ Ⓔ	55. Ⓐ Ⓑ Ⓒ Ⓓ Ⓔ
2. Ⓕ Ⓖ Ⓗ Ⓙ Ⓚ	11. Ⓕ Ⓖ Ⓗ Ⓙ Ⓚ	20. Ⓕ Ⓖ Ⓗ Ⓙ Ⓚ	29. Ⓕ Ⓖ Ⓗ Ⓙ Ⓚ	38. Ⓕ Ⓖ Ⓗ Ⓙ Ⓚ	47. Ⓕ Ⓖ Ⓗ Ⓙ Ⓚ	56. Ⓕ Ⓖ Ⓗ Ⓙ Ⓚ
3. Ⓐ Ⓑ Ⓒ Ⓓ Ⓔ	12. Ⓐ Ⓑ Ⓒ Ⓓ Ⓔ	21. Ⓐ Ⓑ Ⓒ Ⓓ Ⓔ	30. Ⓐ Ⓑ Ⓒ Ⓓ Ⓔ	39. Ⓐ Ⓑ Ⓒ Ⓓ Ⓔ	48. Ⓐ Ⓑ Ⓒ Ⓓ Ⓔ	57. Ⓐ Ⓑ Ⓒ Ⓓ Ⓔ
4. Ⓕ Ⓖ Ⓗ Ⓙ Ⓚ	13. Ⓕ Ⓖ Ⓗ Ⓙ Ⓚ	22. Ⓕ Ⓖ Ⓗ Ⓙ Ⓚ	31. Ⓕ Ⓖ Ⓗ Ⓙ Ⓚ	40. Ⓕ Ⓖ Ⓗ Ⓙ Ⓚ	49. Ⓕ Ⓖ Ⓗ Ⓙ Ⓚ	58. Ⓕ Ⓖ Ⓗ Ⓙ Ⓚ
5. Ⓐ Ⓑ Ⓒ Ⓓ Ⓔ	14. Ⓐ Ⓑ Ⓒ Ⓓ Ⓔ	23. Ⓐ Ⓑ Ⓒ Ⓓ Ⓔ	32. Ⓐ Ⓑ Ⓒ Ⓓ Ⓔ	41. Ⓐ Ⓑ Ⓒ Ⓓ Ⓔ	50. Ⓐ Ⓑ Ⓒ Ⓓ Ⓔ	59. Ⓐ Ⓑ Ⓒ Ⓓ Ⓔ
6. Ⓕ Ⓖ Ⓗ Ⓙ Ⓚ	15. Ⓕ Ⓖ Ⓗ Ⓙ Ⓚ	24. Ⓕ Ⓖ Ⓗ Ⓙ Ⓚ	33. Ⓕ Ⓖ Ⓗ Ⓙ Ⓚ	42. Ⓕ Ⓖ Ⓗ Ⓙ Ⓚ	51. Ⓕ Ⓖ Ⓗ Ⓙ Ⓚ	60. Ⓕ Ⓖ Ⓗ Ⓙ Ⓚ
7. Ⓐ Ⓑ Ⓒ Ⓓ Ⓔ	16. Ⓐ Ⓑ Ⓒ Ⓓ Ⓔ	25. Ⓐ Ⓑ Ⓒ Ⓓ Ⓔ	34. Ⓐ Ⓑ Ⓒ Ⓓ Ⓔ	43. Ⓐ Ⓑ Ⓒ Ⓓ Ⓔ	52. Ⓐ Ⓑ Ⓒ Ⓓ Ⓔ	
8. Ⓕ Ⓖ Ⓗ Ⓙ Ⓚ	17. Ⓕ Ⓖ Ⓗ Ⓙ Ⓚ	26. Ⓕ Ⓖ Ⓗ Ⓙ Ⓚ	35. Ⓕ Ⓖ Ⓗ Ⓙ Ⓚ	44. Ⓕ Ⓖ Ⓗ Ⓙ Ⓚ	53. Ⓕ Ⓖ Ⓗ Ⓙ Ⓚ	

Reading Test

	6. Ⓐ Ⓑ Ⓒ Ⓓ	12. Ⓐ Ⓑ Ⓒ Ⓓ	18. Ⓐ Ⓑ Ⓒ Ⓓ	24. Ⓐ Ⓑ Ⓒ Ⓓ	30. Ⓐ Ⓑ Ⓒ Ⓓ	36. Ⓐ Ⓑ Ⓒ Ⓓ
1. Ⓐ Ⓑ Ⓒ Ⓓ	7. Ⓐ Ⓑ Ⓒ Ⓓ	13. Ⓐ Ⓑ Ⓒ Ⓓ	19. Ⓐ Ⓑ Ⓒ Ⓓ	25. Ⓐ Ⓑ Ⓒ Ⓓ	31. Ⓐ Ⓑ Ⓒ Ⓓ	37. Ⓐ Ⓑ Ⓒ Ⓓ
2. Ⓕ Ⓖ Ⓗ Ⓙ	8. Ⓕ Ⓖ Ⓗ Ⓙ	14. Ⓕ Ⓖ Ⓗ Ⓙ	20. Ⓕ Ⓖ Ⓗ Ⓙ	26. Ⓕ Ⓖ Ⓗ Ⓙ	32. Ⓕ Ⓖ Ⓗ Ⓙ	38. Ⓕ Ⓖ Ⓗ Ⓙ
3. Ⓐ Ⓑ Ⓒ Ⓓ	9. Ⓐ Ⓑ Ⓒ Ⓓ	15. Ⓐ Ⓑ Ⓒ Ⓓ	21. Ⓐ Ⓑ Ⓒ Ⓓ	27. Ⓐ Ⓑ Ⓒ Ⓓ	33. Ⓐ Ⓑ Ⓒ Ⓓ	39 Ⓐ Ⓑ Ⓒ Ⓓ
4. Ⓕ Ⓖ Ⓗ Ⓙ	10. Ⓕ Ⓖ Ⓗ Ⓙ	16. Ⓕ Ⓖ Ⓗ Ⓙ	22. Ⓕ Ⓖ Ⓗ Ⓙ	28. Ⓕ Ⓖ Ⓗ Ⓙ	34. Ⓕ Ⓖ Ⓗ Ⓙ	40. Ⓕ Ⓖ Ⓗ Ⓙ
5. Ⓐ Ⓑ Ⓒ Ⓓ	11. Ⓐ Ⓑ Ⓒ Ⓓ	17. Ⓐ Ⓑ Ⓒ Ⓓ	23. Ⓐ Ⓑ Ⓒ Ⓓ	29. Ⓐ Ⓑ Ⓒ Ⓓ	35. Ⓐ Ⓑ Ⓒ Ⓓ	

Science Test

	6. Ⓐ Ⓑ Ⓒ Ⓓ	12. Ⓐ Ⓑ Ⓒ Ⓓ	18. Ⓐ Ⓑ Ⓒ Ⓓ	24. Ⓐ Ⓑ Ⓒ Ⓓ	30. Ⓐ Ⓑ Ⓒ Ⓓ	36 Ⓐ Ⓑ Ⓒ Ⓓ
1. Ⓐ Ⓑ Ⓒ Ⓓ	7. Ⓐ Ⓑ Ⓒ Ⓓ	13. Ⓐ Ⓑ Ⓒ Ⓓ	19. Ⓐ Ⓑ Ⓒ Ⓓ	25. Ⓐ Ⓑ Ⓒ Ⓓ	31. Ⓐ Ⓑ Ⓒ Ⓓ	37. Ⓐ Ⓑ Ⓒ Ⓓ
2. Ⓕ Ⓖ Ⓗ Ⓙ	8. Ⓕ Ⓖ Ⓗ Ⓙ	14. Ⓕ Ⓖ Ⓗ Ⓙ	20. Ⓕ Ⓖ Ⓗ Ⓙ	26. Ⓕ Ⓖ Ⓗ Ⓙ	32. Ⓕ Ⓖ Ⓗ Ⓙ	38. Ⓕ Ⓖ Ⓗ Ⓙ
3. Ⓐ Ⓑ Ⓒ Ⓓ	9. Ⓐ Ⓑ Ⓒ Ⓓ	15. Ⓐ Ⓑ Ⓒ Ⓓ	21. Ⓐ Ⓑ Ⓒ Ⓓ	27. Ⓐ Ⓑ Ⓒ Ⓓ	33. Ⓐ Ⓑ Ⓒ Ⓓ	39 Ⓐ Ⓑ Ⓒ Ⓓ
4. Ⓕ Ⓖ Ⓗ Ⓙ	10. Ⓕ Ⓖ Ⓗ Ⓙ	16. Ⓕ Ⓖ Ⓗ Ⓙ	22. Ⓕ Ⓖ Ⓗ Ⓙ	28. Ⓕ Ⓖ Ⓗ Ⓙ	34. Ⓕ Ⓖ Ⓗ Ⓙ	40. Ⓕ Ⓖ Ⓗ Ⓙ
5. Ⓐ Ⓑ Ⓒ Ⓓ	11. Ⓐ Ⓑ Ⓒ Ⓓ	17. Ⓐ Ⓑ Ⓒ Ⓓ	23. Ⓐ Ⓑ Ⓒ Ⓓ	29. Ⓐ Ⓑ Ⓒ Ⓓ	35. Ⓐ Ⓑ Ⓒ Ⓓ	

Practice Test

HOW TO TAKE THIS PRACTICE TEST

This Practice Test is a Kaplan-created test, similar to the actual ACT test booklet. Before taking the practice test, find a quiet room where you can work uninterrupted for three hours. Make sure you have a comfortable desk, your calculator, and several No. 2 pencils. Use the answer sheet to record your answers. Once you start the practice test, don't stop until you've finished. Remember: You can review any questions within a section, but you may not jump from one section to another.

You'll find the answers and explanations to the test questions immediately following the test.

ENGLISH TEST
45 Minutes—75 Questions

Directions: In the following five passages, certain words and phrases have been underlined and numbered. You will find alternatives for each underlined portion in the right-hand column. Select the one that best expresses the idea, that makes the statement acceptable in standard written English, or that is phrased most consistently with the style and tone of the entire passage. If you feel that the original version is best, select "NO CHANGE." You will also find questions asking about a section of the passage or about the entire passage. For these questions, decide which choice gives the most appropriate response to the given question. For each question in the test, select the best choice, and fill in the corresponding space on the answer folder. You may wish to read each passage through before you begin to answer the questions associated with it. Most answers cannot be determined without reading several sentences around the phrases in question. Make sure to read far enough ahead each time you choose an alternative.

Passage I

Since primitive times, societies have <u>created,</u>
                                        1
<u>and told</u> legends. Even before the development of written language, cultures would orally pass down these popular stories.

2 These stories served the dual purpose of entertaining audiences and of transmitting values

1. **A.** NO CHANGE
   B. created then subsequently told
   C. created and told
   D. created, and told original

2. Suppose that the author wants to insert a sentence here to describe the different kinds of oral stories told by these societies. Which of the following sentences would best serve that purpose?

   F. These myths and tales varied in substance, from the humorous to the heroic.
   G. These myths and tales were often recited by paid storytellers.
   H. Unfortunately, no recording of the original myths and tales exists.
   J. Sometimes it took several evenings for the full story to be recited.

GO ON TO THE NEXT PAGE

and beliefs from generation to generation. <u>Indeed</u>
                                              3
today we have many more permanent ways of

handing down our beliefs to future generations,

we continue to create and tell legends. In our

technological society, a new form of folk tales has

emerged: <u>the</u> urban legend.
          4
                    [2]
    Urban legends are stories we all have heard;

they are supposed to have really happened, but are

never <u>verifiable however</u>. It seems that the people
         5
involved can never be found. Researchers of the

urban legend call the elusive participant in such

supposed "real-life" events a FOAF—a Friend of a

Friend.
              [3]
    Urban legends have some characteristic

features. They are often humorous in nature with

a surprise <u>ending and a conclusion</u>. One such
                6
legend is the tale of the hunter who was returning

home from an unsuccessful hunting trip. On his

way home, he accidentally hit and killed a deer on

a deserted highway. Even though he knew it was

3. A. NO CHANGE
   B. However,
   C. Indeed,
   D. Although

4. F. NO CHANGE
   G. it is called the
   H. it being the
   J. known as the

5. A. NO CHANGE
   B. verifiable, however.
   C. verifiable, furthermore.
   D. verifiable.

6. F. NO CHANGE
   G. ending.
   H. ending, which is a conclusion.
   J. ending or conclusion.

illegal, he decided to keep the deer, and he <u>loads it</u>
                                              7
<u>in</u> the back of his station wagon. As the hunter

7. **A.** NO CHANGE
   B. loaded it in
   C. is loading it in
   D. had loaded it in

continued driving, the deer, <u>he was</u> only
                             8
temporarily knocked unconscious by the car, woke

up and began thrashing around. The hunter

panicked, stopped the car, ran to the ditch, and

watched the enraged deer destroy his car.

8. **F.** NO CHANGE
   G. which being
   H. that is
   J. which was

[4]
One legend involves alligators in the sewer

systems of major metropolitan areas. According to

the story, before alligators were a protected <u>species,</u>
                                               9
<u>people</u> vacationing in Florida purchased baby
  9

9. **A.** NO CHANGE
   B. species; people
   C. species. People
   D. species people

alligators to take home as souvenirs. <u>Between 1930</u>
                                       10
<u>and 1940, nearly a million alligators in Florida</u>
                      10
<u>were killed for the value of their skin, used to</u>
                      10
<u>make expensive leather products such as boots</u>
                      10
<u>and wallets.</u> After the novelty of having a pet
  10
alligator wore off, many people flushed their baby

souvenirs down toilets. Legend has it that the baby

alligators found a perfect growing and breeding

environment in city sewer systems, where they

thrive to this day on the ample supply of rats.

10. **F.** NO CHANGE
    G. Because their skin is used to make expensive leather products such as boots and wallets, nearly a million alligators in Florida were killed between 1930 and 1940.
    H. Killed between 1930 and 1940, the skin of nearly a million alligators from Florida was used to make expensive leather products such as boots and wallets.
    J. OMIT the underlined portion.

GO ON TO THE NEXT PAGE

[5]

In addition to urban legends that

are told from friend to friend, a growing number

of urban legends are passed along through the

Internet and e-mail. One of the more popular

stories <u>are about</u> a woman who was unwittingly
      11

charged $100 for a cookie recipe she requested at

an upscale restaurant. To get her money's worth,

this <u>woman supposed</u> copied the recipe for the
      12

delicious cookies and forwarded it via e-mail to

everyone she knew.

[6]

Although today's technology enhances our

ability to tell and retell urban legends, the Internet

can also serve as a monitor of urban legends.

<u>Dedicated to commonly told urban legends,</u>
      13

<u>research is done by many websites.</u> According to
      13

those websites, most legends, including the ones

told here, have no basis in reality.

11. **A.** NO CHANGE
    B. would be about
    C. is about
    D. is dealing with

12. **F.** NO CHANGE
    G. woman supposedly
    H. women supposedly
    J. women supposed to

13. **A.** NO CHANGE
    B. Many websites are dedicated to research-ing the validity of commonly told urban legends.
    C. Researching the validity of commonly told urban legends, many websites are dedicated.
    D. OMIT the underlined portion.

> Items 14–15 ask about the preceding passage as a whole.

14. The author wants to insert the following sentence:

    > Other urban legends seem to be designed to instill fear.

    What would be the most logical placement for this sentence?

    F. After the last sentence of Paragraph 2
    G. After the second sentence of Paragraph 3
    H. Before the first sentence of Paragraph 4
    J. After the last sentence of Paragraph 4

15. Suppose that the author had been assigned to write an essay comparing the purposes and topics of myths and legends in primitive societies and in our modern society. Would this essay fulfill that assignment?

    A. Yes, because the essay describes myths and legends from primitive societies and modern society.
    B. Yes, because the essay provides explanations of possible purposes and topics for myths and legends from primitive societies and modern society.
    C. No, because the essay does not provide enough information about the topics of the myths and legends in primitive societies to make a valid comparison.
    D. No, because the essay doesn't provide any information on the myths and legends of primitive societies.

GO ON TO THE NEXT PAGE

Passage II

What does it mean to be successful? <u>Do one</u>
16

measure success by money? If I told you about a

<u>man: working</u> as a teacher, a land surveyor, and a
17
factory worker (never holding any of these jobs

for more than a few years), would that man sound

like a success to you? If I told you that he spent

<u>two solitary years living alone</u> in a small cabin that
18
he built for himself, and that he spent those years

looking at plants and writing in a diary—would

you think of him as a celebrity or an important

figure? What if I told you that <u>he rarely ventured</u>
19
far from the town where he was born, that he was

thrown in jail for refusing to pay his taxes, and

that he died at the age of forty-five? Do any of

these facts seem to point to a man whose life

should be studied and emulated? You may already

know about this man. You may even have read

some of his writings. His name <u>was: Henry David</u>
20
<u>Thoreau, and he</u> was, in addition to the jobs listed
20

16. F. NO CHANGE
    G. Does we
    H. Does one
    J. Did you

17. A. NO CHANGE
    B. man who worked
    C. man and worked
    D. man, which working

18. F. NO CHANGE
    G. two years living alone
    H. two solitary years all by himself
    J. a couple of lonely years living in solitude

19. A. NO CHANGE
    B. he ventured rarely
    C. he has rare ventures
    D. this person was to venture rarely

20. F. NO CHANGE
    G. was Henry David Thoreau and he
    H. was: Henry David Thoreau, who
    J. was Henry David Thoreau, and he

GO ON TO THE NEXT PAGE

above, a poet, an essayist, a naturalist, and a social critic. Although the facts listed about him may not seem to add up to much, he <u>was, in fact a</u>
21
tremendously influential person. Along with writers such as Ralph Waldo Emerson, Mark Twain, and Walt Whitman, Thoreau helped to create the first literature and philosophy that most people identify as <u>unique</u> "American."
22

In 1845, Thoreau built a <u>cabin. Near</u> Walden
23
Pond and remained there for more than two years, living alone, fending for himself, and observing the nature around him. He kept scrupulous notes in his diary, notes that he later distilled into his most famous work titled *Walden*. <u>*Walden* is read</u>
24
<u>by many literature students today.</u>
24
[1] To protest slavery, Thoreau refused to pay his taxes in 1846. [2] Thoreau was a firm believer in the abolition of slavery, and he objected to the practice's extension into the new territories of the

21. **A.** NO CHANGE
B. was, in fact, a
C. was in fact a
D. was in fact, a

22. **F.** NO CHANGE
G. uniquely
H. uniqueness
J. the most unique

23. **A.** NO CHANGE
B. cabin. On
C. cabin, by
D. cabin near

24. **F.** NO CHANGE
G. This book is read by many literature students today.
H. Today, many literature students read *Walden*.
J. OMIT the underlined portion.

GO ON TO THE NEXT PAGE

West. [3] For this act of rebellion, he was thrown in the Concord jail. 25

Thoreau used his writing to spread his message of resistance and activism; he published 26 an essay entitled *Civil Disobedience* (also known as *Resistance to Civil Government*). In it, Thoreau laid out his argument for refusing to obey unjust laws.

Although Thoreau's life was very brief, his 27 works and his ideas continue to touch and influence people. Students all over the country— all over the world—continue to read his essays and hear his unique voice, urging them to lead lives of principle, individuality, and freedom. 28

To be able to live out the ideas that burn in the 29 heart of a person—surely that is the meaning of 29 success.

25. What is the most logical order of sentences in this paragraph?
   A. NO CHANGE
   B. 3, 2, 1
   C. 2, 1, 3
   D. 3, 1, 2

26. F. NO CHANGE
   G. activism and he published
   H. activism; which is why he published
   J. activism to publish

27. A. NO CHANGE
   B. he's
   C. their
   D. those

28. The purpose of this paragraph is to:
   F. explain why Thoreau was put in jail.
   G. prove a point about people's conception of success.
   H. suggest that Thoreau may be misunderstood.
   J. discuss Thoreau's importance in today's world.

29. A. NO CHANGE
   B. one's heart
   C. the heart and soul of a person
   D. through the heart of a person

GO ON TO THE NEXT PAGE

Question 30 asks about the preceding passage as a whole.

30. By including questions throughout the entire first paragraph, the author allows the reader to:

    F. answer each question as the passage proceeds.
    G. think about the meaning of "success."
    H. assess the quality of Thoreau's work.
    J. form an opinion about greed in modern society.

Passage III

[1]

More than half of the world's <u>currently living</u>
                                    31
<u>plant</u> and animal species live in tropical
 31
rainforests. Four square miles of a Central

American rainforest can be home to up to 1,500

different species of flowering plants, 700 species of

trees, 400 species of birds, and 125 species of

mammals. Of these mammals, the sloth is one of

the most unusual.

[2]

Unlike most mammals, the sloth is usually

upside down. A sloth does just about everything

upside down, including sleeping, eating, mating,

and giving birth. <u>Its' unique</u> anatomy allows the
                    32
sloth to spend most of the time hanging from one

tree branch or another, high in the canopy

of a rainforest tree. About the size of a large

31. A. NO CHANGE
    B. currently existing plant
    C. living plant
    D. plant

32. F. NO CHANGE
    G. It's unique
    H. Its unique
    J. Its uniquely

GO ON TO THE NEXT PAGE

domestic cat, the sloth hangs from its unusually
             33
long limbs and long hook-like claws. Specially

designed for limbs, the sloth's muscles
             34
seem to cling to things.
             34

                    [3]
      In fact, a sloth's limbs are so specific adapted
                         35
to upside-down life that a sloth is essentially

incapable of walking on the ground. Instead, they
                                         36
must crawl or drag itself with its massive claws.

This makes it easy to see why the sloth rarely

leaves its home in the trees. Because it
                                37
cannot move swiftly on the ground, the sloth is an

excellent swimmer.
                    [4]
[38] A sloth can hang upside down and, without

---

33. A. NO CHANGE
    B. cat; the
    C. cat. The
    D. cat, but the

34. F. NO CHANGE
    G. The sloth's muscles seem to cling to things for specially designed limbs.
    H. The muscles in a sloth's limbs seem to be specially designed for clinging to things.
    J. OMIT the underlined portion.

35. A. NO CHANGE
    B. so specific and
    C. so specified
    D. so specifically

36. F. NO CHANGE
    G. Instead, it
    H. However, they
    J. In addition, it

37. A. NO CHANGE
    B. Despite
    C. Similarly,
    D. Though

38. The author wants to insert a sentence here to help connect Paragraph 3 and Paragraph 4. Which of the following sentences would best serve that purpose?

    F. Of course, many other animals are also excellent swimmers.
    G. Another unique characteristic of the sloth is its flexibility.
    H. In addition to swimming, the sloth is an incredible climber.
    J. Flexibility is a trait that helps the sloth survive.

GO ON TO THE NEXT PAGE

moving the rest of its <u>body turn</u> its face 180
39

degrees so that it <u>was looking</u> at the ground. A
40
sloth can rotate its forelimbs in all directions, so it

can easily reach the leaves that make up its diet.

The sloth can also roll itself up into a ball in

order to <u>protect and defend itself from predators.</u>
41

<u>The howler monkey, another inhabitant of the</u>
42
<u>rainforest, is not as flexible as the sloth.</u>
42

[5]

The best defense a sloth has from predators

such as jaguars and large snakes, though, is its

camouflage. During the rainy season, a sloth's

thick brown or gray fur is usually covered with a

coat of blue-green <u>algae. Which</u> helps it blend in
43
with its forest surroundings. Another type of

camouflage is the sloth's incredibly slow

movement: it often moves less than 100 feet

during a 24-hour period.

39. **A.** NO CHANGE
    B. body turns
    C. body, it has the capability of turning
    D. body, turn

40. **F.** NO CHANGE
    G. had been looking
    H. will have the ability to be looking
    J. can look

41. **A.** NO CHANGE
    B. protect, and defend itself
    C. protects itself
    D. protect itself

42. **F.** NO CHANGE
    G. Another inhabitant of the rainforest, the howler monkey, is not as flexible as the sloth.
    H. Not as flexible as the sloth is the howler monkey, another inhabitant of the rainforest.
    J. OMIT the underlined portion.

43. **A.** NO CHANGE
    B. algae, which
    C. algae, being that it
    D. algae

[6]

It is this slow movement that earned the sloth its name. *Sloth* is also a word for laziness or an aversion to work. But even though it sleeps an average of 15 hours a day, the sloth isn't necessarily lazy. It just moves, upside down, at its own slow pace through its world of rainforest trees. [44]

44. The author is considering deleting the last sentence of Paragraph 6. This change would:

F. diminish the amount of information provided about the habits of the sloth.

G. make the ending of the passage more abrupt.

H. emphasize the slothful nature of the sloth.

J. make the tone of the essay more consistent.

Question 45 asks about the preceding passage as a whole.

45. The author wants to insert the following description:

An observer could easily be tricked into thinking that a sloth was just a pile of decaying leaves.

What would be the most appropriate placement for this sentence?

A. After the last sentence of Paragraph 1

B. After the third sentence of Paragraph 2

C. Before the last sentence of Paragraph 5

D. Before the first sentence of Paragraph 6

Passage IV

During the summer of 1988, I watched

Yellowstone National Park go up in flames. In

June, <u>fires ignited by lightning</u> had been allowed
        46
to burn unsuppressed because park officials

expected that the usual summer rains would

douse the flames. However, the rains never <u>will</u>
                                            47
<u>have come.</u> A plentiful fuel supply of fallen logs
  47
and pine needles was available, and winds of up to

100 mph whipped the spreading fires along and

carried red-hot embers to other areas, creating

new fires. By the time park officials succumbed to

the pressure of public opinion and <u>decide</u> to try to
                                    48

extinguish the <u>flames. It's</u> too late. The situation
                 49
remained out of control in spite of the efforts of

9,000 fire fighters who were using state-of-the-art

equipment. By September, more than 720,000

acres of Yellowstone had been affected by fire.

46. **F.** NO CHANGE
    G. fires having been ignited by lightning
    H. fires, the kind ignited by lightning,
    J. fires ignited and started by lightning

47. **A.** NO CHANGE
    B. came
    C. were coming
    D. have come

48. **F.** NO CHANGE
    G. are deciding
    H. decided
    J. OMIT the underlined portion.

49. **A.** NO CHANGE
    B. flames, it's
    C. flames, it was
    D. flames; it was

GO ON TO THE NEXT PAGE

Nature was only able to curb the destruction; the
                            50
smoke did not begin to clear until the first snow

arrived on September 11.

        Being that I was an ecologist who has studied
                51
forests for 20 years, I knew that this was not nearly

the tragedy it seemed to be. Large fires are, after

all, necessary in order that the continued health in
                                            52
the forest ecosystem be maintained. Fires thin out
        52
overcrowded areas and allow the sun to reach

species of plants stunted by shade. Ash fertilizes

the soil, and fire smoke kills forest bacteria. In the

case of the lodgepole pine, fire is essential to

reproduction: the pines' cone open only when
                        53
exposed to temperatures greater than 112 degrees.

        The fires in Yellowstone did result in some

loss of wildlife, but overall, the region's animals

proved to be fire-tolerant and fire-adaptive.

However, large animals such as bison were often
    54

50. F. NO CHANGE
   G. Only curbing the destruction by able
       nature
   H. Only nature was able to curb the
       destruction
   J. Nature was able to curb only the
       destruction

51. A. NO CHANGE
   B. Being that I am
   C. I'm
   D. As

52. F. NO CHANGE
   G. for the continued health of the forest
       ecosystem to be maintained.
   H. in order to continue the maintenance of
       the health of the forest ecosystem.
   J. for the continued health of the forest
       ecosystem.

53. A. NO CHANGE
   B. pines cones'
   C. pine's cones
   D. pine's cone

54. F. NO CHANGE
   G. Clearly,
   H. In fact,
   J. Instead,

GO ON TO THE NEXT PAGE

seen <u>grazing, and</u> bedding down in meadows near
              55
burning forests. Also, the fire posed little threat to

the members of any endangered animal species in

the park.

My confidence in the natural resilience of the

forest has been borne out in the years since the

fires ravaged Yellowstone. <u>Judging from the recent</u>
                                              56
<u>pictures of the park,</u> the forest was not destroyed;
          56

<u>it</u> was rejuvenated.
57

55. **A.** NO CHANGE
    B. grazing; and bedding
    C. grazing: and bedding
    D. grazing and bedding

56. **F.** NO CHANGE
    G. Recent pictures of the park show that
    H. Judging by the recent pictures of the park,
    J. As judged according to pictures taken of the park recently,

57. **A.** NO CHANGE
    B. they
    C. the fires
    D. I

GO ON TO THE NEXT PAGE

Items 58 and 59 pose questions about the passage as a whole.

58. The writer is considering inserting the following true statement after the first sentence of the second paragraph:

> Many more acres of forest burned in Alaska in 1988 than in Yellowstone Park.

Would this addition be appropriate for the essay?

- **F.** Yes, the statement would add important information about the effects of large-scale forest fires.
- **G.** Yes, the statement would provide an informative contrast to the Yellowstone fire.
- **H.** No, the statement would not provide any additional information about the effect of the 1988 fire in Yellowstone.
- **J.** No, the statement would undermine the author's position as an authority on the subject of forest fires.

59. Suppose that the writer wishes to provide additional support for the claim that the fire posed little threat to the members of any endangered animal species in the park. Which of the following additions would be most effective?

- **A.** A list of the endangered animals known to inhabit the park
- **B.** A discussion of the particular vulnerability of endangered species of birds to forest fires
- **C.** An explanation of the relative infrequency of such an extensive series of forest fires
- **D.** A summary of reports of biologists who monitored the activity of endangered species in the park during the fire

---

Passage V

[1]

White water rafting <u>being</u> a favorite pastime
       60

of mine for several years. I have drifted down

many challenging North American rivers,

including the Snake, the Green, and the <u>Salmon,</u>
               61
<u>and there are many other rivers in America as</u>
         61
<u>well.</u> I have spent some of my best moments in
 61
dangerous rapids, yet nothing has matched the

60. F. NO CHANGE
   G. have been
   H. has been
   J. was

61. A. NO CHANGE
   B. Salmon, just three of many rivers existing in America.
   C. Salmon; many other rivers exist in North America.
   D. Salmon.

thrill I experienced facing my first <u>rapids, on the</u>
                                            62

<u>Deschutes River.</u>
        62

[2]

My father and I spent the morning floating down

a calm and peaceful stretch of the Deschutes in his

wooden MacKenzie river boat. This trip <u>it being</u>
                                            63

the wooden boat's first time down rapids, as well

as mine. <u>Rapids are rated according to a uniform</u>
                                                    64

<u>scale of relative difficulty.</u>
        64

[3]

<u>Roaring, I was in the boat approaching</u>
                    65

<u>Whitehorse Rapids.</u> I felt much like a novice skier
        65

peering down her first steep slope: I was scared,

but even more excited. The water <u>churned and</u>
                                            66

<u>covering me</u> with a refreshing spray. My father,
        66

towards the stern, controlled the oars. The

carefree expression he usually wore on the river

had been replaced <u>and instead he adopted</u> a look
                            67

of intense concentration as he maneuvered

around boulders dotting our path. To release

tension, we began to holler like kids on a roller

62. **F.** NO CHANGE
    G. rapids: on Deschutes River.
    H. rapids; on the Deschutes River.
    J. rapids on the Deschutes River.

63. **A.** NO CHANGE
    B. it happened that it was
    C. was
    D. being

64. **F.** NO CHANGE
    G. Rated according to a uniform scale,
        rapids are relatively difficult.
    H. (Rapids are rated according to a uniform
        scale of relative difficulty.)
    J. OMIT the underlined portion.

65. **A.** NO CHANGE
    B. It roared, and the boat and I approached
        Whitehorse Rapids.
    C. While the roaring boat was approaching
        Whitehorse Rapids, I could hear the
        water.
    D. I could hear the water roar as we
        approached Whitehorse Rapids.

66. **F.** NO CHANGE
    G. churned, and covering me
    H. churning and covering me
    J. churned, covering me

67. **A.** NO CHANGE
    B. with
    C. by another countenance altogether:
    D. instead with some other expression;

GO ON TO THE NEXT PAGE

coaster, our voices echoing <u>across</u> the water as we
68

lurched violently about.

[4]

Suddenly we came to a jarring halt <u>and we</u>
69

<u>stopped</u>; the left side of the bow was wedged on a
69

large rock. A whirlpool whirled around us; if we

capsized we would be sucked into the undertow.

Instinctively, I threw all of my weight towards the

right side of the tilting boat. Luckily, <u>it was</u> just
70

enough force to dislodge us, and we continued on

down for about ten more minutes of spectacular

rapids.

[5]

Later that day we went through Buckskin

Mary Rapids and Boxcar Rapids. When we pulled

up on the bank that evening, we saw that the boat

had received its first scar: <u>that scar was a</u> small
71

hole on the upper bow from the boulder we had

wrestled with. In the years to come, we went down

many rapids and the boat <u>receiving many</u> bruises,
72

68. F. NO CHANGE
    G. throughout
    H. around
    J. from

69. A. NO CHANGE
    B. which stopped us
    C. and stopped
    D. OMIT the underlined portion.

70. F. NO CHANGE
    G. it's
    H. it is
    J. its

71. A. NO CHANGE
    B. that was a
    C. which was a
    D. a

72. F. NO CHANGE
    G. received many
    H. received much
    J. receives many

but Whitehorse is the most memorable rapids of

all. 73

73. Which of the following concluding sentences would most effectively emphasize the final point made in this paragraph while retaining the style and tone of the narrative as a whole?

A. The brutal calamities that it presented the unwary rafter were more than offset by its beguiling excitement.

B. Perhaps it is true that your first close encounter with white water is your most intense.

C. Or, if not the most memorable, then at least a very memorable one!

D. Call me crazy or weird if you want, but white water rafting is the sport for me.

Items 74 and 75 pose questions about the passage as a whole.

---

74. The writer has been assigned to write an essay that focuses on the techniques of white water rafting. Would this essay meet the requirements of that assignment?

F. No, because the essay's main focus is on a particular experience, not on techniques.

G. No, because the essay mostly deals with the relationship between father and daughter.

H. Yes, because specific rafting techniques are the essay's main focus.

J. Yes, because it presents a dramatic story of a day of white water rafting.

75. Suppose that the writer wants to add the following sentence to the essay:

It was such a peaceful summer day that it was hard to believe dangerous rapids awaited us downstream.

What would be the most logical placement of this sentence?

A. After the last sentence of Paragraph 1

B. After the last sentence of Paragraph 2

C. Before the first sentence of Paragraph 4

D. After the last sentence of Paragraph 4

If you finish before time is called, you may check your work on this section only. Do not turn to any other section in the test. **STOP**

MATH TEST
60 Minutes—60 Questions

Directions: Solve each of the following problems, select the correct answer, and then fill in the corresponding space on your answer sheet.

Don't linger over problems that are too time-consuming. Do as many as you can, then come back to the others in the time you have remaining.

Calculator use is permitted, but some problems can best be solved without a calculator.

Note: Unless otherwise noted, all of the following should be assumed.

1. Illustrative figures are not necessarily drawn to scale.
2. All geometric figures lie in a plane.
3. The term *line* indicates a straight line.
4. The term *average* indicates arithmetic mean.

---

1. In a recent survey, 14 people found their mayor to be "very competent." This number is exactly 20% of the people surveyed. How many people were surveyed?

   A. 28
   B. 35
   C. 56
   D. 70
   E. 84

2. A train traveled at a rate of 90 miles per hour for x hours and then at a rate of 60 miles per hour for y hours. Which expression represents the train's average rate in miles per hour for the entire distance traveled?

   F. $\dfrac{540}{xy}$

   G. $\dfrac{90}{x} \times \dfrac{60}{y}$

   H. $\dfrac{90}{x} + \dfrac{60}{y}$

   J. $\dfrac{90x + 60y}{x + y}$

   K. $\dfrac{150}{x + y}$

DO YOUR FIGURING HERE.

GO ON TO THE NEXT PAGE

3. In a certain string ensemble, the ratio of men to women is 5:3. If there are a total of 24 people in the ensemble, how many women are there?

A. 12
B. 11
C. 10
D. 9
E. 8

4. If $x \neq 0$, and $x^2 - 3x = 6x$, then $x = ?$

F. -9
G. -3
H. $\sqrt{3}$
J. 3
K. 9

5. The two overlapping circles below form three non-overlapping regions, as shown:

What is the maximum number of non-overlapping regions that can be formed by three overlapping circles?

A. 5
B. 6
C. 7
D. 8
E. 9

6. If $x^2 + 6x + 8 = 4 + 10x$, then x equals which of the following?

F. -2
G. -1
H. 0
J. 1
K. 2

DO YOUR FIGURING HERE.

GO ON TO THE NEXT PAGE

7. Nine less than the number c is the same as the number d, and d less than twice c is 20. Which two equations could be used to determine the value of c and d?

   A. $d - 9 = c$
      $d - 2c = 20$

   B. $c - 9 = d$
      $2c - d = 20$

   C. $c - 9 = d$
      $d - 2c = 20$

   D. $9 - c = d$
      $2c - d = 20$

   E. $9 - c = d$
      $2cd = 20$

8. A restaurant's fixed-price special dinner consists of an appetizer, an entrée, and dessert. If the restaurant offers 3 different types of appetizers, 5 different types of entrees, and 4 different types of desserts, how many different ways are there to order a fixed-price special dinner?

   F. 4
   G. 5
   H. 12
   J. 23
   K. 60

9. At a recent audition for a school play, 1 out of 3 students who auditioned were asked to come to a second audition. After the second audition, 75% of those asked to the second audition were offered parts. If 18 students were offered parts, how many students went to the first audition?

   A. 18
   B. 24
   C. 48
   D. 56
   E. 72

DO YOUR FIGURING HERE.

GO ON TO THE NEXT PAGE

10. One number is 5 times another number and
their sum is –60. What is the lesser of the two
numbers?

    F. –5
    G. –10
    H. –12
    J. –48
    K. –50

11. In the figure below, which is composed of
equilateral triangles, what is the greatest
number of parallelograms that can be found?

    A. 6
    B. 9
    C. 12
    D. 15
    E. 18

12. The circle in the figure below is inscribed in a
square with a perimeter of 16 inches. What is
the area of the shaded region?

    F. 4π
    G. $16 - 2\pi$
    H. $16 - 4\pi$
    J. $8 - 2\pi$
    K. $8 - 4\pi$

DO YOUR FIGURING HERE.

GO ON TO THE NEXT PAGE

13. How many positive integers less than 50 are multiples of 4 but not multiples of 6?

    A. 4
    B. 6
    C. 8
    D. 10
    E. 12

14. What is the value of $f(3)$ where $f(x) = (8 - 3x)(x^2 - 2x - 15)$?

    F. -30
    G. -18
    H. 12
    J. 24
    K. 30

15. A class contains five juniors and five seniors. If one member of the class is assigned at random to present a paper on a certain subject, and another member of the class is randomly assigned to assist him, what is the probability that both will be juniors?

    A. $\dfrac{1}{10}$

    B. $\dfrac{1}{5}$

    C. $\dfrac{2}{9}$

    D. $\dfrac{2}{5}$

    E. $\dfrac{1}{2}$

DO YOUR FIGURING HERE.

GO ON TO THE NEXT PAGE

16. In triangle *XYZ* below, $\overline{XS}$ and $\overline{SZ}$ are 3 and 12 units, respectively. If the area of triangle *XYZ* is 45 square units, how many units long is altitude $\overline{YS}$?

DO YOUR FIGURING HERE.

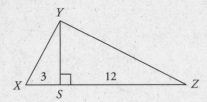

F.   3
G.   6
H.   9
J.   12
K.   15

17. At which *y*-coordinate does the line described by the equation $6y - 3x = 18$ intersect the *y*-axis?

A.   18
B.   9
C.   6
D.   3
E.   2

18. If $x^2 - y^2 = 12$ and $x - y = 4$, what is the value of $x^2 + 2xy + y^2$?

F.   3
G.   8
H.   9
J.   12
K.   16

GO ON TO THE NEXT PAGE

19. What is the area in square units of the figure below?

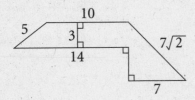

A. 147
B. 108.5
C. 91
D. 60.5
E. $39 + 7\sqrt{2}$

20. A carpenter is cutting wood to make a new bookcase with a board that is 12 feet long. If the carpenter cuts off 3 pieces, each of which is 17 inches long, how many inches long is the remaining fourth and final board? (A foot contains 12 inches.)

F. 36
G. 51
H. 93
J. 108
K. 144

21. If $x^2 - 4x - 6 = 6$, what are the possible values for x?

A. 4, 12
B. −6, 2
C. −6, −2
D. 6, 2
E. 6, −2

22. If −3 is a solution for the equation $x^2 + kx - 15 = 0$, what is the value of k?

F. 5
G. 2
H. −2
J. −5
K. cannot be determined from the information given

GO ON TO THE NEXT PAGE

23. If the lengths, in inches, of all three sides of a triangle are integers, and one side is 7 inches long, what is the smallest possible perimeter of the triangle, in inches?

    A. 9
    B. 10
    C. 12
    D. 15
    E. 18

24. If $0° < \theta < 90°$ and $\sin \theta = \dfrac{\sqrt{11}}{2\sqrt{3}}$ then $\cos \theta = ?$

    F. $\dfrac{1}{2\sqrt{3}}$

    G. $\dfrac{1}{\sqrt{11}}$

    H. $\dfrac{2}{\sqrt{3}}$

    J. $\dfrac{2\sqrt{3}}{\sqrt{11}}$

    K. $\dfrac{11}{2\sqrt{3}}$

25. Which of the following expressions is equivalent to $\dfrac{\sqrt{3+x}}{\sqrt{3-x}}$ for all x such that $-3 < x < 3$?

    A. $\dfrac{3-x}{3+x}$

    B. $\dfrac{3+x}{3-x}$

    C. $\dfrac{-3\sqrt{3+x}}{3-x}$

    D. $\dfrac{\sqrt{9-x^2}}{3-x}$

    E. $\dfrac{\sqrt{x^2-9}}{3+x}$

DO YOUR FIGURING HERE.

GO ON TO THE NEXT PAGE

26. In a certain cookie jar containing only macaroons and gingersnaps, the ratio of macaroons to gingersnaps is 2 to 5. Which of the following could be the total number of cookies in the cookie jar?

DO YOUR FIGURING HERE.

F.   24
G.   35
H.   39
J.   48
K.   52

27. What is the sum of $\frac{3}{16}$ and .175?

A.   .3165
B.   .3500
C.   .3625
D.   .3750
E.   .3875

28. What is the maximum possible area, in square inches, of a rectangle with a perimeter of 20 inches?

F.   15
G.   20
H.   25
J.   30
K.   40

29. $\dfrac{\dfrac{3}{2}+\dfrac{7}{4}}{\left(\dfrac{15}{8}-\dfrac{3}{4}\right)-\left(\dfrac{4+3}{-4+3}\right)}$ =?

A. $\frac{3}{8}$

B. $\frac{2}{5}$

C. $\frac{9}{13}$

D. $\frac{5}{2}$

E. $\frac{8}{3}$

GO ON TO THE NEXT PAGE

30. If $x - 15 = 7 - 5(x - 4)$, then $x = ?$

    F. 0

    G. 2

    H. 4

    J. 5

    K. 7

DO YOUR FIGURING HERE.

31. The sketch below shows the dimensions of a flower garden. What is the area of this garden in square meters?

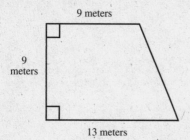

9 meters

9 meters

13 meters

    A. 31

    B. 85

    C. 99

    D. 101

    E. 117

32. What is the slope of the line described by the equation $6y - 3x = 18$?

    F. -2

    G. $-\dfrac{1}{2}$

    H. $\dfrac{1}{2}$

    J. 2

    K. 3

GO ON TO THE NEXT PAGE

KAPLAN

33. Line m passes through the point $(4, 3)$ in the standard (x, y) coordinate plane, and is perpendicular to the line described by the equation $y = -\frac{4}{5}x + 6$. Which of the following equations describes line m?

DO YOUR FIGURING HERE.

A. $y = \frac{5}{4}x + 2$

B. $y = -\frac{5}{4}x + 6$

C. $y = \frac{4}{5}x - 2$

D. $y = -\frac{4}{5}x + 2$

E. $y = \frac{5}{4}x - 2$

34. Line t in the standard (x, y) coordinate plane has a y-intercept of -3 and is parallel to the line having the equation $3x - 5y = 4$. Which of the following is an equation for line t?

F. $y = -\frac{3}{5}x + 3$

G. $y = -\frac{5}{3}x - 3$

H. $y = \frac{3}{5}x + 3$

J. $y = \frac{5}{3}x + 3$

K. $y = \frac{3}{5}x - 3$

35. If $y = mx + b$, which of the following equations expresses x in terms of y, m, and b?

A. $x = \frac{y - b}{m}$

B. $x = \frac{b - y}{m}$

C. $x = \frac{y + b}{m}$

D. $x = \frac{y}{m} - b$

E. $x = \frac{y}{m} + b$

GO ON TO THE NEXT PAGE

36. In the figure below, $\overline{AB} = 20$, $\overline{BC} = 15$, and $\angle ADB$ and $\angle ABC$ are right angles. What is the length of $\overline{AD}$?

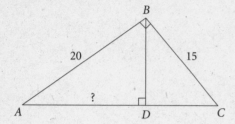

   F.   9
   G.   12
   H.   15
   J.   16
   K.   25

37. In the standard (x, y) coordinate plane shown in the figure below, points A and B lie on line m, and point C lies below it. The coordinates of points A, B, and C are $(0, 5)$, $(5, 5)$, and $(3, 3)$, respectively. What is the shortest possible distance from point C to a point on line m?

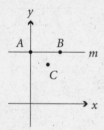

   A.   2
   B. $2\sqrt{2}$
   C.   3
   D. $\sqrt{13}$
   E.   5

DO YOUR FIGURING HERE.

GO ON TO THE NEXT PAGE

38. For all $x \neq 8$, $\dfrac{x^2 - 11x + 24}{8 - x} = ?$

   F. $8 - x$

   G. $3 - x$

   H. $x - 3$

   J. $x - 8$

   K. $x - 11$

DO YOUR FIGURING HERE.

39. Points A and B lie in the standard (x, y) coordinate plane. The (x, y) coordinates of A are $(2, 1)$ and the (x, y) coordinates of B are $(-2, -2)$. What is the distance from A to B?

   A. $3\sqrt{2}$

   B. $3\sqrt{3}$

   C. 5

   D. 6

   E. 7

40. In the figure below, $\overline{AB}$ and $\overline{CD}$ are both tangent to the circle as shown, and $ABCD$ is a rectangle with side lengths $2x$ and $5x$ as shown. What is the area of the shaded region?

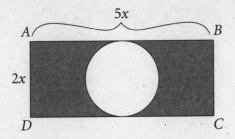

   F. $10\pi x^2$

   G. $10x^2 - \pi x^2$

   H. $10x^2 - 2\pi x$

   J. $9\pi x^2$

   K. $6\pi x^2$

GO ON TO THE NEXT PAGE

DO YOUR FIGURING HERE.

41. If $0° < \theta < 90°$ and $\cos \theta = \dfrac{5\sqrt{2}}{8}$, then $\tan \theta = ?$

    A. $\dfrac{5}{\sqrt{7}}$

    B. $\dfrac{\sqrt{7}}{5}$

    C. $\dfrac{\sqrt{14}}{8}$

    D. $\dfrac{8}{\sqrt{14}}$

    E. $\dfrac{8}{5\sqrt{2}}$

42. Consider fractions of the form $\dfrac{7}{n}$, where n is an integer. How many integer values of n make this fraction greater than .5 and less than .8?

    F. 3
    G. 4
    H. 5
    J. 6
    K. 7

GO ON TO THE NEXT PAGE

43. The circumference of circle X is 12π and the circumference of circle Y is 8π. What is the greatest possible distance between two points, one which lies on the circumference of circle X and one of which lies on the circumference of circle Y?

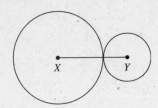

- **A.** 6
- **B.** 10
- **C.** 20
- **D.** 10π
- **E.** 20π

44. $\sqrt{(x^2 + 4)^2} - (x + 2)(x - 2) = ?$

- **F.** $2x^2$
- **G.** $x^2 - 8$
- **H.** $2(x - 2)$
- **J.** 0
- **K.** 8

45. If $s = -3$, then $s^3 + 2s^2 + 2s = ?$

- **A.** -15
- **B.** -10
- **C.** -5
- **D.** 5
- **E.** 33

46. How many different numbers are solutions for the equation $2x + 6 = (x + 5)(x + 3)$?

- **F.** 0
- **G.** 1
- **H.** 2
- **J.** 3
- **K.** Infinitely many

DO YOUR FIGURING HERE.

GO ON TO THE NEXT PAGE

47. In square *ABCD* below, *AC* = 8. What is the perimeter of *ABCD*?

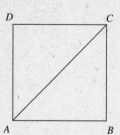

DO YOUR FIGURING HERE.

A. $4\sqrt{2}$

B. 8

C. $8\sqrt{2}$

D. 16

E. $16\sqrt{2}$

48. The front surface of a fence panel is shown below with the lengths labeled representing inches. The panel is symmetrical along its center vertical axis. What is the surface area of the front surface of the panel in square inches?

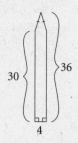

F. 144

G. 132

H. 120

J. 80

K. $64 + 6\sqrt{5}$

GO ON TO THE NEXT PAGE

49. In the figure below, *O* is the center of the circle, and *C*, *D*, and *E* are points on the circumference of the circle. If ∠*OCD* measures 70° and ∠*OED* measures 45°, what is the measure of ∠*CDE*?

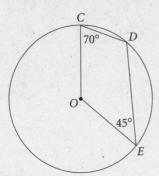

   A. 25°
   B. 45°
   C. 70°
   D. 90°
   E. 115°

50. Which of the following systems of equations does NOT have a solution?

   F. $x + 3y = 19$
       $3x + y = 6$

   G. $x + 3y = 19$
       $x - 3y = 13$

   H. $x - 3y = 19$
       $3x - y = 7$

   J. $x - 3y = 19$
       $3x + y = 6$

   K. $x + 3y = 6$
       $3x + 9y = 7$

51. What is the 46th digit to the right of the decimal point in the decimal equivalent of $\frac{1}{7}$?

   A. 1
   B. 2
   C. 4
   D. 7
   E. 8

52. Which of the following inequalities is equivalent to $-2 - 4x \leq -6x$?

   F. $x \geq -2$
   G. $x \geq 1$
   H. $x \geq 2$
   J. $x \leq -1$
   K. $x \leq 1$

53. If $x > 0$ and $y > 0$, $\dfrac{\sqrt{x}}{x} + \dfrac{\sqrt{y}}{y}$ is equivalent to which of the following?

   A. $\dfrac{2}{\sqrt{xy}}$

   B. $\dfrac{\sqrt{x} + \sqrt{y}}{\sqrt{xy}}$

   C. $\dfrac{x + y}{xy}$

   D. $\dfrac{\sqrt{x} + \sqrt{y}}{\sqrt{x + y}}$

   E. $\dfrac{x + y}{\sqrt{xy}}$

DO YOUR FIGURING HERE.

GO ON TO THE NEXT PAGE

54. In the diagram below, $\overline{CD}$, $\overline{BE}$, and $\overline{AF}$ are all parallel and are intersected by two transversals as shown. What is the length of $\overline{EF}$?

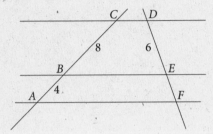

DO YOUR FIGURING HERE.

F. 2

G. 3

H. 4

J. 6

K. 9

55. What is the area, in square units, of the square whose vertices are located at the (x, y) coordinate points indicated in the figure below?

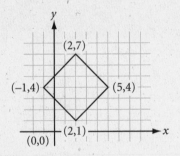

A. 9

B. 12

C. 16

D. 18

E. 24

56. Compared to the graph of $y = \cos \theta$, the graph of $y = 2 \cos \theta$ has:

    F. twice the period and the same amplitude.
    G. half the period and the same amplitude.
    H. twice the period and half the amplitude.
    J. half the amplitude and the same period.
    K. twice the amplitude and the same period.

57. Brandy has a collection of comic books. If she adds 15 to the number of comic books in her collection and multiplies the sum by 3, the result will be 65 less than 4 times the number of comic books in her collection. How many comic books are in her collection?

    A. 50
    B. 85
    C. 110
    D. 145
    E. 175

58. One empty cylinder has three times the height and twice the diameter of another empty cylinder. How many fillings of the smaller cylinder would be equivalent to one filling of the larger cylinder?

    (Note: The volume of a cylinder of radius r and height h is $\pi r^2 h$.)

    F. 6
    G. $6\sqrt{2}$
    H. 12
    J. 18
    K. 24

DO YOUR FIGURING HERE.

GO ON TO THE NEXT PAGE

59. What is the perimeter of a 30°- 60°- 90° triangle with a long leg of 12 inches?

   A. $6\sqrt{3} + 12$
   B. $4\sqrt{3} + 18$
   C. $8\sqrt{3} + 18$
   D. $12\sqrt{3} + 12$
   E. $12\sqrt{3} + 18$

60. A baseball team scores an average of x points in its first n games and then scores y points in its next and final game of the season. Which of the following represents the team's average score for the entire season?

   F. $x + \dfrac{y}{n}$

   G. $x + \dfrac{y}{n + 1}$

   H. $\dfrac{x + ny}{n + 1}$

   J. $\dfrac{nx + y}{n + 1}$

   K. $\dfrac{n(x + y)}{n + 1}$

DO YOUR FIGURING HERE.

If you finish before time is called, you may check your work on this section only. Do not turn to any other section in the test.

STOP

READING TEST
35 Minutes–40 Questions

Directions: This test contains four passages, each followed by several questions. After reading a passage, select the best answer to each question and fill in the corresponding oval on your answer sheet. You are allowed to refer to the passages while answering the questions.

Passage I

Emma Woodhouse, handsome, clever, and rich, with a comfortable home and happy disposition, seemed to unite some of *Line* the best blessings of existence. She had lived
(5) nearly twenty-one years in the world with very little to distress or vex her. She was the youngest of the two daughters of a most affectionate, indulgent father, and had, in consequence of her sister's marriage, been
(10) mistress of his house from a very early period. Her mother had died too long ago for her to have more than an indistinct remembrance of her caresses, and her place had been taken by an excellent governess
(15) who had fallen little short of a mother in affection.

Sixteen years had Miss Taylor been in Mr. Woodhouse's family, less as a governess than a friend, very fond of both daughters, but
(20) particularly of Emma. Between them it was more the intimacy of sisters. Even before Miss Taylor had ceased to hold the nominal office of governess, the mildness of her temper had hardly allowed her to impose
(25) any restraint. The shadow of authority being now long passed away, they had been living together as friend and friend very mutually attached, and Emma doing just what she liked, highly esteeming Miss Taylor's
(30) judgment, but directed chiefly by her own. The real evils, indeed, of Emma's situation were the power of having rather too much her own way, and a disposition to think a little too well of herself; these were the
(35) disadvantages which threatened alloy to her many enjoyments. The danger, however, was at present so unperceived, that they did not by any means rank as misfortunes with her.

Sorrow came—a gentle sorrow—but not
(40) at all in the shape of any disagreeable consciousness. Miss Taylor married. It was Miss Taylor's loss which first brought grief. It was on the wedding-day of this beloved friend that Emma first sat in mournful
(45) thought of any continuance. The wedding over, and the bride-people gone, she and her father were left to dine together, with no prospect of a third to cheer a long evening. Her father composed himself to sleep after
(50) dinner, as usual, and she had then only to sit and think of what she had lost.

The marriage had every promise of happiness for her friend. Mr. Weston was a man of unexceptionable character, easy
(55) fortune, suitable age, and pleasant manners. There was some satisfaction in considering with what self-denying, generous friendship she had always wished and promoted the match, but it was a black morning's work for
(60) her. The want of Miss Taylor would be felt every hour of every day. She recalled her past kindness—the kindness, the affection of sixteen years—how she had taught her and how she had played with her from five years
(65) old—how she had devoted all her powers to attach and amuse her in health—and how

→

GO ON TO THE NEXT PAGE

she had nursed her through the various illnesses of childhood. A large debt of gratitude was owing here, but the (70) intercourse of the last seven years, the equal footing and perfect unreserve which had soon followed Isabella's marriage, on their being left to each other, was yet a dearer, tenderer recollection. She had been a friend (75) and companion such as few possessed: intelligent, well-informed, useful, gentle, knowing all the ways of the family, interested in all its concerns, and peculiarly interested in her, in every pleasure, every scheme of (80) hers—one to whom she could speak every thought as it arose, and who had such an affection for her as could never find fault.

How was she to bear the change? It was true that her friend was going only half a (85) mile from them, but Emma was aware that great must be the difference between a Mrs. Weston, only half a mile from them, and a Miss Taylor in the house. With all her advantages, natural and domestic, she was (90) now in great danger of suffering from intellectual solitude.

This passage is an adapted excerpt from Jane Austen's novel *Emma*. In this passage, Emma confronts a change in her previously happy life.

1. According to the passage, what are the greatest disadvantages facing Emma?

   A. Her father is not a stimulating conversationalist, and she is bored.
   B. She is lonely and afraid that Mrs. Weston will not have a happy marriage.
   C. She is used to having her way too much, and she thinks too highly of herself.
   D. She misses the companionship of her mother, her sister, and Miss Taylor.

2. The name of Emma's sister is:

   F. Mrs. Weston.
   G. Isabella.
   H. Miss Taylor.
   J. Mrs. Woodhouse.

3. As described in the passage, Emma's relationship with Miss Taylor can be characterized as:

   A. similar to a mother-daughter relationship.
   B. similar to the relationship of sisters or best friends.
   C. weaker than Emma's relationship with her sister.
   D. stronger than Miss Taylor's relationship with her new husband.

4. As used in line 33, *disposition* can most closely be defined as:

   F. a tendency.
   G. control.
   H. placement.
   J. transfer.

5. Which of the following are included in Emma's memories of her relationship with Miss Taylor?

   I. Miss Taylor taking care of Emma during childhood illnesses
   II. Miss Taylor's interest in all of the concerns of Emma's family
   III. Miss Taylor teaching her mathematics
   IV. Miss Taylor scolding her for being selfish

   A. I, III, and IV only
   B. I and III only
   C. II, III, and IV only
   D. I and II only

GO ON TO THE NEXT PAGE

6. It is most reasonable to infer from Emma's realization that "great must be the difference between a Mrs. Weston, only half a mile from them, and a Miss Taylor in the house" (lines 86–88) that:

F. Miss Taylor will no longer be a part of Emma's life.

G. Emma is happy about the marriage because now she will have more freedom.

H. Emma regrets that her relationship with Miss Taylor will change.

J. Emma believes that her relationship with Miss Taylor will become stronger.

7. Based on the passage, Emma could best be described as:

A. sweet and naïve.

B. self-centered and naïve.

C. self-centered and headstrong.

D. unappreciative and bitter.

8. The passage suggests that the quality Emma values most in a friend is:

F. charisma.

G. devotion.

H. honesty.

J. intelligence.

9. How does Emma view Mr. Weston?

A. She thinks that he is an excellent match, and it required considerable self-sacrifice not to pursue him herself.

B. She considers him to be a respectable if somewhat average match for her friend.

C. She sees him as an intruder who has carried away her best friend in "a black morning's work" (line 59).

D. She believes he is an indulgent, easily swayed man, reminiscent of her father.

10. From the passage, it can be inferred that Emma is accustomed to:

F. behaving according to the wishes of her affectionate father.

G. taking the advice of Miss Taylor when faced with deciding upon a course of action.

H. doing as she pleases without permission from her father or governess.

J. abiding by strict rules governing her behavior.

GO ON TO THE NEXT PAGE

Passage II

Learning and its result, memory, are processes by which we retain acquired information, emotions, and impressions that
Line can influence our behavior. At the
(5) psychological level, memory is not a single process. Sensory memory, the first of three main systems of memory, describes the momentary lingering of perceptual information as it is initially sensed and
(10) briefly recorded. When an image strikes the eyes it lingers in the visual system for an instant while the image is interpreted, and is quickly overwritten by new information. In the visual system this is called *iconic memory*,
(15) in the auditory system it is *echoic memory*, and in reference to touch it is *haptic memory*.

If sensory information is processed it can move into the second main system of memory, working memory. This was once
(20) known as short-term memory (and that term is still popularly used). But working memory is viewed as a more accurate term, since this system not only stores information for short periods of time, but also enables
(25) the use and manipulation of information processed there. However, only a limited number of items can be held in working memory (the average for most people is seven), and decay of the memory occurs
(30) rapidly, although it can be held longer if the information is mentally or vocally repeated. Unless we make a conscious effort to retain it, a working memory may disappear forever.

Long-term memory is the most
(35) comprehensive of the three, with apparent infinite capacity. Memories recorded in long-term memory are never lost, although at times there may be difficulty accessing them. There are three independent
(40) categories of long-term memory which interact extensively: *episodic* involves personal memories and details of daily life, and is closely identified with its time and place; *semantic* contains facts and general
(45) knowledge that are not tied to when or how they were learned; and *procedural* retains skills used to perform certain activities that eventually may not require conscious effort.

Although the main systems of memory
(50) are widely accepted, controversy continues about memory formation and retrieval. It was once believed that for a memory to enter long-term memory it must first be held in working memory. However, this idea has
(55) been challenged by an alternate theory suggesting that sensory memories can be directly entered into long-term memory through a pathway that runs parallel to, rather than in series with, working memory.
(60) Memories therefore can register simultaneously in both systems.

Likewise, all agree that the retrieval of long-term memories is facilitated by repetition, but there is no agreement about
(65) the accuracy of these memories. For many years the scientific community viewed human memory as similar to computer memory, with the mind recording each detail just as it was presented. However, there
(70) is a growing consensus that our memory is sometimes flawed. An inference or assumption made by an individual when a memory is created may later be recalled as fact, or the mind may fill in details that were
(75) originally missing. Moreover, when we try to recall a particular memory, an unrelated memory may alter it through a process called interference. There is even evidence that an entirely false memory can be incorporated as
(80) a memory indistinguishable from true memories. Although for most purposes these discrepancies are harmless, concerns regarding the accuracy of human memory

GO ON TO THE NEXT PAGE

challenge the reliability of eyewitness
(85) testimony.

11. The main purpose of the passage is to:

    A. describe the main memory systems and
       why they are increasingly controversial.

    B. describe the main memory systems and
       some views of memory formation and
       retrieval.

    C. demonstrate that early ideas about
       memory formation and retrieval were
       incorrect.

    D. demonstrate that theories about the
       main memory systems are incorrect.

12. Based on information in the passage, which
    of the following would be recalled from
    semantic long-term memory?

    F. Ballet steps
    G. A childhood birthday
    H. Multiplication tables
    J. Riding a bicycle

13. It can be reasonably inferred from the
    passage that, if a man in a car accident is
    unable to remember details of his life and
    family, but does remember how to perform
    his job, his:

    A. episodic memories have been lost.
    B. episodic memories have become
       inaccessible.
    C. procedural memories have been lost.
    D. procedural memories have become
       inaccessible.

14. The fact that the scientific community once
    viewed human memory as similar to
    computer memory is mentioned in the last
    paragraph in order to:

    F. illustrate that memory is now viewed as
       complex rather than mechanical.

    G. explain that memory is now viewed as
       an exact record of events.

    H. illustrate that memory is always
       inaccurate.

    J. explain that memories are formed the
       same way computers encode data.

15. If a person reads, "The baseball hit the
    window," and, when asked to recall the
    sentence, remembers "The baseball broke the
    window," according to the passage this is
    probably an example of:

    A. interference altering a memory.
    B. a memory that became inaccessible.
    C. a reader's assumption altering a
       memory.
    D. a completely false memory being
       created.

16. According to the passage, all the following are
    examples of episodic memory EXCEPT:

    F. the meal you ate last night
    G. the name of an old classmate
    H. the year your class won a trophy
    J. the face of a stranger passed on the
       street

GO ON TO THE NEXT PAGE

17. Based on information in the passage the term *short-term memory* was most likely replaced with *working memory* in order to:

    A. refute the idea that memories in this category degrade quickly.

    B. emphasize that memories in this category can be manipulated.

    C. show that memories in this category become long-term memories.

    D. demonstrate that echoic memories are held in the visual system.

18. As it is used in the passage, the word *iconic* (line 14) most nearly means relating to:

    F. something sacred.

    G. a symbolic representation.

    H. visual sensory memory.

    J. a picture that represents a computer command.

19. According to the passage, most of the scientific community now agrees that:

    A. there are really four main categories of memory, not three.

    B. memories held in long-term memory remain forever.

    C. memories must be held in working memory before long-term memory.

    D. repetition does not affect the duration of memory.

20. According to the passage, which of the following is a characteristic of working memory?

    F. A slight echo in the ear

    G. Quick replacement by new sensory information

    H. Rapid forgetting

    J. Infinite capacity

GO ON TO THE NEXT PAGE

Passage III

There can be little doubt that women artists have been most prominent in photography and that they have made their greatest contribution in this field. One
(5) reason for this is not difficult to ascertain. As several historians of photography have pointed out, photography, being a new medium outside the traditional academic framework, was wide open to women and
(10) offered them opportunities that the older fields did not....

All these observations apply to the first woman to have achieved eminence in photography, and that is Julia Margaret
(15) Cameron.... Born in 1815 in Calcutta into an upper-middle-class family and married to Charles Hay Cameron, a distinguished jurist and member of the Supreme Court of India, Julia Cameron was well known as a brilliant
(20) conversationalist and a woman of personality and intellect who was unconventional to the point of eccentricity. Although the mother of six children, she adopted several more and still found time to
(25) be active in social causes and literary activities. After the Camerons settled in England in 1848 at Freshwater Bay on the Isle of Wight, she became the center of an artistic and literary circle that included such
(30) notable figures as the poet Alfred Lord Tennyson and the painter George Frederick Watts. Pursuing numerous activities and taking care of her large family, Mrs. Cameron might have been remembered as
(35) still another rather remarkable and colorful Victorian lady had it not been for the fact that, in 1863, her daughter presented her with photographic equipment, thinking her mother might enjoy taking pictures of her
(40) family and friends. Although forty-eight years old, Mrs. Cameron took up this new hobby with enormous enthusiasm and

dedication. She was a complete beginner, but within a very few years she developed into
(45) one of the greatest photographers of her period and a giant in the history of photography. She worked ceaselessly as long as daylight lasted and mastered the technical processes of photography, at that time far
(50) more cumbersome than today, turning her coal house into a darkroom and her chicken house into a studio. To her, photography was a "divine art," and in it she found her vocation. In 1864, she wrote triumphantly
(55) under one of her photographs, "My First Success," and from then until her death in Ceylon in 1874, she devoted herself wholly to this art.

Working in a large format (her portrait
(60) studies are usually about 11 inches by 14 inches) and requiring a long exposure (on the average five minutes), she produced a large body of work that stands up as one of the notable artistic achievements of the
(65) Victorian period. The English art critic Roger Fry believed that her portraits were likely to outlive the works of artists who were her contemporaries. Her friend Watts, then a very celebrated portrait painter, inscribed on
(70) one of her photographs, "I wish I could paint such a picture as this." ...Her work was widely exhibited, and she received gold, silver, and bronze medals in England, America, Germany, and Austria. No other
(75) female artist of the nineteenth century achieved such acclaim, and no other woman photographer has ever enjoyed such success.

Her work falls into two main categories on which her contemporaries and people
(80) today differ sharply. Victorian critics were particularly impressed by her allegorical pictures, many of them based on the poems of her friend and neighbor Tennyson.... Contemporary taste much prefers her
(85) portraits and finds her narrative scenes

GO ON TO THE NEXT PAGE

sentimental and sometimes in bad taste. Yet, not only Julia Cameron, but also the painters of that time loved to depict subjects such as *The Five Foolish Virgins* or *Pray God, Bring*
(90) *Father Safely Home*. Still, today her fame rests upon her portraits for, as she herself said, she was intent upon representing not only the outer likeness but also the inner greatness of the people she portrayed.
(95) Working with the utmost dedication, she produced photographs of such eminent Victorians as Tennyson, Browning, Carlyle, Trollope, Longfellow, Watts, Darwin, Ellen Terry, Sir John Herschel, who was a close
(100) friend of hers, and Mrs. Duckworth, the mother of Virginia Woolf.

This passage is excerpted from *A History of Women Artists* by Hugo Munsterberg. (© 1975 by Hugo Munsterberg. Reprinted by permission of Clarkson N. Potter, Inc., a division of Crown Publishers, Inc.)

21. Which of the following conclusions can be reasonably drawn from the passage's discussion of Julia Margaret Cameron?

    A. She was a traditional homemaker until she discovered photography.
    B. Her work holds a significant place in the history of photography.
    C. She was unable to achieve in her lifetime the artistic recognition she deserved.
    D. Her eccentricity has kept her from being taken seriously by modern critics of photography.

22. According to the passage, Cameron is most respected by modern critics for her:

    F. portraits.
    G. allegorical pictures.
    H. use of a large format.
    J. service in recording the faces of so many twentieth-century figures.

23. The author uses which of the following methods to develop the second paragraph (lines 12–58)?

    A. A series of anecdotes depicting Cameron's energy and unconventionality
    B. A presentation of factual data demonstrating Cameron's importance in the history of photography
    C. A description of the author's personal acquaintance with Cameron
    D. A chronological account of Cameron's background and artistic growth

24. As it is used in the passage, *cumbersome* (line 50) most closely means:

    F. difficult to manage.
    G. expensive.
    H. intense.
    J. enjoyable.

25. When the author says that Cameron had found "her vocation" (line 54), his main point is that photography:

    A. offered Cameron an escape from the confines of conventional social life.
    B. became the main interest of her life.
    C. became her primary source of income.
    D. provided her with a way to express her religious beliefs.

26. The main point of the third paragraph is that Cameron:

    F. achieved great artistic success during her lifetime.

    G. is the greatest photographer who ever lived.

    H. was considered a more important artist during her lifetime than she is now.

    J. revolutionized photographic methods in the Victorian era.

27. According to the passage, the art of photography offered women artists more opportunities than did other art forms because it:

    A. did not require expensive materials.

    B. allowed the artist to use family and friends for subject matter.

    C. was non-traditional.

    D. required little artistic skill.

28. *The Five Foolish Virgins* and *Pray God, Bring Father Safely Home* are examples of:

    F. portraits of celebrated Victorians.

    G. allegorical subjects of the sort that were popular during the Victorian era.

    H. photographs in which Cameron sought to show a subject's outer likeness and inner greatness.

    J. photographs by Cameron that were scoffed at by her contemporaries.

29. According to the passage, which of the following opinions of Cameron's work was held by Victorian critics but is NOT held by modern critics?

    A. Photographs should be based on poems.

    B. Her portraits are too sentimental.

    C. Narrative scenes are often in bad taste.

    D. Her allegorical pictures are her best work.

30. The author's treatment of Cameron's development as a photographer can best be described as:

    F. admiring.

    G. condescending.

    H. neutral.

    J. defensive.

GO ON TO THE NEXT PAGE

Passage IV

The harbor seal, Phoca vitulina, lives amphibiously along the northern Atlantic and Pacific coasts. This extraordinary
Line mammal, which does most of its fishing at
(5) night when visibility is low and in places where noise levels are high, has developed several unique adaptations that have sharpened its acoustic and visual acuity. The need for such adaptations has been
(10) compounded by the varying behavior of sound and light in each of the two habitats of the harbor seal—land and water.

While the seal is on land, its ear operates much like the human ear, with sound waves
(15) traveling through air and entering the inner ear through the auditory canal. The directions from which sounds originate are distinguishable because the sound waves arrive at each inner ear at different times. In
(20) water, however, where sound waves travel faster than they do in air, the ability of the brain to differentiate arrival times between each ear is severely reduced. Yet it is crucial for the seal to be able to pinpoint the exact
(25) origins of sound in order to locate both its offspring and its prey. Therefore, the seal has developed an extremely sensitive quadrophonic hearing system, composed of a specialized band of tissue that extends
(30) down from the ear to the inner ear. In water, sound is conducted to the seal's inner ear by this special band of tissue, making it possible for the seal to identify the exact origins of sounds.

(35) The eye of the seal is also uniquely adapted to operate in both air and water. The human eye, adapted to function primarily in air, is equipped with a cornea, which aids in the refraction and focusing of light onto the
(40) retina. As a result, when a human eye is submerged in water, light rays are further refracted and the image is blurry. The seal's cornea, however, refracts light as water does. Therefore, in water, light rays are transmitted
(45) by the cornea without distortion, and are clearly focused on the retina. In air, however, the cornea is astigmatic, resulting in a distortion of incoming light rays. The seal compensates for this by having a stenopaic
(50) pupil, which constricts into a vertical slit. Since the astigmatism is most pronounced in the horizontal plane of the eye, the vertical pupil serves to minimize its effect on the seal's vision.

(55) Since the harbor seal hunts for food under conditions of low visibility, some scientists believe it has echolocation systems akin to those of bats, porpoises, and dolphins. This kind of natural radar involves the emission
(60) of high frequency sound pulses that reflect off obstacles such as predators, prey, or natural barriers. The reflections are received as sensory signals by the brain, which processes them into an image. The animal,
(65) blinded by unfavorable lighting conditions, is thus able to perceive its surroundings. Such echolocation by harbor seals is suggested by the fact that they emit "clicks," high frequency sounds produced in short,
(70) fast bursts that occur mostly at night, when visibility is low.

Finally, there is speculation that the seal's whiskers, or vibrissae, which are unusually well developed and highly sensitive to
(75) vibrations, act as additional sensory receptors. Scientists speculate that the vibrissae may sense wave disturbances produced by nearby moving fish, allowing the seal to home in on and capture prey.

GO ON TO THE NEXT PAGE

31. The harbor seal's eye compensates for the distortion of light rays on land by means of its:

    A. vibrissae
    B. cornea
    C. stenopaic pupil
    D. echolocation

32. The passage implies that a harbor seal's vision is:

    F. inferior to a human's vision in the water, but superior to it on land.
    G. superior to a human's vision in the water, but inferior to it on land.
    H. inferior to a human's vision both in the water and on land.
    J. equivalent to a human's vision both in the water and on land.

33. According to the passage, scientists think vibrissae help harbor seals to catch prey by:

    A. improving underwater vision.
    B. sensing vibrations in the air.
    C. camouflaging predator seals.
    D. detecting underwater movement.

34. According to the passage, the speed of sound in water is:

    F. faster than the speed of sound in air.
    G. slower than the speed of sound in air.
    H. the same as the speed of sound in air.
    J. unable to be determined exactly.

35. According to the passage, which of the following have contributed to the harbor seal's need to adapt its visual and acoustic senses?

    I. Night hunting
    II. The need to operate in two habitats
    III. A noisy environment

    A. I and II only
    B. II and III only
    C. I and III only
    D. I, II, and III

36. Which of the following claims expresses the writer's opinion and not a fact?

    F. The human eye is adapted to function primarily in air.
    G. When the seal is on land, its ear operates like a human ear.
    H. The "clicks" emitted by the harbor seal mean it uses echolocation.
    J. The need for adaptation is increased if an animal lives in two habitats.

37. The passage suggests that the harbor seal lives in:

    A. cold ocean waters with accessible coasts.
    B. all areas with abundant fish populations.
    C. most island and coastal regions.
    D. warm coastlines with exceptionally clear waters.

38. According to the passage, a special band of tissue extending from the ear to the inner ear enables the harbor seal to:

    F. make its distinctive "clicking" sounds.
    G. find prey by echolocation.
    H. breathe underwater.
    J. determine where a sound originated.

GO ON TO THE NEXT PAGE

39. The author compares harbor seal sensory organs to human sensory organs primarily in order to:

    A. point out similarities among mammals.

    B. explain how the seal's sensory organs function.

    C. prove that seals are more adaptively successful than humans.

    D. prove that humans are better adapted to their environment than seals.

40. According to the passage, one way in which seals differ from humans is:

    F. that sound waves enter the inner ear through the auditory canal.

    G. the degree of refraction of light by their corneas.

    H. they focus light rays on the retina.

    J. they have adapted to live in a certain environment.

If you finish before time is called, you may check your work on this section only. Do not turn to any other section in the test. **STOP**

SCIENCE TEST
35 Minutes—40 Questions

Directions: Each of the following seven passages is followed by several questions. After reading each passage, decide on the best answer to each question and fill in the corresponding oval on your answer sheet. You are allowed to refer to the passages while answering the questions. Calculator use is not allowed on this test.

Passage I

The table below contains some physical properties of common optical materials. The refractive index of a material is a measure of the amount by which light is bent upon entering the material. The transmittance range is the range of wavelengths over which the material is transparent.

Physical Properties of Optical Materials				
Material	Refractive index for light of 0.589 µm	Transmittance range (µm)	Useful range for prisms (µm)	Chemical resistance
Lithium fluoride	1.39	0.12–6	2.7–5.5	Poor
Calcium fluoride	1.43	0.12–12	5–9.4	Good
Sodium chloride	1.54	0.3–17	8–16	Poor
Quartz	1.54	0.20–3.3	0.20–2.7	Excellent
Potassium bromide	1.56	0.3–29	15–28	Poor
Flint glass*	1.66	0.35–2.2	0.35–2	Excellent
Cesium iodide	1.79	0.3–70	15–55	Poor

*Flint glass is lead oxide doped quartz.

1. According to the table, which material(s) will transmit light at 25 µm?

    A. Potassium bromide only
    B. Potassium bromide and cesium iodide
    C. Lithium fluoride and cesium iodide
    D. Lithium fluoride and flint glass

2. A scientist hypothesizes that any material with poor chemical resistance would have a transmittance range wider than 10 µm. The properties of which of the following materials contradicts this hypothesis?

    F. Lithium fluoride
    G. Flint glass
    H. Cesium iodide
    J. Quartz

GO ON TO THE NEXT PAGE

3. When light travels from one medium to another, total internal reflection can occur if the first medium has a higher refractive index than the second. Total internal reflection could occur if light were travelling from:

    A. lithium fluoride to flint glass.
    B. potassium bromide to cesium iodide.
    C. quartz to potassium bromide.
    D. flint glass to calcium fluoride.

4. Based on the information in the table, how is the transmittance range related to the useful prism range?

    F. The transmittance range is always narrower than the useful prism range.
    G. The transmittance range is narrower than or equal to the useful prism range.
    H. The transmittance range increases as the useful prism range decreases.
    J. The transmittance range is wider than and includes within it the useful prism range.

5. The addition of lead oxide to pure quartz has the effect of:

    A. decreasing the transmittance range and the refractive index.
    B. decreasing the transmittance range and increasing the refractive index.
    C. increasing the transmittance range and the useful prism range.
    D. increasing the transmittance range and decreasing the useful prism range.

Passage II

Osmosis is the diffusion of a solvent (often water) across a semipermeable membrane from the side of the membrane with a lower concentration of dissolved material to the side with a higher concentration of dissolved material. The result of osmosis is an equilibrium—an even distribution—on both sides of the membrane. In order to prevent osmosis, external pressure must be applied to the side with the higher concentration of dissolved material. Osmotic pressure is the external pressure required to prevent osmosis. The apparatus shown below was used to measure osmotic pressure in the following experiments.

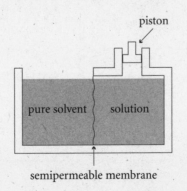

Experiment 1

Aqueous (water-based) solutions containing different concentrations of sucrose were placed in the closed side of the apparatus. The open side was filled with water. The sucrose solutions also contained a blue dye that binds to the sucrose. The osmotic pressure created by the piston was measured for each solution at various temperatures. The results are given in Table 1.

Table 1

Concentration of sucrose solution (mol/L)	Temperature (K)	Osmotic pressure (atm)
1.00	298.0	24.47
0.50	298.0	12.23
0.10	298.0	2.45
0.05	298.0	1.22
1.00	348.0	28.57
0.50	348.0	14.29
0.10	348.0	2.86
0.05	348.0	1.43

Experiment 2

Sucrose solutions of 4 different organic solvents were investigated in the same manner as in Experiment 1 with all trials at 298 K. The results are shown in Table 2.

Table 2

Solvent	Concentration of sucrose solution (mol/L)	Osmotic pressure (atm)
Ethanol	0.50	12.23
Ethanol	0.10	2.45
Acetone	0.50	12.23
Acetone	0.10	2.45
Diethyl ether	0.50	12.23
Diethyl ether	0.10	2.45
Methanol	0.50	12.23
Methanol	0.10	2.45

GO ON TO THE NEXT PAGE

6. According to the experimental results, osmotic pressure is dependent upon the:

   F.   solvent and temperature only.

   G. solvent and concentration only.

   H. temperature and concentration only.

   J.   solvent, temperature, and concentration.

7. According to Experiment 2, if methanol was used as a solvent, what pressure must be applied to a 0.5 mol/L solution of sucrose at 298 K to prevent osmosis?

   A. 24.46 atm

   B. 12.23 atm

   C. 2.45 atm

   D. 1.23 atm

8. A 0.10 mol/L aqueous sucrose solution is separated from an equal volume of pure water by a semipermeable membrane. If the solution is at a pressure of 1 atm and a temperature of 298 K, the sucrose solution:

   F.   will diffuse across the semipermeable membrane from the sucrose solution side to the pure water side.

   G. will diffuse across the semipermeable membrane from the pure water side to the sucrose solution side.

   H. will not diffuse across the semipermeable membrane.

   J.   will diffuse across the semipermeable membrane, but the direction of diffusion cannot be determined.

9. In Experiment 1, the scientists investigated the effect of:

   A. solvent and concentration on osmotic pressure.

   B. volume and temperature on osmotic pressure.

   C. concentration and temperature on osmotic pressure.

   D. temperature on atmospheric pressure.

10. Which of the following conclusions can be drawn from the experimental results?

   I.   Osmotic pressure is independent of the solvent used.

   II. Osmotic pressure is only dependent upon the temperature of the system.

   III. Osmosis occurs only when the osmotic pressure is exceeded.

   F.   I only

   G. III only

   H. I and II only

   J.   I and III only

11. What was the most likely purpose of the dye placed in the sucrose solutions in Experiments 1 and 2?

   A. The dye showed when osmosis was completed.

   B. The dye showed the presence of ions in the solutions.

   C. The dye was used to make the experiment more colorful.

   D. The dye was used to make the onset of osmosis visible.

Passage III

A chemist investigating the influence of molecular weight and structure on the boiling point (transition from solid to gaseous state) of different compounds recorded the data in the tables below. Two types of compounds were investigated: organic carbon compounds (shown in Table 1) and inorganic compounds (shown in Table 2).

Table 1

Straight-Chain Hydrocarbons		
Molecular formula	Molar weight* (g/mol)	Boiling point (°C)
CH_4	16	−162
C_2H_6	30	−88
C_3H_8	44	−42
C_4H_{10}	58	0
C_5H_{12}	72	36
C_8H_{18}	114	126
$C_{20}H_{42}$	282	345

*Molar weight is the weight of one mole, or an *Avogadro's Number* of molecules ($\approx 6 \times 10^{23}$), in grams.

Table 2

Other Substances (Polar and Non-Polar)		
Molecular formula	Molar weight (g/mol)	Boiling point (°C)
N_2*	28	−196
SiH_4*	32	−112
GeH_4*	77	−90
Br_2*	160	59
CO**	28	−192
PH_3**	34	−85
AsH_3**	78	−55
ICl**	162	97

* *Non-Polar*: molecule's charge is evenly distributed

**Polar: molecule's negative and positive charges are partially separated

GO ON TO THE NEXT PAGE

12. Which of the following straight-chain hydrocarbons would NOT be a gas at room temperature?

    F. C_2H_6
    G. C_3H_8
    H. C_4H_{10}
    J. C_5H_{12}

13. Which of the following conclusions is supported by the observed results?

    I.   Boiling point varies directly with molecular weight.
    II. Boiling point varies inversely with molecular weight.
    III. Boiling point is affected by molecular structure.

    A. I only
    B. II only
    C. I and III only
    D. II and III only

14. Based on the data in Table 1, the boiling point of the straight-chain hydrocarbon C_6H_{14} (molecular weight 86 g/mol) is most likely:

    F. 30° C.
    G. 70° C.
    H. 130° C.
    J. impossible to predict.

15. Based on the data in Table 2, as molecular weight increases, the difference between the boiling points of polar and non-polar substances of similar molecular weight:

    A. increases.
    B. decreases.
    C. remains constant.
    D. varies randomly.

16. A polar substance with a boiling point of 0° C is likely to have a molar weight closest to which of the following:

    F. 58
    G. 80
    H. 108
    J. 132

17. Which of the following places the compound types in ascending order according to the rate at which the boiling point increases with increasing molar weight?

    A. straight-chain hydrocarbons, non-polar inorganic compounds, polar inorganic compounds
    B. straight-chain hydrocarbons, polar inorganic compounds, non-polar inorganic compounds
    C. non-polar inorganic compounds, straight-chain hydrocarbons, polar inorganic compounds
    D. non-polar inorganic compounds, polar inorganic compounds, straight-chain hydrocarbons

GO ON TO THE NEXT PAGE

Passage IV

A series of experiments was performed to study the environmental factors affecting the size and number of leaves on the *Cyas* plant.

Experiment 1

Five groups of 25 *Cyas* seedlings, all from 2–3 cm tall, were allowed to grow for 3 months, each group at a different humidity level. All of the groups were kept at 75° F and received 9 hours of sunlight a day. The average leaf lengths, widths, and densities are given in Table 1.

Table 1

% Humidity	Average length (cm)	Average width (cm)	Average density* (leaves/cm)
15	5.6	1.6	0.13
35	7.1	1.8	0.25
55	9.8	2.0	0.56
75	14.6	2.6	0.61
95	7.5	1.7	0.52

*Number of leaves per 1 cm of plant stalk

Experiment 2

Five new groups of 25 seedlings, all from 2–3 cm tall, were allowed to grow for 3 months, each group receiving different amounts of sunlight at a constant humidity of 55%. All other conditions were the same as in Experiment 1. The results are listed in Table 2.

Table 2

Sunlight (hrs/day)	Average length (cm)	Average width (cm)	Average density* (leaves/cm)
0	5.3	1.5	0.32
3	12.4	2.4	0.59
6	11.2	2.0	0.56
9	8.4	1.8	0.26
12	7.7	1.7	0.19

*Number of leaves per 1 cm of plant stalk

GO ON TO THE NEXT PAGE

Experiment 3

Five new groups of 25 seedlings, all from 2–3 cm tall, were allowed to grow at a constant humidity of 55% for 3 months at different daytime and nighttime temperatures. All other conditions were the same as in Experiment 1. The results are shown in Table 3.

Table 3

Day/Night temperature (°F)	Average length (cm)	Average width (cm)	Average density* (leaves/cm)
85/85	6.8	1.5	0.28
85/65	12.3	2.1	0.53
65/85	8.1	1.7	0.33
75/75	7.1	1.9	0.45
65/65	8.3	1.7	0.39

*Number of leaves per 1 cm of plant stalk

18. Which of the following conclusions can be made based on the results of Experiment 2 alone?

    F. The seedlings do not require long daily periods of sunlight to grow.

    G. The average leaf density is independent of the humidity the seedlings receive.

    H. The seedlings need more water at night than during the day.

    J. The average length of the leaves increases as the amount of sunlight increases.

19. Seedlings grown at a 40% humidity level under the same conditions as in Experiment 1 would have average leaf widths closest to:

    A. 1.6 cm.
    B. 1.9 cm.
    C. 2.2 cm.
    D. 2.5 cm.

20. According to the experimental results, under which set of conditions would a *Cyas* seedling be most likely to produce the largest leaves?

    F. 95% humidity and 3 hours of sunlight
    G. 75% humidity and 3 hours of sunlight
    H. 95% humidity and 6 hours of sunlight
    J. 75% humidity and 6 hours of sunlight

21. Which variable remained constant throughout all of the experiments?

    A. The number of seedling groups
    B. The percent of humidity
    C. The daytime temperature
    D. The nighttime temperature

22. It was assumed in the design of the 3 experiments that all of the *Cyas* seedlings were:

    F. more than 5 cm tall.
    G. equally capable of germinating.
    H. equally capable of producing flowers.
    J. equally capable of further growth.

23. As a continuation of the 3 experiments listed, it would be most appropriate to next investigate:

    A. how many leaves over 6.0 cm long there are on each plant.
    B. which animals consume *Cyas* seedlings.
    C. how the mineral content of the soil affects the leaf size and density.
    D. what time of year the seedlings have the darkest coloring.

Passage V

The resistance (R) of a conductor is the extent to which it opposes the flow of electricity. Resistance depends not only on the conductor's resistivity (ρ), but also on the conductor's length (L) and cross-sectional area (A). The resistivity of a conductor is a physical property of the material that varies with temperature.

A research team designing a new appliance was researching the best type of wire to use in a particular circuit. The most important consideration was the wire's resistance. The team studied the resistance of wires made from four metals—gold (Au), aluminum (Al), tungsten (W), and iron (Fe). Two lengths and two gauges (diameters) of each type of wire were tested at 20° C. The results are recorded in the table below.

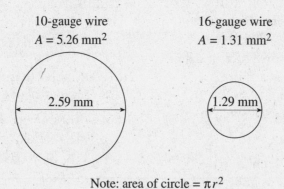

10-gauge wire
$A = 5.26 \text{ mm}^2$
2.59 mm

16-gauge wire
$A = 1.31 \text{ mm}^2$
1.29 mm

Note: area of circle $= \pi r^2$

GO ON TO THE NEXT PAGE

Material	Resistivity ($\mu\Omega \supseteq cm$)	Length (cm)	Cross-sectional area (mm^2)	Resistance ($\mu\Omega$)
Au	2.44	1.0	5.26	46.4
Au	2.44	1.0	1.31	186.0
Au	2.44	2.0	5.26	92.8
Au	2.44	2.0	1.31	372.0
Al	2.83	1.0	5.26	53.8
Al	2.83	1.0	1.31	216.0
Al	2.83	2.0	5.26	107.6
Al	2.83	2.0	1.31	432.0
W	5.51	1.0	5.26	105.0
W	5.51	1.0	1.31	421.0
W	5.51	2.0	5.26	210.0
W	5.51	2.0	1.31	842.0
Fe	10.00	1.0	5.26	190.0
Fe	10.00	1.0	1.31	764.0
Fe	10.00	2.0	5.26	380.0
Fe	10.00	2.0	1.31	1,528.0

24. Of the wires tested, resistance increases for any given material as which parameter is decreased?

   F.   Length
   G.   Cross-sectional area
   H.   Resistivity
   J.   Gauge

25. Given the data in the table, which of the following best expresses resistance in terms of resistivity (ρ), cross-sectional area (A), and length (L)?

   A. $\dfrac{\rho A}{L}$

   B. $\dfrac{\rho L}{A}$

   C. $\rho A L$

   D. $\dfrac{A L}{\rho}$

26. Which of the following wires would have the highest resistance?

   F.   A 1-cm aluminum wire with a cross-sectional area of 3.31 mm^2
   G.   A 2-cm aluminum wire with a cross-sectional area of 3.31 mm^2
   H.   A 1-cm tungsten wire with a cross-sectional area of 0.33 mm^2
   J.   A 2-cm tungsten wire with a cross-sectional area of 0.33 mm^2

GO ON TO THE NEXT PAGE

27. According to the information given, which of the following statements is (are) correct?

    I.   10-gauge wire has a larger diameter than 16-gauge wire.

    II.   Gold has a higher resistivity than tungsten.

    III.   Aluminum conducts electricity better than iron.

A. I only

B. II only

C. III only

D. I and III only

28. Which of the following graphs best represents the relationship between the resistivity of a tungsten wire and its length?

F.

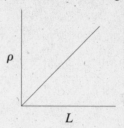

G.

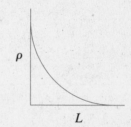

H.

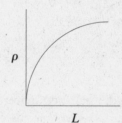

J.

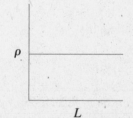

GO ON TO THE NEXT PAGE

KAPLAN

Passage VI

Siamese cats have a genotype for dark fur, but the enzymes that produce the dark coloring function best at temperatures below the cat's normal body temperature. A Siamese cat usually has darker fur on its ears, nose, paws, and tail, because these parts have a lower temperature than the rest of its body. If a Siamese cat spends more than one hour a day for six consecutive days outdoors (an "outdoor" cat) during very cold weather, darker fur grows in other places on its body. If a Siamese cat does not spend this amount of time outdoors, it is an "indoor" cat. The amount of dark fur on its body remains constant throughout the year.

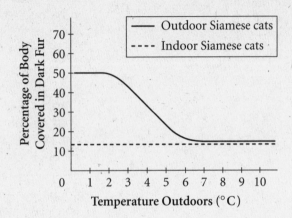

29. A particular Siamese cat goes outdoors a total of 3 hours per week during the coldest part of the year. One could predict that the percentage of its body covered by dark fur would be closest to:

    A. 0%
    B. 10%
    C. 40%
    D. 60%

30. According to the graph, what is the most likely temperature outside if outdoor Siamese cats have 45% of their bodies covered in dark fur?

    F. 0° C
    G. 3° C
    H. 6° C
    J. 9° C

31. If a Siamese cat that lived indoors was lost and later found with dark fur over 30% of its body, which of the following could be inferred about the period during which it was missing:

    I.   It was living in an area where temperatures fell below 5° C.
    II. It spent more time outdoors than indoors.
    III. It was missing for at least 6 days.

    A. I and II only
    B. I and III only
    C. II and III only
    D. I, II, and III

GO ON TO THE NEXT PAGE

32. If a Siamese cat has dark fur over 10% of its body, which of the following must be true about the cat?

   F. It lives indoors.

   G. It lives in an area where the temperature outdoors is usually 7° C or higher.

   H. It either lives indoors or it lives in an area where the temperature outdoors is usually 7° C or higher.

   J. None of the above

33. If a researcher wants to find out how fur color is affected by the amount of time a Siamese cat spends outside in cold weather, which experiment would be the most helpful?

   A. The "indoor" cats in the original experiment should be used as the control group and their fur color should be compared to a group of Siamese cats spending six hours or more a day outside in cold weather for six consecutive days.

   B. A new group of Siamese cats should be formed and kept outside two or more hours a day at varying temperatures. Their fur color at different outdoor temperatures should be compared to the "outdoor" cats already charted.

   C. Siamese cats should be split into two groups, one group spending only one hour per day outside for six consecutive days in cold weather, and the other group spending at least two hours a day outside for six consecutive days in the same weather.

   D. No new experiment is needed. The data already gathered shows that the more time a Siamese cat spends outside in cold weather, the darker its fur will be.

GO ON TO THE NEXT PAGE

Passage VII

Bovine spongiform encephalopathy (BSE) is caused by an unconventional pseudovirus that eventually kills infected cattle. BSE is diagnosed post mortem from the diseased cavities that appear in brain tissue, and is associated with the use in cattle feed of ground-up meat from scrapie-infected sheep. A series of experiments was performed to determine the mode of transmission of BSE. The results are given in the table below.

Experiment 1

Sixty healthy cows were divided into two equal groups. Group A's feed included meat from scrapie-free sheep; and Group B's feed included meat from scrapie-infected sheep. Eighteen months later, the two groups were slaughtered and their brains examined for BSE cavities.

Experiment 2

Researchers injected ground-up sheep brains directly into the brains of two groups of thirty healthy cows. The cows in Group C received brains from scrapie-free sheep. The cows in Group D received brains from scrapie-infected sheep. Eighteen months later, both groups were slaughtered and their brains examined for diseased cavities.

Group	Mode of transmission	Scrapie present	Number of cows infected with BSE*
A	feed	no	1
B	feed	yes	12
C	injection	no	0
D	injection	yes	3

*As determined visually by presence/absence of spongiform encephalopathy

34. Which of the following hypotheses was investigated in Experiment 1?

    F. The injection of scrapie-infected sheep brains into cows' brains causes BSE.

    G. The ingestion of wild grasses causes BSE.

    H. The ingestion of scrapie-infected sheep meat causes scrapie.

    J. The ingestion of scrapie-infected sheep meat causes BSE.

35. What is the purpose of Experiment 2?

    A. To determine whether BSE can be transmitted by injection

    B. To determine whether BSE can be transmitted by ingestion

    C. To determine whether ingestion or injection is the primary mode of BSE transmission

    D. To determine the healthiest diet for cows

GO ON TO THE NEXT PAGE

36. Which of the following assumptions is made by the researchers in Experiments 1 and 2?

   F. Cows do not suffer from scrapie.

   G. A year and a half is a sufficient amount of time for BSE to develop in a cow.

   H. Cows and sheep suffer from the same diseases.

   J. Cows that eat scrapie-free sheep meat will not develop BSE.

37. A researcher wishes to determine whether BSE can be transmitted through scrapie-infected goats. Which of the following experiments would best test this?

   A. Repeating Experiment 1, using a mixture of sheep and goat meat in Group C's feed

   B. Repeating Experiments 1 and 2, replacing sheep with healthy goats

   C. Repeating Experiments 1 and 2, replacing healthy sheep with healthy goats and scrapie-infected sheep with scrapie-infected goats

   D. Repeating Experiment 2, replacing healthy cows with healthy goats

38. What is the control group in Experiment 1?

   F. Group A

   G. Group B

   H. Group C

   J. Group D

39. Which of the following conclusions is (are) supported by the experiments?

   I. Cows that are exposed to scrapie-infected sheep are more likely to develop BSE than cows that are not.

   II. BSE is only transmitted by eating scrapie-infected sheep meat.

   III. A cow that eats scrapie-infected sheep meat is more likely to develop BSE than a cow that is injected with scrapie-infected sheep brains.

   A. II only

   B. III only

   C. I and III only

   D. II and III only

40. Which of the following statements is consistent with the results of Experiment 1?

   F. All cows that are fed scrapie-infected sheep meat develop BSE.

   G. All cows that are injected with scrapie-infected sheep brains develop BSE.

   H. Some cows that are fed scrapie-infected sheep meat develop BSE.

   J. Some cows that are injected with scrapie-infected sheep brains develop BSE.

If you finish before time is called, you may check your work on this section only. Do not turn to any other section in the test.

STOP

ANSWER KEY

English Test

1. C	31. D	61. D
2. F	32. H	62. J
3. D	33. A	63. C
4. F	34. H	64. J
5. D	35. D	65. D
6. G	36. G	66. J
7. B	37. D	67. B
8. J	38. G	68. F
9. A	39. D	69. D
10. J	40. J	70. F
11. C	41. D	71. D
12. G	42. J	72. G
13. B	43. B	73. B
14. H	44. G	74. F
15. C	45. C	75. B
16. H	46. F	
17. B	47. B	
18. G	48. H	
19. A	49. C	
20. J	50. H	
21. B	51. D	
22. G	52. J	
23. D	53. C	
24. J	54. H	
25. C	55. D	
26. F	56. H	
27. A	57. A	
28. J	58. H	
29. B	59. D	
30. G	60. H	

Math Test

1. D	31. C
2. J	32. H
3. D	33. E
4. K	34. K
5. C	35. A
6. K	36. J
7. B	37. A
8. K	38. G
9. E	39. C
10. K	40. G
11. D	41. B
12. H	42. H
13. C	43. C
14. H	44. K
15. C	45. A
16. G	46. G
17. D	47. E
18. H	48. G
19. D	49. E
20. H	50. K
21. E	51. E
22. H	52. K
23. D	53. B
24. F	54. G
25. D	55. D
26. G	56. K
27. C	57. C
28. H	58. H
29. B	59. D
30. K	60. J

ANSWER KEY CONTINUED

Reading Test

1. C	31. C
2. G	32. G
3. B	33. D
4. F	34. F
5. D	35. D
6. H	36. H
7. C	37. A
8. G	38. J
9. B	39. B
10. H	40. G
11. B	
12. H	
13. B	
14. F	
15. C	
16. J	
17. B	
18. H	
19. B	
20. H	
21. B	
22. F	
23. D	
24. F	
25. B	
26. F	
27. C	
28. G	
29. D	
30. F	

Science Test

1. B	31. B
2. F	32. H
3. D	33. C
4. J	34. J
5. B	35. A
6. H	36. G
7. B	37. C
8. G	38. F
9. C	39. B
10. F	40. H
11. D	
12. J	
13. C	
14. G	
15. A	
16. H	
17. D	
18. F	
19. B	
20. G	
21. A	
22. J	
23. C	
24. G	
25. B	
26. J	
27. D	
28. J	
29. B	
30. G	

Answers and Explanations

ENGLISH TEST

Passage I

1. C

(C) is the most correct and concise answer choice. (A) uses an unnecessary comma. (B) is unnecessarily wordy. (D) is redundant—if the societies created the legends, there is no need to describe the legends as original.

2. F

The question stem gives an important clue to the best answer: the purpose of the inserted sentence is "to describe the different kinds" of stories. (F) is the only choice that does this. (G) explains how the stories were told. (H) explains why more is not known about the stories. (J) describes the length of some stories.

3. D

Answer choices (A), (B), and (C) create run-on sentences. (D) describes a relationship that makes sense between our "many more permanent ways of handing down our beliefs" and the fact that "we continue to create and tell legends." It also creates a complete sentence.

4. F

Answer choices (G), (H), and (J) are unnecessarily wordy.

5. D

In addition to other problems, answer choices (A), (B), and (C) are redundant or unnecessarily wordy. Because the contrasting word *but* is already used, *however* is repetitive and should be eliminated.

6. G

Answer choices (F), (H), and (J) are all redundant. The word *conclusion* is unnecessary because it expresses the same thing as the word *ending*, which has already been used.

7. B

(B) is the only choice that stays consistent with the verb tense established by *knew* and *decided*.

8. J

(F) creates a run-on sentence and also makes it seem that the hunter, not the deer, "was only temporarily knocked unconscious by the car." (G) and (H) use incorrect verb tenses.

9. A

(B) is incorrect because the words preceding the semicolon could not be a complete sentence on their own. (C) would create a sentence fragment. (D) would create a run-on sentence.

10. J

Regardless of the sequence of the words, the information provided in choices (F), (G), and (H) is irrelevant to the passage's topic of urban legends.

11. C

The subject of the sentence is *One*, so the verb must be singular. (B) and (D) use incorrect verb tenses.

12. G

(F) creates a sentence that does not make sense. (H) and (J) use the plural *women* instead of the singular *woman*.

13. B

(B) most clearly expresses the idea that several websites research "the validity of commonly told urban legends." Because this information is relevant to the topic of urban legends, "OMIT the underlined portion" is not the best answer.

14. H

Paragraph 3 describes an urban legend that is "humorous in nature." Paragraph 4 describes a rather frightening legend: alligators living underneath the city in the sewer system. The sentence, "Other urban legends seem to be designed to instill fear" is an appropriate topic sentence for Paragraph 4, and it also serves as a needed transition between Paragraph 3 and Paragraph 4.

15. C

Although the third and fourth sentences of Paragraph 1 provide some general information about the purpose and topics of the myths and legends of primitive societies, no specifics are given. This makes (C) the best answer.

Passage II

16. H

The choices here would be *do you* or *does one*. The latter appears as an answer choice.

17. B

(A) incorrectly uses a colon. (C) and (D) are grammatically incorrect.

18. G

Solitary and *alone* are redundant in the same sentence. (H) and (J) also have redundancy.

19. A

The underlined portion is clearest the way it is written.

20. J

The colon is incorrect, so eliminate (F) and (H). Because it is a compound sentence, a comma is needed before *and*.

21. B

In fact is nonessential—it should be set off by commas.

22. G

American (an adjective) is the word being modified. Therefore, the adverb form of *unique* is needed.

23. D

Near Walden Pond ... is a long sentence fragment. The best way to fix the error is to simply combine the sentences.

24. J

This paragraph and the ones that immediately follow outline Thoreau's life. His influence on the people of today is not discussed until the end of the essay. Therefore, the underlined sentence does not belong.

25. C

Sentence 3 comes immediately after Sentence 1. (C) is the only choice that lists it this way.

26. F

There are two independent clauses on both sides of the semicolon, so the sentence is punctuated correctly. (G) needs a comma before *and*. (H) is incorrect because the second half of the sentence is not an independent clause. (J) does not make sense.

27. A

A possessive pronoun is needed because the works belong to Thoreau. Eliminate (B) and (D). (C) relates to more than one person, so it is incorrect as well.

28. J

This paragraph is all about what Thoreau means to us today.

29. B

(A), (C), and (D) are excessively wordy.

30. G

The use of questions forces the reader to think about the answers. (F) is too literal, and (J) is too broad for the topic of the essay. (H) is incorrect because the author establishes the quality of Thoreau's work.

Passage III

31. D

Because the word *live* is used later in the sentence, (A), (B), and (C) contain redundant information.

32. H

In this sentence, the *its* must be possessive because the *unique anatomy* belongs to the sloth. The word describing *anatomy* must be an adjective, not an adverb.

33. A

The comma is correctly used in (A) to separate the nonessential descriptive phrase *about the size of a large domestic cat* from the rest of the sentence.

34. H

The information about the sloth's limbs is relevant to the topic, so it should not be omitted. (H) makes the most sense in the context of the passage.

35. D

Adapted needs to be modified by an adverb, so (D) is the best answer choice.

36. G

Instead describes the right relationship between the two sentences. The pronouns must be consistent, and since *its* is already used in the sentence, (G) is the best answer choice.

37. D

(D) is the only choice that correctly describes the relationship between the sloth's inability to "move swiftly on the ground" and its ability to swim.

38. G

(G) connects the sloth's unique characteristics discussed in Paragraph 3 with the description of its flexibility in Paragraph 4.

39. D

(D) correctly uses the second comma necessary to separate the phrase *without moving the rest of its body* from the rest of the sentence. (C) can be eliminated because it is unnecessarily wordy.

40. J

(J) is the only choice that contains a consistent verb tense.

41. D

(A) and (B) contain redundant information. (C) uses an incorrect form of the verb.

42. J

This information about the howler monkey is irrelevant to the topic of the passage.

43. B

(A) creates a sentence fragment. (C) is unnecessarily wordy and awkward. (D) creates a run-on sentence.

44. G

The last sentence serves as a conclusion for the entire passage, and removing it would make the ending more abrupt.

45. C

The description of the sloth's "camouflage" is in Paragraph 5.

Passage IV

46. F

The underlined portion is best left as is. The other answer choices make the sentence unnecessarily wordy.

47. B

The verb tense must agree with the tense that has been established up to this point. The passage is in past tense, so the past tense choice (B) is correct.

48. H

Like the question before, the simple past tense is correct.

49. C

(A) creates a sentence fragment and uses an incorrect verb tense. (B) also uses the wrong verb tense. (D) incorrectly uses a semicolon, as the words preceding the semicolon do not constitute an independent clause.

50. H

In the context of the rest of the passage, only (H) makes sense. The fire fighters' attempts to extinguish the flames failed; only nature could stop the fire with the first snowfall.

51. D

(A) and (B) are unnecessarily wordy and awkward. (C) creates a run-on sentence.

52. J

All of the other answer choices are unnecessarily wordy and/or repetitive.

53. C

From the word *open*, you can determine that the best answer will contain *cones*. This makes (C) the only possible answer, as the apostrophe is incorrectly used in (B).

54. H

This is the only answer choice that makes sense in the context of the passage. The sighting of the large animals near burning forests is used as evidence that the animals of the region were "fire-tolerant and fire-adaptive."

55. D

The comma in (A) is unnecessary because the sentence has a list of only two examples, not three. The semicolon in (B) is incorrectly used because *and bedding down* does not begin an independent clause. The colon in (C) is incorrectly used because it is not being used to introduce or emphasize information.

56. H

The problem with *judging from the recent pictures of the park* is that the phrase is modifying *forest*, and a forest obviously can't judge anything. The phrase would have been okay if the sentence read, "Judging from the recent pictures of the park, I think that the forest was not destroyed." In this case the phrase modifies *I*, the author, who is capable of judging. Choice G takes care of the problem by rewriting the sentence so that the modifying phrase is gone.

57. A

The pronoun refers to *forest*.

58. H

The introduction of information about fires in Alaska is unwarranted, so (F) and (G) can be eliminated. (J) is incorrect because the additional information would actually uphold the author's position as an authority.

59. D

The reports mentioned in (D) would substantiate the author's claims much more so than any of the other answer choices.

Passage V

60. H

(F) creates a sentence fragment, and (G) incorrectly uses a plural verb with a singular subject. The context of the paragraph makes (H) a better choice than (J).

61. D

The final part of the sentence, "...and there are many other rivers in America as well," is completely irrelevant to the rest of the sentence and the paragraph, in which the author discusses white water rafting and the rivers she's rafted.

62. J

The phrase *on the Deschutes River* is essential information and, therefore, should not be set off by a comma. (G) and (H) incorrectly use the colon and semicolon, respectively.

63. C

(A) and (D) create sentence fragments, and (B) is extremely awkward.

64. J

This sentence is irrelevant to the topic of the passage.

65. D

This sentence makes it sound as though the author was roaring, not the rapids; *roaring* is a misplaced modifier. (B) doesn't fix the problem because the reader has no idea what *it* refers to. (D) is the clearest choice.

66. J

The word *cover* must either be in past tense, or the structure of the sentence must change. (J) does the latter.

67. B

(B) is the simplest, most concise way of expressing the idea. Replacing *and instead he adopted* with *with* makes the sentence much less awkward.

68. F

(G) and (J) make it sound as though the author is in the water. (F) expresses the idea better than (H).

69. D

The phrase *and we stopped* is redundant because *we came to a jarring halt* says the same thing much more expressively. Omit the underlined portion.

70. F

It was is fine here because the author is telling her story in the past tense. (G) and (H) are the present tense, and (J) incorrectly introduces the possessive form.

71. D

The other answer choices are unnecessarily wordy; the simplest choice is the best.

72. G

The participle *receiving* has to be changed into a verb in the past tense, *received*, in order to be consistent with *went*. (G) is correct as opposed to (H) because the number of bruises something has can be counted, which necessitates *many bruises*, not *much bruises*.

73. B

(A) wouldn't work as a concluding sentence because its style and tone are off; nowhere in the passage does the writer use language such as *brutal calamities* and *beguiling excitement*. Also, the writer and her father were not "unwary rafters." (C) contradicts the writer's main theme that nothing was as memorable as her first ride through the rapids. The tone in (D), "call me crazy or weird...," is much different from the writer's. (B) is the choice that closely matches the author's style and tone while restating the main theme of the passage.

74. F

This essay relates a personal experience of the writer: her first time rafting down the rapids. There is very little mention of the techniques of white water rafting, so the essay would not meet the requirements of the assignment. (G) is wrong because the essay does not focus on the relationship between father and daughter, but on their first rafting experience together.

75. B

The sentence is a preface of things to come, so it must appear towards the beginning of the essay. That eliminates (C) and (D). The second paragraph is about the peaceful setting, so (B) is the most sensible answer.

MATH TEST

1. D

You know that 14 people are 20% of the total, and you need to find 100% of the total. You could set up an equation, or you could multiply 14 by 5, since 100% is 5 times as much as 20%. The number of people surveyed is 14×5, or 70.

2. J

One safe way to answer this question is by picking numbers. For instance, if you let $x = 2$ and $y = 3$, the train would have traveled $90 \times 2 + 60 \times 3 = 360$ miles in 5 hours, or $\frac{360}{5} = 72$ miles per hour. If you then plug $x = 2$ and $y = 3$ into the answer choices looking for 72, it's clear that the correct answer is (J). No other answer choice equals 72 when $x = 2$ and $y = 3$.

3. D

If the ratio of men to women is 5:3, then the ratio of women to the total is 3:8. Since you know the total number of string players is 24, you can set up the equation $\frac{3}{8} = \frac{x}{24}$ to find that $x = 9$. Also, without setting up the proportion, you could note that the total number of players is 3 times the ratio total, so the number of women will be 3 times the part of the ratio that represents women.

4. K

In a pinch you could backsolve on this question, but this one is fairly easy to solve algebraically, like so:

$$x^2 - 3x = 6x$$
$$x^2 = 9x$$

Now you can divide both sides by x because $x \neq 0$:

$$\frac{x^2}{x} = \frac{9x}{x}$$

$$x = 9$$

5. C

With visual perception problems such as this one, the key is to play around with possibilities as you try to draw a solution. Eventually, you should be able to come up with a picture like this:

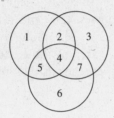

6. K

This problem could be solved algebraically, but look at the answer choices. They are all simple numbers, making this a great opportunity for backsolving. Begin with choice (H).

Plugging in 0, you get:

$$(0)^2 + 6(0) + 8 = 4 + 10(0)$$

$$8 = 4$$

Since 8 does not equal 4, you know this isn't the correct answer. But it is difficult to know which answer to try next. Should you aim higher or lower? If you're unsure of which direction to go, just try whatever looks easiest. Choice (J), 1, looks like a good candidate:

$$(1)^2 + 6(1) + 8 = 4 + 10(1)$$

$$1 + 6 + 8 = 4 + 10$$

$$15 = 14$$

So (J) doesn't work either, but it looks like the numbers are getting closer so you're going in the right direction. Try out choice (K) just to be sure.

$$(2)^2 + 6(2) + 8 = 4 + 10(2)$$

$$4 + 12 + 8 = 4 + 20$$

$$24 = 24$$

Choice (K) is the correct answer.

7. B

Translate piece by piece:

"Nine less than c" indicates subtraction: $c - 9$.

"Nine less than c is the same as the number d": $c - 9 = d$. There's one equation.

"d less than" also indicates subtraction: $- d$.

"d less than twice c is 20": $2c - d = 20$. There's the second equation.

Choice (B) matches what we found.

8. K

To determine the total number of possible arrangements on a question like this one, simply determine the number of possibilities for each component, and then multiply them together. There are 3 types of appetizers, 5 types of entrees, and 4 types of desserts. Therefore there are $3 \times 5 \times 4 = 60$ ways to order a dinner, and choice (K) is correct.

9. E

Backsolving is a great technique to use for this problem. Start with (C). The director asked one out of 3 students to come to the second audition and $\frac{1}{3}$ of 48 is 16, so 16 students were invited to a second audition. Then 75% of 16, which is $\frac{3}{4}(16) = 12$ students were offered parts. The question states that 18 students were offered parts, so you already know that (C) is too small. You can also eliminate (A) and (B). Since the director invited $\frac{1}{3}$ of the students to a second audition, the number of students at the first audition must be divisible by 3. (You can't have a fraction of a student.) That eliminates (D), which leaves only (E).

10. K

Begin by translating the English into math: $x + 5x = -60$, $6x = -60$, so $x = -10$, and the two numbers are -10 and -50. Thus the lesser number is -50.

By the way, this is where most people mess up. They forget that the "lesser" of two negative numbers is the negative number with the larger absolute value (since *less* means *to the left of* on the number line):

11. D

You're looking for the total number of parallelograms that can be found among the triangles, and parallelograms could be formed two ways from these triangles, either from two adjacent triangles, or from four adjacent triangles, like so:

Begin by looking for the smaller parallelograms. If you look for parallelograms leaning in the same direction as the one we drew, you'll find three. But there are two other possible orientations for the smaller parallelogram; it could be flipped horizontally, or it could be rotated 90 degrees so that one triangle sits atop the other in the form of a diamond; both of these orientations also have three parallelograms, for a total of nine smaller parallelograms.

Now look for larger parallelograms. Perhaps the easiest way to count these is to look along the sides of the larger composite triangle. You should be able to spot two of the larger parallelograms along each side, one originating at each vertex, for a total of six larger parallelograms. Thus there are a total of $9 + 6 = 15$ parallelograms in all.

12. H

The square has a perimeter of 16 inches, so each side of the square is 4 inches, and the area of the square is, therefore, 16 square inches. If the side of the square is 4 inches, then the diameter of the circle is also 4 inches. The radius of the circle is then 2 inches. The area of the circle is 4π square inches. The area of the shaded region is then $16 - 4\pi$ square inches.

13. C

The safest strategy is simply to list out the possibilities. It's also helpful to realize that multiples of both 4 and 6 are multiples of 12 (the least common multiple between the two), so skip over all multiples of 12:

4, 8, ~~12~~, 16, 20, ~~24~~, 28, 32, ~~36~~, 40, 44, ~~48~~

So there are 8 in all.

14. H

Don't be intimidated by the expression $f(x)$. In this case, that just means that you should plug in the number that appears in the parentheses for the x in the expression they have given you. So, if $f(x) = (8 - 3x)(x^2 - 2x - 15)$, $f(3) = (8 - 3(3))((3)^2 - 2(3) - 15)$. Once you get to this point, just remember PEMDAS. $(8 - 3(3))((3)^2 - 2(3) - 15) = (8 - 9)(9 - 6 - 15) = (-1)(-12) = 12$, choice (H).

15. C

A class contains five juniors and five seniors. If one member of the class is assigned at random to present a paper on a certain subject, and another member of the class is randomly assigned to assist him, then:

The probability that the first student picked will be a junior $= \dfrac{\text{\# of Juniors}}{\text{Total \# of Students}} = \dfrac{5}{10} = \dfrac{1}{2}$. The probability that the second student picked will be a junior, given that the first student picked was a junior $= \dfrac{\text{\# of Juniors Remaining}}{\text{Total \# of Students Remaining}}$.

So the probability that both students will be juniors $= \dfrac{1}{2} \times \dfrac{4}{9} = \dfrac{2}{9}$.

16. G

Since the formula to find the area of a triangle is $\dfrac{1}{2}$ (*base*)(*height*), you can plug in the base and area to find the height. You know that the area of this triangle is 45 units and that the base is $3 + 12 = 15$. Let x be the length of altitude $\overline{YS}$. Plug these into the area formula to get $45 = \dfrac{15x}{2}$. Solve for x to get $x = 6$.

17. D

The y-coordinate is the point on which the x value is zero, so plug $x = 0$ into the equation:

$$6y - 3(0) = 18$$
$$6y = 18$$
$$y = 3$$

18. H

This question involves common quadratics, so the key is to write these quadratic expressions in their other forms. For instance $x^2 - y^2 = 12$, so $(x + y)(x - y) = 12$. Since $x - y = 4$, $(x + y)(4) = 12$, so $x + y = 3$. Finally, $x^2 + 2xy + y^2 = (x + y)^2 = (3)^2 = 9$.

19. D

This shape must be divided into 3 simple shapes. By drawing downward two perpendicular line segments from the endpoints of the side which is 10 units long, you are left with a 3×10 rectangle, a triangle with a base of 4 and a height of 3, and a triangle with a base of 7 and a hypotenuse of $7\sqrt{2}$. The rectangle has an area of $3 \times 10 = 30$ square units. The smaller triangle has an area of $\dfrac{4 \times 3}{2} = 6$ square units. The larger triangle is a 45°-45°-90° triangle, so the height must be 7. Therefore, it has an area of $\dfrac{7 \times 7}{2} = 24.5$ square units. The entire shape has an area of $6 + 30 + 24.5 = 60.5$ square units.

20. H

Although backsolving is certainly possible with this problem, it's probably quicker to solve with arithmetic. The board is 12 feet long, which means it is $12 \times 12 = 144$ inches. The carpenter cuts off $3 \times 17 = 51$ inches. That leaves $144 - 51 = 93$ inches.

21. E

To answer this question, begin by setting the right side of equation to equal zero:

$$x^2 - 4x - 6 = 6$$
$$x^2 - 4x - 12 = 0$$

Now use reverse-FOIL to factor the left side of the equation:

$$(x - 6)(x + 2) = 0$$

Thus either $x - 6 = 0$ or $x + 2 = 0$, so $x = 6$ or -2.

22. H

Here's another question that tests your understanding of FOIL, but you have to be careful. The question states that -3 is a possible solution for the equation $x^2 + kx - 15 = 0$, so in its factored form, one set of parentheses with a factor inside must be $(x + 3)$. Since the last term in the equation in its expanded form is -15, that means that the entire factored equation must read $(x + 3)(x - 5) = 0$, which in its expanded form is $x^2 - 2x - 15 = 0$. Thus $k = -2$.

23. D

To solve this problem you need to understand the triangle inequality theorem, which states: The sum of the lengths of any two sides of a triangle is always greater then the length of the third side. Therefore, the other sides of this triangle must add up to more than 7. You know from the problem that every side must be an integer. That means that the sides must add up to at least 8 inches (4 inches and 4 inches, or 7 inches and 1 inch, for example). The smallest possible perimeter is $7 + 8 = 15$.

24. F

It's time to use SOHCAHTOA, and drawing a triangle might help as well. If the sine of θ (opposite side over hypotenuse) is $\dfrac{\sqrt{11}}{2\sqrt{3}}$, then one of the legs of the right triangle is $\sqrt{11}$ and the hypotenuse is $2\sqrt{3}$. Now apply the Pythagorean theorem to come up the other (adjacent) leg: $(\sqrt{11})^2 + (n)^2 = (2\sqrt{3})^2$, so $11 + n^2 = 12$, so $11 + n^2 = 12$, which means that $n^2 = 1$, and $n = 1$, Thus cosine (adjacent side over hypotenuse) θ is $\dfrac{1}{2\sqrt{3}}$.

25. D

Take a quick look at the answer choices before simplifying an expression like this one. Notice that none of these choices contain a radical sign in their

denominators. So when you simplify the expression, try to eliminate that radical sign. Your calculations should look something like this:

$$\frac{\sqrt{3+x}}{\sqrt{3-x}} \times \frac{\sqrt{3-x}}{\sqrt{3-x}} = \frac{\sqrt{(3+x)(3-x)}}{\sqrt{(3-x)^2}} =$$

$$\frac{\sqrt{9 - 3x + 3x - x^2}}{3 - x} = \frac{\sqrt{9 - x^2}}{3 - x}.$$

So choice (D) is correct.

26. G

If the ratio of the parts is 2:5, then the ratio total is $2 + 5 = 7$. Thus the actual total number of cookies must be a multiple of 7. The only answer choice that's a multiple of 7 is (G), 35.

27. C

This question is a great opportunity to use your calculator. Notice that all your answer choices are decimals. In order to solve, convert $\dfrac{3}{16}$ into a decimal and add that to .175. $\dfrac{3}{16} = .1875$, so the sum equals $.1875 + .175 = .3625$. So choice (C) is correct.

28. H

Remember that if you are given a perimeter for a rectangle, the rectangle with the greatest area for that perimeter will be a square. So we are looking for the area of a square with a perimeter of 20. The perimeter of a square equals $4s$, where s is the length of one side of the square. If $4s = 20$, then $s = 5$. The area of the square equals $s^2 = 5^2 = 25$, choice (H).

29. B

Be careful on this one. You can't start plugging numbers into your calculator without paying attention to the order of operations. This one is best solved on your own.

$$\frac{\dfrac{3}{2}+\dfrac{7}{4}}{\left(\dfrac{15}{8}-\dfrac{3}{4}\right)-\left(\dfrac{4+3}{-4+3}\right)}=\frac{\dfrac{3}{2}+\dfrac{7}{4}}{\left(\dfrac{9}{8}\right)-\left(\dfrac{7}{-1}\right)}=$$

$$\frac{\dfrac{13}{4}}{\dfrac{9}{8}+\dfrac{7}{1}}=\frac{\dfrac{13}{4}}{\dfrac{65}{8}}=\frac{13}{4}\times\frac{8}{65}=\frac{2}{5}$$

30. K

You could solve this algebraically for x as follows:

$$x - 15 = 7 - 5(x - 4)$$
$$x - 15 = 7 - 5x + 20$$
$$x - 15 = -5x + 27$$
$$6x = 42$$
$$x = 7$$

Remember also that if you are ever stuck, you can try to backsolve with the answer choices. Here if you try them all out, only 7 works:

$$7 - 15 = 7 - 5(7 - 4)$$
$$-8 = 7 - 5(3)$$
$$-8 = 7 - 15$$
$$-8 = -8$$

31. C

Break strange figures like this one up into shapes that are more familiar and easier to handle. In this case, the quadrilateral can be split into a square and a right triangle. The square is 9×9, so the area of

that part of the figure is 81 square meters. The right triangle has a height of 9 and a base of 4, so the area of the triangle would be $\frac{1}{2}bh = \frac{1}{2}(4 \times 9) = \frac{1}{2}(36)$ = 18 square meters. So the total area of the figure is (81 + 18) square meters = 99 square meters, choice (C).

32. H

The easiest way to solve this question is to put it in the form $y = mx + b$, in which case m equals the slope. In other words, you want to isolate y:

$$6y - 3x = 18$$
$$6y = 3x + 18$$
$$y = \frac{3x + 18}{6}$$
$$y = \frac{1}{2}x + 3$$

So the slope equals $\frac{1}{2}$.

33. E

To answer this question you have to know that perpendicular lines on the standard (x, y) coordinate plane have slopes that are negative reciprocals of each other. In other words, the line described by the equation $y = -\frac{4}{5}x + 6$ has a slope of $-\frac{4}{5}$, so a line perpendicular to it has a slope of $\frac{5}{4}$. Looking at the answer choices, you can immediately eliminate (B), (C), and (D). Now just plug in the coordinates you're given, $(4, 3)$, into one of the remaining equations. Try choice (A).

$$3 = \frac{5}{4}(4) + 2$$

$$3 = 5 + 2$$

This does not compute, so the answer must be (E). (Try it out if you're not convinced.)

34. K

Since the problem gives you the y-intercept, it is easy to look at the answer choices and rule out (F), (H), and (J). Put the equation from the question in slope-intercept form to find its slope:

$$3x - 5y = 4$$

$$-5y = -3x + 4$$

$$y = \frac{-3x + 4}{-5}$$

$$y = \frac{3}{5}x - \frac{4}{5}$$

Since line t is parallel, it has the same slope. This matches (K).

35. A

To solve for x in the equation $y = mx + b$, isolate x on one side of the equation. Begin by subtracting b from both sides. You will be left with $y - b = mx$. Then divide both sides by m, and you will be left with $x = \frac{y - b}{m}$, choice (A).

36. J

In this figure there are many right triangles, and many similar triangles. If you know to be on the lookout for 3-4-5 triangles, it should be easy to spot that triangle ABC has sides of 15-20-25, so $\overline{AC}$ is 25. Now turn your attention to triangle ABD. Since it's a right triangle that shares $\angle BAC$ with triangle ABC, it too must be a 3-4-5 triangle. So if the hypotenuse is 20, the shorter leg $(\overline{BD})$ must have a

length of 12, and the longer leg $(\overline{AD})$ must have a length of 16.

37. A

The shortest distance to line m will be a line perpendicular to m. So, the distance will be the difference between the y-coordinates of point C and the nearest point on line m. Since every point on m has a y-coordinate of 5, and point C has a y-coordinate of 3, the difference is 2.

38. G

Perhaps the easiest approach here is to pick numbers. Pick a simple number such as $x = 2$. Thus

$$\frac{x^2 - 11x + 24}{8 - x} = \frac{(2)^2 - 11(2) + 24}{8 - 2} = \frac{4 - 22 + 24}{6}$$

$= \frac{6}{6} = 1$. So 1 is your target number. When you plug $x = 2$ into the answer choices, the only choice that gives you 1 is (G).

39. C

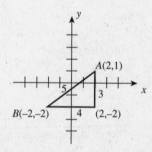

It may help you to draw a picture. Draw a right triangle into the coordinate plane as we've done above. Note that the distance between the two points represents the hypotenuse of the triangle. The legs of the triangle have lengths of 3 and 4, so the distance between the two points must be 5, choice (C).

40. G

To find the area of the shaded region, you must subtract the area of the circle from the area of the rectangle. Since the sides of the rectangle are $2x$ and $5x$, it has an area of $2x \cdot 5x = 10x^2$. By examining the diagram, you can see that the circle has a diameter of $2x$, so it has a radius of x. Its area is, therefore, πx^2. The shaded region, therefore, has an area of $10x^2 - \pi x^2$.

41. B

Since you are not given a diagram for this problem, it's best to draw a quick sketch of a right triangle to help keep the sides separate in your mind. Mark one of the acute angles θ. Since $\cos \theta = \dfrac{5\sqrt{2}}{8}$, mark the adjacent side $5\sqrt{2}$ and the hypotenuse as 8. (Remember SOHCAHTOA.) Use the Pythagorean theorem to find that the side opposite θ is $\sqrt{14}$. The problem asks you to find $\tan \theta$. Tangent $= \dfrac{\text{opposite}}{\text{adjacent}}$, so $\tan \theta = \dfrac{\sqrt{14}}{5\sqrt{2}}$, which can be simplified to $\dfrac{\sqrt{7}}{5}$.

42. H

This question is one where your calculator can come in handy. Divide 7 by integer values for n, and look for values between .5 and .8. Begin by looking for the integer values of n where $\dfrac{7}{n}$ is greater than .5. If $n = 14$, then $\dfrac{7}{n} = .5$, so n must be less than 14.

Work through values of n until you get to the point where $\dfrac{7}{n} \geq .8$. When $n = 9$, $\dfrac{7}{n} = .778$, but when $n = 8$, $\dfrac{7}{n} = .875$. So the integer values that work for n in this case are $n = 9, 10, 11, 12,$ and 13. Five integer values work, so choice (H) is correct.

43. C

The points are as far apart as possible when separated by a diameter of X and a diameter of Y.

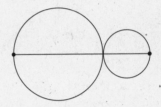

The circumference of a circle is $\pi \times$ (diameter), so the diameter of circle X is 12 and the diameter of circle Y is 8. The greatest possible distance between points then is $12 + 8 = 20$.

44. K

Begin by getting rid of the square root sign. If $y \geq 0$, then $\sqrt{y^2} = y$, so $\sqrt{(x^2 + 4)^2} = x^2 + 4$. $(x + 2)(x - 2) = x^2 - 4$, so you now have $(x^2 + 4) - (x^2 - 4) = ?$ Get rid of the parentheses and you have $x^2 + 4 - x^2 + 4 = x^2 - x^2 + 4 + 4 = 8$.

45. A

Here you need to substitute -3 for s and solve. That gives you the expression $(-3)^3 + 2(-3)^2 + 2(-3)$, which equals $-27 + 18 - 6$, or -15. If you missed this problem, you probably made a mistake with the signs of the numbers.

46. G

Be careful on this one. Begin by simplifying the equation by FOILing one side:

$$2x + 6 = (x + 5)(x + 3)$$
$$2x + 6 = x^2 + 8x + 15$$

Then get the right side of the equation to equal zero: $x^2 + 6x + 9 = 0$.

The left side of this equation is the perfect square $(x + 3)^2$, so $(x + 3)^2 = 0$, which has only one solution, $x = -3$. Choice (G) is correct.

47. E

This is a great eyeballing question. The perimeter is greater than $\overline{AC}$, so you can get rid of choices (A) and (B). It appears to be quite a bit greater than $\overline{AC}$, more than twice as great, so choices (C) and (D) are out as well. That only leaves choice (E).

If you wanted to solve this the conventional way, since the perimeter is the sum of the lengths of all the sides of the square, you need to find the length of the square's sides. Let the length of each of the square's sides be x. $\overline{AC}$ divides the square into two right triangles, so we can apply the Pythagorean theorem: $\overline{AB}^2 + \overline{BC}^2 = \overline{AC}^2$. Since $\overline{AB}$ and $\overline{BC}$ are sides of the square they have the same length. We can write that as $x^2 + x^2 = \overline{AC}^2$. $\overline{AC} = 8$, so $2x^2 = 8^2$; $2x^2 = 64$; $x^2 = 32$; $x = \sqrt{32} = \sqrt{16 \times 2} = 4\sqrt{2}$. So each side of the square is $4\sqrt{2}$, and the perimeter of the square is $4 \times 4\sqrt{2} = 16\sqrt{2}$.

48. G

To find the area of this complex shape, you could divide it into 2 simple shapes by drawing a line 30 inches up, parallel to the horizontal base. This leaves you with a 4×30 rectangle and a triangle

with height of 6 and a base of 4. The rectangle has an area of $4 \times 30 = 120$ square inches, and the triangle has an area of $\frac{4 \times 6}{2} = 12$ square inches. That makes a total of $120 + 12 = 132$ square inches.

49. E

Drawing $\overline{OD}$ divides quadrilateral $OCDE$ into two triangles, OCD and ODE. Both triangles are isosceles because $\overline{OC}$, $\overline{OD}$, and $\overline{OE}$ are all radii of circle O. Angles ODC and OCD have equal measures, since they're opposite equal sides, so $\angle ODC$ measures 70°. Similarly, $\angle ODE$ measures 45°. Together, angles ODC and ODE make up $\angle CDE$, so its measure is 70° + 45° = 115°.

50. K

Remember that lines intersect at the point that is a solution to both equations. So, equations with no common solution don't intersect—they have the same slope and are parallel. To solve this problem, search through the answer choices to find the pair of equations representing lines with the same slope. If you write the equations in (K) in slope-intercept form, you'll get $y = -\frac{1}{3}x + 2$, $y = -\frac{1}{3}x + \frac{7}{9}$, so the slope is clearly the same for both equations.

51. E

To solve a repeating decimal question, begin by determining the pattern of the decimal on your calculator. $\frac{1}{7} = 0.142857142857 \ldots$, so you know that this fraction repeats every 6 decimal places. Since we are looking for the 46th decimal place, we need to determine where in the 6-term pattern we would be at the 46th place. Divide 46 by 6, and look for the remainder. The remainder in this case is 4, so we are looking for the fourth term in the sequence, which is 8, choice (E).

52. K

Remember that you treat an inequality exactly like an equality, except that you need to flip the sign when you multiply or divide by a negative number. In this problem, you start with the inequality $-2 - 4x \leq -6x$. Add $4x$ to both sides to get $-2 \leq -2x$. Divide by -2 and flip the sign to get $1 \geq x$, which matches (K).

53. B

For this problem, it would probably be easiest to

pick numbers. Since you will be taking the square

root of the numbers, it's easiest to pick perfect

squares, like 4 and 9. $\dfrac{\sqrt{4}}{4} + \dfrac{\sqrt{9}}{9} = \dfrac{2}{4} + \dfrac{3}{9} = \dfrac{1}{2} +$

$\dfrac{1}{3} = \dfrac{5}{6}$. When you plug 4 and 9 into the answer

choices, only (B) gives you $\dfrac{5}{6}$.

54. G

When transversals intersect parallel lines, corresponding line segments on the transversals are proportional. In other words, $\dfrac{\overline{DE}}{CB} = \dfrac{\overline{EF}}{BA}$. Thus $\dfrac{6}{8} = \dfrac{\overline{EF}}{4} = $, so $\overline{EF} = 3$.

55. D

Divide the square into two right triangles by drawing the diagonal from (2, 7) to (2, 1). Remember that the area of each triangle is half its base times its height. Treat the diagonal as the base of a triangle. Its length is the distance from (2, 7) to

(2, 1). Since the x-coordinates are the same, that distance is simply the difference between the y-coordinates. $7 - 1$, or 6. The diagonal bisects the square, so the height of the triangle is half the distance from $(-1, 4)$ to $(5,4)$. We already know that a diagonal of this square is 6, so half the distance is 3. Therefore, the base and height of either triangle are 6 and 3, so the area of each triangle is $\dfrac{6 \times 3}{2}$ or 9 square units. The square is made up of two such triangles and so has twice the area, or 18 square units.

56. K

Compared to the graph of $y = \cos\theta$, the graph of $y = 2\cos\theta$ would have twice the amplitude and the same period, choice (K). Here you are doubling y, which represents the vertical coordinates, but the θ coordinates stay the same. The amplitude of a trigonometric equation refers to how high or low the curve moves from the horizontal axis. The period refers to the distance required to complete a single wave along the horizontal axis.

57. C

To solve this problem with algebra, you need to translate each phrase into mathematics. Translated, the problem is $3(x + 15) = 4x - 65$. Solve for x to get 110. Alternatively, you could backsolve.

58. H

The volume of a cylinder is $\pi r^2 h$, so pick numbers to make this question more concrete and plug them into this volume formula. Let's say the smaller cylinder has a height of 1 and a radius of 1 (diameter of 2), for a volume of $\pi(1)^2 \times 1 = \pi$. The larger cylinder would then have a height of 3 and a radius of 2 (diameter of 4), for a volume of $\pi(2)^2 \times 3 = 12\pi$. Thus it would take 12 fillings of the smaller cylinder to fill the larger cylinder.

59. D

Draw a picture of the triangle, and carefully apply your knowledge of the ratio of the lengths of the sides of a 30°-60°-90° triangle ($x : x\sqrt{3} : 2x$). So if the longer leg has a length of 12, the shorter leg has a length of $\dfrac{12}{\sqrt{3}} = \dfrac{12\sqrt{3}}{\sqrt{3} \times \sqrt{3}} = \dfrac{12\sqrt{3}}{3} = 4\sqrt{3}$.

Thus the hypotenuse is twice this, or $8\sqrt{3}$. So the perimeter is the sum of the three sides, or $4\sqrt{3} + 12 + 8\sqrt{3} = 12\sqrt{3} + 12$.

60. J

Remember the average formula on this one. The average formula states, Average $= \dfrac{\text{Sum of the terms}}{\text{Number of terms}}$. So to find the total average, find the total sum and divide it by the total number of terms. If a team averages x points in n games, then it scored nx points in n games. In the final game of the season, it scored y points. So the total sum of points for the season is $nx + y$, and the total number of games is $n + 1$. So the team's average score for the entire season is $\dfrac{nx + y}{n + 1}$, choice (J).

READING TEST

Passage I

1. C
The answer can be found in lines 31–36: "The real evils, indeed, of Emma's situation were the power of having rather too much her own way, and a disposition to think a little too well of herself; these were the disadvantages which threatened alloy to her many enjoyments."

2. G
Isabella's name is given in line 72.

3. B
The answer can be found in lines 20–21: "Between them it was more the intimacy of sisters."

4. F
As it is used in the sentence, *disposition* means "tendency" or "inclination." It would not make sense for Emma to have (G) control, (H) placement, or (J) transfer "to think a little too well of herself" (lines 33–34).

5. D
The answer can be found in lines 61–68: "She recalled her past kindness—the kindness, the affection of sixteen years—how she had taught her and ... how she had devoted all her powers to attach and amuse her in health—and how she had nursed her through the various illnesses of childhood."

6. H
Miss Taylor will continue to be a part of Emma's life, but they will not be as close because Miss Taylor no longer lives with Emma and because Miss Taylor will be primarily concerned with her husband's, not Emma's, well-being.

7. C
Emma is self-centered, as evidenced by her description of her relationship with Miss Taylor.

Among Miss Taylor's admirable qualities, Emma includes the fact that Miss Taylor was "interested in her, in every pleasure, every scheme of hers—one to whom she could speak every thought as it arose, and who had such an affection for her as could never find fault" (lines 78–82). Emma is also clearly headstrong. She is described as "having rather too much her own way" (lines 32–33).

8. G

Emma's description of her friendship with Miss Taylor suggests that Emma most highly values devotion in her friends.

9. B

The description of Mr. Weston is in lines 52–55: "The marriage had every promise of happiness for her friend. Mr. Weston was a man of unexceptional character, easy fortune, suitable age, and pleasant manners." None of the other choices match this description.

10. H

The answer to the question is in lines 28–30: "Emma doing just what she liked, highly esteeming Miss Taylor's judgment, but directed chiefly by her own."

Passage II

11. B

The passage presents the three main systems of memory and states that these systems are widely accepted—so eliminate (A)—but gives alternate theories about the way long-term memories are formed and possible flaws in the process. Although the passage mentions two early ideas about memory that were too simplistic (C) and (D), this is not the main focus of the passage.

12. H

Described in paragraph three, semantic memory holds facts and general knowledge, like the multiplication tables (H). Ballet steps (F) and riding a bicycle (J) would be in procedural memory, a childhood memory (G) would be in episodic.

13. B

All the information you need is in paragraph three. Memories of one's personal life would be held in episodic memory, therefore the man's episodic memory was affected. Eliminate (C) and (D). Long-term memories are "never lost," but they may become inaccessible, therefore the author would most likely agree that the man's episodic memories had become inaccessible to him.

14. F

While memory was once viewed as relatively simple and automatic with memories being held exactly as they were originally received, it is now believed that many factors alter the way memories are formed and retrieved. (G) and (J) contradict this. (H) is too extreme.

15. C

In the last paragraph the author states that assumptions and inferences can affect memory. A person might assume that if the ball hits a window the window will break. Interference (A) is when one, unrelated memory alters another. The memory described in the question is not inaccessible (B), but wrong. And most of the memory is still correct, not false (D).

16. J

This detail question requires very careful reading. Refresh your memory by looking at *episodic* in paragraph three. It's in long-term memory, and involves personal events closely identified with a time and place. (F), G, and (H) fit that idea closely. If you're unsure, look at the description of working (short-term) memory in paragraph two. You'll see that it includes those things briefly remembered and then lost forever—like the face of a stranger passed on the street.

17. B

Paragraph two describes this change in terminology. The term *short-term memory* did not accurately describe all the functions of this category of memory. *Working memory* is more accurate since, although these memories degrade quickly—eliminating (A)—these memories can also be used and manipulated as described in the second paragraph. (C) and (D) confuse information in other paragraphs.

18. H

Don't panic. All you have to do is look at the line where this term is defined for you. The term doesn't relate to any of the usual meanings of the word *icon*.

19. B

The second sentence in paragraph three states, "Memories recorded in long-term memory are never lost…." Although absolute statements are often too extreme to be correct in Reading, when the passage explicitly supports an absolute statement don't be afraid to choose it. You might choose (A) if you mistook "short-term" and "working" memory for two separate categories. (C) is contradicted in paragraph four, and (D) is contradicted at the end of paragraph two and again at the start of paragraph five.

20. H

Paragraph two states that working memories decay rapidly, which means that they are quickly forgotten. (F) and (G) relate to sensory memory. (J) is characteristic of long-term memory.

Passage III

21. B

In lines 12–14 Julia Margaret Cameron is described as "the first woman to have achieved eminence in photography." The other answer choices contradict information supplied in the passage.

22. F

The answer to this question can be found in lines 84–85: "Contemporary taste much prefers her portraits…" and in lines 90–91: "today her fame rests upon her portraits…".

23. D

The dates used in the passage tell you that this is a chronological account; the author begins with Cameron's birth in 1815, tells of her marriage and then her move to England in 1848, points out that she received her first photographic equipment in 1863, describes one of her photographs from 1864, and then concludes the paragraph with her death in 1874.

24. F

The dictionary definition of *cumbersome* is "difficult to handle because of weight or bulk." (F) most closely fits this definition, and it is the only answer choice that makes sense within the context of the sentence.

25. B

(A) contradicts information from the passage, which suggests that Cameron led anything but a conventional life. Neither the money that Cameron earned as a photographer nor her religious beliefs are discussed in the passage, making (C) and (D) incorrect answers.

26. F

Lines 62–65 say, "She produced a large body of work that stands up as one of the notable artistic achievements of the Victorian period." To say that she is "the greatest photographer who ever lived" goes beyond anything stated or implied in the passage. The third paragraph does not compare her importance as an artist during her lifetime to her importance today. The passage also does not state that she "revolutionized" any photographic methods.

27. C

The answer to this question can be found in lines 7–11: "photography, being a new medium outside the traditional academic framework, was wide open to women and offered them opportunities that the older fields did not…".

28. G

These titles refer to allegorical pictures, as described in lines 80–83: "Victorian critics were particularly impressed by her allegorical pictures, many of them based on the poems of her friend and neighbor Tennyson…."

29. D

The answer to this question can be found in lines 84–86: "Contemporary taste much prefers her portraits and finds her narrative scenes sentimental and sometimes in bad taste."

30. F

The author says that Cameron "achieved eminence" (line 13) in her field, that she "devoted herself wholly to this art" (lines 57–58), and that "no other woman photographer has ever enjoyed such success" (lines 76–77). Only (F) fits these descriptions.

Passage IV

31: C

For details about the eye, look at paragraph three. Only the cornea and stenopaic pupil are relevant, eliminating (A) and (D). But the cornea (B) is helpful underwater, not on land.

32. G

The eye is covered in paragraph three. The seal's cornea improves vision in the water (note the comparison to human underwater vision), but distorts light moving through the air. Another adaptation was then needed to "minimize" distortion,

but that doesn't mean distortion is completely eliminated, so the seal's vision in the air is distorted, (G).

33. D

The vibrissae are discussed only in the last paragraph. They sense wave disturbances made by nearby moving fish, so (D) is correct.

34. F

This is stated in the second paragraph, where the seal's hearing is discussed.

35. D

This appears in the first paragraph, which introduces the influences on the seal's adaptations. They include that the seal "does most of its fishing at night," that "noise levels are high," and that these factors are compounded by the seal's "two habitats."

36. H

Locating each of these claims in the passage, we find that (H) is "suggested" and the subject of speculation, rather than stated as fact. All the others are given in support of claims.

37. A

We find in the first paragraph that they live along the northern Atlantic and Pacific coasts. Since they live in both the land and water, the coastlines must be accessible. We can infer that the waters are cold rather than warm, eliminate (D). (B) and (C) are too broad.

38. J

This feature is mentioned at the end of paragraph two. It shouldn't be confused with echolocation, which is discussed in paragraph four, but not connected with any particular sensory organ.

39. B

The entire passage is about how seal's sensory organs have adapted to life on land and in the water, making (B) the best choice. Generally, we are told about differences, not similarities, between the two, eliminating (A). The relative success of human and seal adaptation to their environments isn't discussed (C) and (D).

40. G

In paragraph three, we see that human corneas refract light badly in water, and seal's corneas perform well.

SCIENCE TEST

Passage I

1. B

To answer this question, you have to examine the third column of the table, transmittance range. For a material to transmit light at a wavelength of 25 μm, its transmittance range—the range of wavelengths over which the material is transparent—must include 25 μm. Only potassium bromide (0.3–29 μm) and cesium iodide (0.3–70 μm) have transmittance ranges that include 25 μm, so (B) is correct.

2. F

The material that contradicts this hypothesis is going to have poor chemical resistance, but a transmittance range less than 10 μm. Lithium fluoride (F) fits the bill: its chemical resistance is poor, and its transmittance range is less than 6 μm wide. (G) and (J) are wrong because both flint glass and quartz have excellent chemical resistance. (H) is out because cesium iodide has a transmittance range nearly 70 μm wide.

3. D

The correct answer is a pair of materials in which the refractive index of the first material is greater than that of the second. In (A), (B), and (C), the refractive index of the first material is less than that of the second. In (D), however, flint glass has a refractive index of 1.66 while calcium fluoride's refractive index is only 1.43. That makes (D) the correct answer.

4. J

The easiest way to answer this question is to use the first couple of materials and test each hypothesis on them. (F) and (G) are incorrect because the transmittance range of lithium fluoride is wider than its useful prism range. Comparing the data on lithium fluoride and calcium fluoride rules out (H) because transmittance range does NOT increase as useful prism range decreases. In fact, looking down the rest of the table, you see that transmittance range seems to decrease as useful prism range decreases. (J) is the only one left, and the data on lithium fluoride and calcium fluoride as well as all the other materials confirms that the transmittance range is always wider than, and includes within it, the useful prism range.

5. B

According to the footnote to the table, quartz infused with lead oxide is flint glass. A comparison of the properties of pure quartz and flint glass shows that the transmittance range of flint glass is narrower than that of quartz but that its refractive index is greater. This supports (B).

Passage II

6. H

Use the results of both experiments to answer this question. The answer choices all involve temperature, concentration, and solvent in different combinations. To determine whether osmotic pressure is dependent upon a variable, look for a pair of trials in which all conditions except for that variable are identical. In doing so, you see that temperature and concentration affect osmotic pressure, but solvent does not.

7. B

Find methanol at 0.5 mol/L, which is in Table 2. The text above the table states that all the trials were conducted under the same temperature (298 K). Therefore, simply look across the row that you identified. The osmotic pressure is 12.23, (B).

8. G

To figure out whether or not the sucrose solution will diffuse across the membrane under the conditions described in the question, go back to the definition of osmotic pressure given in the introduction. Once the external pressure reaches the osmotic pressure, osmosis will not occur. In order for osmosis to occur, the external pressure must be less than the osmotic pressure of the solution. The solution in this question is a 0.1 mol/L aqueous sucrose solution at 298 K; those conditions correspond to an osmotic pressure of 2.45 atm. Since the external pressure is 1 atm, which is less than the osmotic pressure, osmosis will occur. From the definition of osmosis in the passage, it is clear that the solution will diffuse from the side of the membrane with a lower concentration of dissolved material, in this case pure water, to the side with a higher concentration, in this case sucrose solution. (G) is correct.

9. C

To determine what the scientists investigated in Experiment 1, look at what they varied and what they measured. In Experiment 1, the scientists varied the concentration and the temperature of sucrose solutions, and they measured the osmotic pressure. Therefore, they were investigating the effect of concentration and temperature on osmotic pressure (C). Watch out for (A): it states what was investigated in Experiment 2, not Experiment 1.

10. F

The results in Table 2 indicate that osmotic pressure doesn't depend on the solvent, as discussed in the explanation to Question 1. So Statement I is a valid conclusion, and (G) can be eliminated. Statement II is false. The results in Table 1 indicate that osmotic pressure is dependent on concentration as well as temperature. So (H) can be ruled out. Now consider Statement III. It is not a valid conclusion because osmotic pressure is the pressure required to prevent osmosis, so osmosis occurs only if the external pressure is less than the osmotic pressure.

11. D

To answer questions that ask about the design of an experiment, look at what the scientists are trying to measure. You're told that osmotic pressure is the pressure required to prevent osmosis. In order to measure the osmotic pressure of a solution, scientists need to be able to tell when osmosis begins. If you have two clear solutions with sucrose dissolved in one of them, how can you tell when there's any movement of solvent between the two of them? If the sucrose is dyed, the color of the solvent will start to turn blue when osmosis starts, i.e., when solvent moves across the membrane to create an equilibrium. Therefore, (D) is correct.

Passage III

12. J

Even if you do not know how many °C are equivalent to room temperature, you can eliminate all of the incorrect answer choices. Choices (F), (G), and (H) all reach a boiling point at low temperatures and, therefore, would all be gases at room temperature. (J), at 36° C, is the only logical choice.

13. C

To answer this question, you have to look for trends in each table and draw conclusions. This can be done by looking at the values in each category and seeing how they vary with respect to each other. If you look at Tables 1 and 2, you can see that there is a direct variation between boiling point and molecular weight: as one increases, the other increases. Therefore, Statement I is correct, Statement II is false, and you can eliminate (B) and (D). Now consider Statement III. To investigate the relationship between molecular structure and boiling point, you have to keep the third variable—molecular weight—constant. Look at the data for two compounds with different molecular structures but the same molecular weight: N_2 and CO; their boiling points differ. Therefore, Statement III is correct, and (C) is the correct response.

14. G

In order to answer this question, you need to establish where C_6H_{14} would fit in Table 1. It is clear from Table 1 that the boiling point increases as the molecular weight increases, so the boiling point of C_6H_{14} will be between the boiling points of molecules with greater and lesser molecular weights. The molecular weight of C_6H_{14} is 86 g/mol, so it will lie between those hydrocarbons with molecular weights of 72 g/mol and 114 g/mol. Therefore, its boiling point will be between 36° C and 126° C. (G), with a value of 70° C, is the only choice that lies between these two boiling points.

15. A

N_2, a non-polar molecule, and CO, a polar molecule, have identical molecular weights and their boiling points differ by only 4° C. SiH_4 (non-polar) and PH_3 (polar) have nearly identical molecular weights as well, but the difference between their boiling points is 27° C—much greater than the difference between the boiling points of N_2 and CO, which have lower molecular weights than SiH_4 and PH_3. The difference between the boiling points of polar and non-polar substances of similar molecular weight increases as molecular weight increases, so (A) is correct.

16. H

If you refer to Table 2, you'll see that for polar substances, as the molar weight goes from 78 to 162, the boiling point goes from –55°C to 97° C. You know the molar weight has to be somewhere between 78 and 162, so (F) is clearly out, and (G), 80, is too close to 78 to be the answer. You would expect the molar weight to be closer to 78 than 162, since 0 is closer to –55 than 97. Therefore (J), 132, is out, and (H) is the answer.

17. D

To figure this out, it is best to examine how much the boiling point rises when dealing with similar molar weight gains. For instance, you can roughly compare rates by looking at what happens to straight-chain hydrocarbons when the molar weight goes from 30 to 72 (boiling point change of 124° C), to what happens to non-polar inorganic compounds when the molar weight goes from 32 to 77 (boiling point change of 22° C), to what happens to polar inorganic compounds when the molar weight goes from 34 to 78 (boiling point change of 30° C). From these figures it is clear that the rate at which the boiling point increases with increasing molar weight is the least for non-polar inorganic compounds, and greatest for straight-chain hydrocarbons, so (D) is correct.

Passage IV

18. F

The question refers to Experiment 2 only, so the correct answer will involve sunlight. Table 2 shows that the average length of the leaves increased from 5.3 cm to 12.4 cm as the amount of sunlight increased from 0 to 3 hours per day. But as the amount of sunlight increased further, leaf size decreased. Therefore, (J) is incorrect. Neither humidity (G) nor water (H) is relevant to Experiment 2.

19. B

Table 1 gives leaf widths at 35% and 55% humidity as 1.8 cm and 2.0 cm, respectively. The leaf width at 40% humidity would most likely be between those two figures. (B) is the only choice within that range.

20. G

All the answer choices involve humidity and sunlight, which were investigated in Experiments 1 and 2, respectively. In Table 1, leaf length and width were greatest at 75% humidity. In Table 2, they were greatest at 3 hours per day of sunlight. Combining those two conditions, as in (G), would probably produce the largest leaves.

21. A

This question relates to the method of the study. Each experiment begins with a statement that 5 groups of seedlings were used. Therefore, (A) is correct. The other answer choices list variables that were manipulated.

22. J

(J) is an assumption that underlies the design of all three experiments. If the seedlings were not equally capable of further growth, then changes in leaf size and density could not be reliably attributed to researcher-controlled changes in humidity, sunlight, and temperature. (F) is wrong because all the seedlings were 2–3 cm tall. The seedlings' abilities to germinate (G) or to produce flowers (H) were not mentioned in the passage.

23. C

Each of the three experiments investigated a different factor. To produce the most useful new data, researchers would probably vary a fourth condition. Soil mineral content would be an appropriate factor to examine. None of the other choices relate directly to the purpose of the experiments as expressed in Paragraph 1 of the passage.

Passage V

24. G

According to the table, decreasing the cross-sectional area of a given wire always increases resistance, so (G) is correct. (H) is wrong because resistivity, displayed in the second column, is constant for each material and thus cannot be responsible for variations in resistance for any given material. Gauge varies inversely with cross-sectional area, so (J) is incorrect.

25. B

Because resistance varies inversely with cross-sectional area A, as discussed in the previous explanation, the correct answer to this question must place A in the denominator. The only choice that does so is (B).

26. J

Compare the choices two at a time. The wires in (F) and (G) are made of the same material and have the same cross-sectional area; only their length is different. Doubling the length doubles the resistance, so (G) would have a higher resistance than (F). By similar reasoning, (J) would have a higher resistance than (H). Even though the research team didn't test wire with a 0.33 mm^2 cross-sectional area, it's safe to assume that the tungsten wire would have a higher resistance than the aluminum one.

27. D

The larger circle represents 10-gauge wire; its diameter is 2.59 mm. The smaller circle has a diameter of only 1.29 mm, but it represents 16-gauge wire, so Statement I is true, and you can eliminate choices (B) and (C) without even checking Statements II or III. To check Statement III, the table shows that the resistance of an iron (Fe) wire is much higher than that of an aluminum (Al) wire with the same length and cross-sectional area. The first sentence of Paragraph 1 defined the resistance of a conductor as "the extent to which it opposes the flow of electricity." Since iron has a higher resistance than aluminum, iron must not conduct electricity as well. Therefore, Statement III is true, and (D) is correct.

28. J

The data indicate that the resistivity of a material doesn't change when wire length changes. Therefore, the graph of resistivity versus length for tungsten (or any other) wire is a horizontal line.

Passage VI

29. B

The key to this question is determining whether the cat in question is an outdoor or indoor cat. This cat goes outdoors a total of three hours per week, whereas an outdoor cat would spend at least six hours outdoors per week. Therefore, this cat is an indoor cat, and the percentage of dark fur on its body would remain just above 10%.

30. G

You can draw a line from 45° across to the solid line representing outdoor cats. If you draw a line from that intersection straight down to the *x*-axis, you will hit 3°.

31. B

If the cat grew dark fur over 30% of its body, it must have been an "outdoor" cat as defined in the passage, and, according to the table, been exposed to temperature below 5° C (statement I). To be an outdoor cat, a cat does not have to spend more time outdoors than indoors (statement II) but it has to spend time outdoors for 6 consecutive days (statement III).

32. H

If a Siamese cat does not have dark fur over more than 10% of its body, then it must *either* be an indoor cat *or* live in an area where it is not regularly exposed to temperatures below 7° C.

33. C

Choice (A) is wrong because the "indoor" cats will not help us, since they don't go outside. (B) is not a good choice because the "outdoor" cats of the original experiment cannot be used as a control group: The time they spent outside was not monitored—we only know that they spent more than one hour outside a day. (D) is incorrect because the data already gathered only showed that outdoor cats turn darker in cold weather than indoor cats and doesn't provide any data about how varying the amount of time outdoors affects fur color. The correct answer is (C): a completely new experiment would have to be set up.

Passage VII

34. J

In Experiment 1, the researchers vary what is fed to the cows by giving them meat from scrapie-free sheep and from scrapie-infected sheep. The cows are later examined for signs of BSE. One common type of wrong answer choice for Experiment questions are choices, such as choice (G) for this question, that include factors that are outside the parameters of the experiment.

35. A

In Experiment 2, the researchers vary what is injected into cows' brains. Any answer choice that discusses ingestion as a focus of this experiment is wrong. This eliminates (B), (C), and (D). Often, wrong answer choices for Experiment questions, such as choice (B) for this question, will include the appropriate information from the wrong experiment.

36. G

By examining the method used in a given experiment, one can determine the assumptions the researchers made in carrying out the experiment and the sources of error. Often error enters the experiment because of the assumptions researchers make. In Experiments 1 and 2, the researchers examined the brains of cows a year and a half after the cows were fed scrapie-infected sheep meat or were injected with scrapie-infected sheep brains. If a year and a half is not a sufficient amount of time for BSE to develop, some of the cows that were counted as not infected might have developed BSE if they had been given more time.

37. C

To answer this question, you need to determine how to test whether BSE can be transmitted via scrapie-infected goats. To test this one would compare the effects of feeding cows scrapie-free goat meat with the effects of feeding cows scrapie-infected goat meat and compare the effects of injecting cows with scrapie-free goat brains with the effects of injecting them with scrapie-infected goat brains.

38. F

Remember that control groups are used as standards of comparison. The control group used in Experiment 1 is the group that is fed scrapie-free sheep meat. If the same proportion of Group A developed BSE as that of Group B, then the researchers would not have any evidence to support the hypothesis that the ingestion of scrapie-infected sheep meat causes BSE.

39. B

Since the proportion of the group of cows that ate scrapie-infected sheep meat and developed BSE was greater than the proportion of the group that were injected with scrapie-infected sheep brains and developed BSE, one can conclude that a cow that eats scrapie-infected sheep meat is more likely to develop BSE than a cow that is injected with scrapie-infected sheep brains. Mere exposure to scrapie-infected sheep, as opposed to ingestion thereof, is never studied in either experiment, so conclusion I can be eliminated.

40. H

To answer this question, consider only the results of Experiment 1. In Experiment 1, the researcher varies what is fed to the cows. The number of cows that developed BSE after eating scrapie-infected sheep meat was much greater than the number of cows that developed BSE after eating scrapie-free sheep meat. This is evidence that the ingestion of scrapie-infected sheep meat causes the development of BSE.

Section Five

ACT RESOURCES

ACT RESOURCES

Last-Minute Tips

LAST-MINUTE TIPS PREVIEW

Testing Timeframe
- Three Days Before the Test
- Two Days Before the Test
- The Night Before the Test
- The Morning of the Test
- During the Test
- After the Test

Is it starting to feel like your whole life is a buildup to the ACT? You've known about it for years, you've worried about it for months, and now you've spent at least a few hours in solid preparation for it. As the test gets closer, you may find your anxiety is on the rise. But you really shouldn't worry. After the preparation you've received from this book, you're in good shape for Test Day.

To calm any pretest jitters you may have (and assuming you've left yourself at least some breathing time before your ACT), let's go over a few last-minute strategies for the couple of days before and after the test.

TESTING TIMEFRAME

Three Days Before the Test

If you've left yourself enough time, take this book's Practice Test under timed conditions. You can also use an actual ACT or one of the practice tests contained in Kaplan's other ACT books.

Try to use all of the techniques and tips you've learned in this book. Take control. Approach the test strategically and creatively.

Warning

Don't take a full practice ACT unless you have at least 48 hours left before the test! Doing so will probably exhaust you, hurting your scoring potential on the actual test! You wouldn't run a marathon the day before the real thing, would you?

Two Days Before the Test

Go over the results of your practice test. Don't worry too much about your score or whether you got a specific question right or wrong. Remember the practice test doesn't count. But do examine your performance on specific questions with an eye to how you might get through each one faster and with greater accuracy on the actual test to come.

After reviewing the results of your practice test, see what your "problem areas" are. Go back to the relevant sections of this book and study the techniques and strategies that will help you succeed in those areas on Test Day.

This is the day to do your last studying—review a couple of the more difficult principles we've covered, do a few more practice problems, and call it quits. It doesn't pay to make yourself crazy right before the test. Besides, you've prepared. You'll do well.

The Night Before the Test

Don't study!

Get together an "ACT survival kit" containing the following items:
- A watch
- At least three sharpened No. 2 pencils
- A pencil sharpener
- Two erasers
- Photo ID card
- Your admission ticket
- A snack—there's a break, and you'll probably get hungry

Know exactly where you're going and how you're getting there. It's probably a good idea to visit your test center sometime before Test Day, so that you know what to expect on the big day.

Read a good book, take a bubble bath, watch TV. Exercise can be a good idea early in the afternoon. Working out makes it easier to sleep when you're nervous, and it also makes many people feel better. Of course, don't work so hard that you can't get up the next day!

Take It Easy

Don't study the night before the test. Relax!

Get a good night's sleep. Go to bed early and allow for some extra time to get ready in the morning.

The Morning of the Test

- Dress in layers so that you can adjust to the temperature of the test room.
- Eat breakfast. Make it something substantial, but not anything too heavy or greasy. Don't drink a lot of coffee if you're not used to it; bathroom breaks cut into your time, and too much caffeine—or any other kind of drug—is a bad idea.
- Read something. Warm up your brain with a newspaper or a magazine. Don't let the ACT be the first thing you read that day.
- Be sure to get there early. Allow yourself extra time for traffic, mass-transit delays, and any other possible problems. If you can, go to the test with a friend (even if he or she isn't taking the test). It's nice to have somebody supporting you right up to the last minute.

During the Test

Don't get rattled. If you find your confidence slipping, remind yourself that you know the test; you know the strategies; you know the material tested. You're in great shape, as long as you relax!

Even if something goes really wrong, don't panic. If the test booklet is defective—two pages are stuck together or the ink has run—try to stay calm. Raise your hand, and tell the proctor you need a new book. If you accidentally misgrid your answer page or put the answers in the wrong section, again don't panic. Raise your hand, and tell the proctor. He or she might be able to arrange for you to re-grid your test after it's over, when it won't cost you any time.

After the Test

Once the test is over, put it out of your mind. If you don't plan to take the ACT again, shelve this book and start thinking about more interesting things.

You might walk out of the ACT thinking that you blew it. This is a normal reaction. Lots of people—even the highest scorers—feel that way. You tend to remember the questions that stumped you, not the many that you knew.

If you really did blow the test, you can take it again and no admissions officer will be the wiser. Odds are, though, you didn't really blow it. Most people only remember their disasters on the test; they don't remember the numerous small victories that kept piling up the points. And no test experience is going to be perfect. If you were distracted by the proctor's hacking cough this time around, next time you may be even more distracted by construction noise, or a cold, or the hideous lime-green sweater of the person sitting in front of you.

Cancelling Your Score

Don't cancel your score unless you have a good, solid reason. But if you have a good reason, do it.

Finishing the ACT is an accomplishment. Celebrate!

ACT RESOURCES

Stress Management

STRESS MANAGEMENT PREVIEW

Making the Most of Your Prep Time
- Identify the Sources of Stress
- Take Stock of Your Strengths and Weaknesses
- Imagine Yourself Succeeding
- Exercise Your Frustrations Away
- Take a Deep Breath . . .
- . . . and Keep Breathing
- Quick Tips for the Days Just Before the Exam
- Stress Tips
- Handling Stress During the Test

The countdown has begun. Your date with THE TEST is looming on the horizon. Anxiety is on the rise. Butterflies in your stomach have gone ballistic. Perhaps you feel as if the last thing you ate has turned into a lead ball. Your thinking is getting cloudy. Maybe you think you won't be ready. Maybe you already know your stuff, but you're going into panic mode anyway. Worst of all, you're not sure of what to do about it.

Don't worry! It is possible to tame that anxiety and stress—before and during the ACT or any other test. We'll show you how. You won't believe how quickly and easily you can deal with that killer anxiety.

MAKING THE MOST OF YOUR PREP TIME

Lack of control is one of the prime causes of stress. A ton of research shows that if you don't have a sense of control over what's happening in your life you can easily end up feeling helpless and hopeless. So, just having concrete things to do and to think about—taking control—will help reduce your stress. This section shows you how to take control during the days leading up to the test.

Identify the Sources of Stress

In the space provided, jot down anything you identify as a source of your test-related stress. The idea is to pin down that free-floating anxiety so that you can take control of it. Here are some common examples to get you started.

- I always freeze up on tests.
- I'm nervous about the math (or the grammar or reading comp, etcetera).
- I need a good/great score to go to Acme University.
- My older brother/sister/best friend/girl- or boyfriend did really well. I must match their scores or do better.
- My parents, who are paying for school, will be really disappointed if I don't test well.
- I'm afraid of losing my focus and concentration.
- I'm afraid I'm not spending enough time preparing.
- I study like crazy but nothing seems to stick in my mind.
- I always run out of time and get panicky.
- I feel as though thinking is becoming like wading through thick mud.

Sources of Stress

_____

_____

_____

_____

_____

Take a few minutes to think about the things you've just written down. Then put them in some sort of order. List the statements you most associate with your stress and anxiety first, and put the least disturbing items last. Chances are, the top of the list is a fairly accurate description of exactly how you react to test anxiety, both physically and mentally. The later items usually describe your fears (disappointing mom and dad, looking bad, etcetera). As you write the list, you're forming a hierarchy of items so you can deal first with the anxiety-provokers that bug you most. Very often, taking care of the major items from the top of the list goes a long way towards relieving overall testing anxiety. You probably won't have to bother with the stuff you placed last.

Take Stock of Your Strengths and Weaknesses

Take one minute to list the areas of the ACT or any other test that you are good at. They can be general ("world history") or specific ("Nevada from 1850 to 1875"). Put down as many as you can think of, and if possible, time yourself. Write for the entire time; don't stop writing until you've reached the one-minute stopping point.

Strong Test Subjects

_____

_____

_____

_____

_____

Next, take one minute to list areas of the test you're not so good at, just plain bad at, have failed at, or keep failing at. Again, keep it to one minute, and continue writing until you reach the cutoff. Don't be afraid to identify and write down your weak spots! In all probability, as you do both lists you'll find you are strong in some areas and not so strong in others. Taking stock of your assets and liabilities lets you know the areas you don't have to worry about, and the ones that will demand extra attention and effort.

Weak Test Subjects

_____

_____

_____

_____

_____

Facing your weak spots gives you some distinct advantages. It helps a lot to find out where you need to spend extra effort. Increased exposure to tough material makes it more familiar and less intimidating. (After all, we mostly fear what we don't know and are probably afraid to face.) You'll feel better about yourself because you're dealing directly with areas of the test that bring on your anxiety. You can't help feeling more confident when you know you're actively strengthening your chances of earning a higher overall score.

Now, go back to the "good" list, and expand it for two minutes. Take the general items on that first list and make them more specific; take the specific items and expand them into more general conclusions. Naturally, if anything new comes to mind jot it down. Focus all of your attention and effort on your strengths. Don't underestimate yourself or your abilities. Give yourself full credit. At the same time, don't list strengths you don't really have; you'll only be fooling yourself.

Expanding from general to specific might go as follows. If you listed "world history" as a broad topic you feel strong in, you would then narrow your focus to include areas of this subject about which you are particularly knowledgeable. Your areas of strength might include modern European history, the events leading up to World War I, the Bolshevik revolution, etcetera.

Whatever you know comfortably (that is, almost as well as you know the back of your hand) goes on your "good" list. Okay. You've got the picture. Now, get ready, check your starting time, and start writing down items on your expanded "good" list.

Strong Test Subjects: An Expanded List

_____

_____

_____

_____

_____

After you've stopped, check your time. Did you find yourself going beyond the two minutes allotted? Did you write down more things than you thought you knew? Is it possible you know more than you've given yourself credit for? Could that mean you've found a number of areas in which you feel strong?

You just took an active step toward helping yourself. Notice any increased feelings of confidence? Enjoy them.

Here's another way to think about your writing exercise. Every area of strength and confidence you can identify is much like having a reserve of solid gold at Fort Knox. You'll be able to draw on your reserves as you need them, and you can use your reserves to solve difficult questions, maintain confidence, and keep test stress and anxiety at a distance. The encouraging thing is that every time you recognize another area of strength, succeed at coming up with a solution, or get a good score on a test, you increase your reserves. And, there is absolutely no limit to how much self-confidence you can have or how good you can feel about yourself.

Imagine Yourself Succeeding

This next little group of exercises is both physical and mental. It's a natural follow-up to what you've just accomplished with your lists.

First, get yourself into a comfortable sitting position in a quiet setting. Wear loose clothes. If you wear glasses, take them off. Then, close your eyes and breathe in a deep, satisfying breath of air. Really fill your lungs until your rib cage is fully expanded and you can't take in any more. Then, exhale the air completely. Imagine you're blowing out a candle with your last little puff of air. Do this two or three more times, filling your lungs to their maximum and emptying them totally. Keep your eyes closed, comfortably but not tightly. Let your body sink deeper into the chair as you become even more comfortable.

Strategy

Forcing relaxation is like asking yourself to flap your arms and fly. You can't do it, and every push and prod only gets you more frustrated. Relaxation is something you don't work at. You simply let it happen. Think about it. When was the last time you tried to force yourself to go to sleep, and it worked?

With your eyes shut you can notice something very interesting. You're no longer dealing with the worrisome stuff going on in the world outside of you. Now you can concentrate on what happens *inside* you. The more you recognize your own physical reactions to stress and anxiety, the more you can do about them. You may not realize it, but you've begun to regain a sense of being in control.

Let images begin to form on the "viewing screens" on the back of your eyelids. You're experiencing visualizations from the place in your mind that makes pictures. Allow the images to come easily and naturally; don't force them. Imagine yourself in a relaxing situation. It might be in a special place you've visited before or one you've read about. It can be a fictional location that you create in your imagination, but a real-life memory of a place or situation you know is usually better. Make it as detailed as possible and notice as much as you can.

Stay focused on the images as you sink farther back into your chair. Breathe easily and naturally. You might have the sensations of any stress or tension draining from your muscles and flowing downward, out your feet and away from you.

Take a moment to check how you're feeling. Notice how comfortable you've become. Imagine how much easier it would be if you could take the test feeling this relaxed and in this state of ease. You've coupled the images of your special place with sensations of comfort and relaxation. You've also found a way to become relaxed simply by visualizing your own safe, special place.

Now, close your eyes and start remembering a real-life situation in which you did well on a test. If you can't come up with one, remember a situation in which you did something (academic or otherwise) that you were really proud of—a genuine accomplishment. Make the memory as detailed as possible. Think about the sights, the sounds, the smells, even the tastes associated with this experience. Remember how confident you felt as you accomplished your goal. Now start thinking about the upcoming test. Keep your thoughts and feelings in line with that prior, successful experience. Don't make comparisons between them. Just imagine taking the upcoming test with the same feelings of confidence and relaxed control.

This exercise is a great way to bring the test down to earth. You should practice this exercise often, especially when the prospect of taking the exam starts to bum you out. The more you practice it, the more effective the exercise will be for you.

Exercise Your Frustrations Away

Whether it is jogging, walking, biking, mild aerobics, pushups, or a pickup basketball game, physical exercise is a very effective way to stimulate both your mind and body and to improve your ability to think and concentrate. A surprising number of students get out of the habit of regular exercise, ironically because they're spending so much time prepping for the exam. Also, sedentary people—this is medical fact—get less oxygen to the blood and hence to the head than active people. You can live fine with a little less oxygen; you just can't think as well.

Any big test is a bit like a race. Thinking clearly at the end is just as important as having a quick mind early on. If you can't sustain your energy level in the last sections of the exam, there's too good a chance you could blow it. You need a fit body that can weather the demands any big exam puts on you. Along with a good diet and adequate sleep, exercise is an important part of keeping yourself in fighting shape and thinking clearly for the long haul.

There's another thing that happens when students don't make exercise an integral part of their test preparation. Like any organism in nature, you operate best if all your "energy systems" are in balance. Studying uses a lot of energy, but it's all mental. When you take a study break, do something active instead of raiding the fridge or vegging-out in front of the TV. Take a 5- to 10-minute activity break for every 50 or 60 minutes that you study. The physical exertion gets your body into the act which helps to keep your mind and body in sync. Then, when you finish studying for the night and hit the sack you won't lie there, tense and unable to sleep, because your head is overtired and your body wants to pump iron or run a marathon.

One warning about exercise, however: It's not a good idea to exercise vigorously right before you go to bed. This could easily cause sleep onset problems. For the same reason, it's also not a good idea to study right up to bedtime. Make time for a "buffer period" before you go to bed: For 30 to 60 minutes, just take a hot shower, meditate, simply veg out.

Take a Deep Breath . . .

Here's another natural route to relaxation and invigoration. It's a classic isometric exercise that you can do whenever you get stressed out—just before the test begins, even *during* the test. It's very simple and takes just a few minutes.

Close your eyes. Starting with your eyes and—without holding your breath—gradually tighten every muscle in your body (but not to the point of pain) in the following sequence:

1. Close your eyes tightly.
2. Squeeze your nose and mouth together so that your whole face is scrunched up. (If it makes you self-conscious to do this in the test room, skip the face-scrunching part.)
3. Pull your chin into your chest, and pull your shoulders together.
4. Tighten your arms to your body, then clench your fists.
5. Pull in your stomach.
6. Squeeze your thighs and buttocks together, and tighten your calves.
7. Stretch your feet, then curl your toes (watch out for cramping in this part).

At this point, every muscle should be tightened. Now, relax your body, one part at a time, *in reverse order*, starting with your toes. Let the tension drop out of each muscle. The entire process might take five minutes from start to finish (maybe a couple of minutes during the test). This clenching and unclenching exercise should help you to feel very relaxed.

. . . and Keep Breathing

Conscious attention to breathing is an excellent way of managing that ACT test stress (or any stress, for that matter). The majority of people who get into trouble during tests take shallow breaths. They breathe using only their upper chests and shoulder muscles, and may even hold their breath for long periods of time. Conversely, the test taker who by accident or design keeps breathing normally and rhythmically is likely to be more relaxed and in better control during the entire test experience.

So, now is the time to get into the habit of relaxed breathing. Do the next exercise to learn to breathe in a natural, easy rhythm. By the way, this is another technique you can use during the test to collect your thoughts and ward off excess stress. The entire exercise should take no more than three to five minutes.

With your eyes still closed, breathe in slowly and deeply through your nose. Hold the breath for a bit, and then release it through your mouth. The key is to breathe slowly and deeply by using your diaphragm (the big band of muscle that spans your body just above your waist) to draw air in and out naturally and effortlessly. Breathing with your diaphragm encourages relaxation and helps minimize tension. Try it and notice how relaxed and comfortable you feel.

Quick Tips for the Days Just Before the Exam

- The best test takers do less and less as exam day approaches. Taper off on your study schedule and take it easy on yourself. You want to be relaxed and ready on test day. Give yourself time off, especially the evening before the exam. By that time, if you've studied well, everything you need to know is firmly stored in your memory banks.

- Positive self-talk can be extremely liberating and invigorating, especially as the test looms closer. Tell yourself things such as, "I *choose* to take this test" rather than "I *have* to"; "I *will* do well" rather than "I *hope* things go well"; "I *can*" rather than, "I *cannot*." Be aware of negative, self-defeating thoughts and images and immediately counter any you become aware of. Replace them with affirming statements that encourage your self-esteem and confidence. Create and practice doing visualizations that build on your positive statements.

- Get your act together sooner rather than later. Have everything (including choice of clothing) laid out days in advance. Most important, *know where the test will be held and the easiest, quickest way to get there.* You will gain great peace of mind if you know that all the little details—gas in the car, directions, etcetera—are firmly in your control before test day.

- Experience the test site a few days in advance. This is very helpful if you are especially anxious. If at all possible, find out what room your part of the alphabet is assigned to, and try to sit there (by yourself) for a while. Better yet, bring some practice material and do at least a section or two, if not an entire practice test, in that room. In this case, familiarity doesn't breed contempt, it generates comfort and confidence.

- Forego any practice on the day before the test. It's in your best interest to marshal your physical and psychological resources for 24 hours or so. Even race horses are kept in the paddock and treated like princes the day before a race. Keep the upcoming test out of your consciousness; go to a movie, take a pleasant hike, or just relax. Don't eat junk food or tons of sugar. And—of course—get plenty of rest the night before. Just don't go to bed too early. It's hard to fall asleep earlier than you're used to, and you don't want to lie there thinking about the test.

- When you dress on test day, do it in loose layers. That way you'll be prepared no matter what the temperature of the room is. (An uncomfortable temperature will just distract you from the job at hand.) And, if you have an item of clothing that you tend to feel "lucky" or confident in—a shirt, a pair of jeans, whatever—wear it. A little totem couldn't hurt.

Stress Tips

- Don't work in a messy or cramped area. Before you sit down to study, clear yourself a nice, open space. And make sure you have books, paper, pencils—whatever tools you will need—within easy reach.

- Don't study on your bed, especially if you have problems with insomnia. Your mind may start to associate the bed with work, and make it even harder for you to fall asleep.

- A lamp with a 75-watt bulb is optimal for studying. But don't keep it so close that you create a glare.

- If you want to play music, keep it low and in the background. Music with a regular, mathematical rhythm—reggae, for example—aids the learning process. A recording of ocean waves is also soothing.

Handling Stress During the Test

The biggest stress monster will be test day itself. Fear not; there are methods of quelling your stress during the test.

- Keep moving forward instead of getting bogged down in a difficult question. You don't have to get everything right to achieve a fine score. The best test takers skip difficult material in search of the easier stuff. They mark the ones that require extra time and thought. This strategy buys time and builds confidence so you can handle the tough stuff later.

- Don't be thrown if other test takers seem to be working more busily and furiously than you are. Continue to spend your time patiently but doggedly thinking through your answers; it's going to lead to better results. Don't mistake the other people's sheer activity for progress and higher scores.

- *Keep breathing!* Weak test takers forget to breathe properly as the test proceeds. They start holding their breath without realizing it, or they breathe erratically or arrhythmically. Improper breathing interferes with clear thinking.

- Some quick isometrics during the test—especially if concentration is wandering or energy is waning—can help. Try this: Put your palms together and press intensely for a few seconds. Concentrate on the tension you feel through your palms, wrists, forearms, and up into your biceps and shoulders. Then, quickly release the pressure. Feel the difference as you let go. Focus on the warm relaxation that floods through the muscles. Now you're ready to return to the task.

- Here's another isometric exercise that will relieve tension in both your neck and eye muscles. Slowly rotate your head from side to side, turning your head and eyes to look as far back over each shoulder as you can. Feel the muscles stretch on one side of your neck as they contract on the other. Repeat five times in each direction.

With what you've just learned here, you're armed and ready to do battle with the ACT—or any other test. This book and your studies will give you the information you'll need to answer the questions. It's all firmly planted in your mind. You also know how to deal with any excess tension that might come along, both when you're studying for and taking the exam. You've experienced everything you need to tame your test anxiety and stress. You *are* going to get a great score.

NOTES

NOTES

NOTES

NOTES

NOTES

NOTES

NOTES

Introducing a smarter way to learn.

- Focused, practice-based learning
- Concepts for everyday life
- Recognition and recall exercises
- Quizzes throughout

Available wherever books are sold.

www.kaptest.com
www.simonsays.com

Problem: Studying
Solution: